A Short Course in Technical Trading

Founded in 1807, John Wiley & Sons is the oldest independent publishing company in the United States. With offices in North America, Europe, Australia, and Asia, Wiley is globally committed to developing and marketing print and electronic products and services for our customers' professional and personal knowledge and understanding.

The Wiley Trading series features books by traders who have survived the market's ever changing temperament and have prospered—some by reinventing systems, others by getting back to basics. Whether a novice trader, professional, or somewhere in-between, these books will provide the advice and strategies needed to prosper today and well into the future.

For a list of available titles, visit our Web site at www.WileyFinance.com.

A Short Course in Technical Trading

PERRY J. KAUFMAN

WILEY

John Wiley & Sons, Inc.

For general information on our other products and services, or technical support, please contact our Customer Care Department within the United States at 800-762-2974, outside the United States at 317-572-3993 or fax 317-572-4002.

Wiley also publishes its books in a variety of electronic formats. Some content that appears in print may not be available in electronic books.

For more information about Wiley products, visit our web site at www.wiley.com.

ISBN 0-471-26848-8

10 9 8 7 6 5 4 3 2 1

Contents

Preface

Trading is all about making money. Technical trading uses chart patterns, indicators, some simple math, and clear rules to make money. There are many successful traders who use instinct, but I believe they've got a computer going inside their heads, looking for patterns and signals that tell them prices are going to surge ahead or stop and reverse. Experience teaches you what works and what doesn't work.

In this course we're going to take some simple ideas and turn them into successful trading. If you can't turn an idea into profitable returns, then you're wasting your time. Trading is really all about making money.

I was fortunate to have stumbled into this industry in 1970. As far as I know, no one studies to be a trader—it just happens. You watch stock or gold prices going up or down because of a series of front-page news events, and somehow you decide that here is a profit opportunity. You open a brokerage account and make a trade. Win or lose, you can't stop. It can be the fastest way to making or losing a fortune. When you start out, you have the overwhelming feeling of participating in the ideal of Free Trade. You are making the price and you are trying to beat the market—the collective action of all the other buyers and sellers. It's exhilarating.

When I was asked to teach a graduate course in technical analysis at Baruch College in the spring of 2002, my first thought was, "Technical analysis just isn't enough." The students need to come away with a skill that they can use and build on in the future. We were still immersed in the Enron collapse, and the press was exposing the conflicts of interest between the market analysts and the investment banking departments inside the major brokerage houses. All of a sudden, we couldn't trust the information that was basic to making a buy or sell decision.

Using technical analysis is an unbiased way of evaluating a stock, index, or futures market. If the price is going down, it doesn't matter if the analyst is reporting that the company is undervalued, or that the *pro forma* performance shows a potential profit in six months—the timing is not right to buy.

However, technical analysis isn't enough. It doesn't tell you how to trade. There is a big gap between analyzing the market and trading, and it is filled with trading losses. How can you bridge that gap without making every mistake yourself? You can learn from someone with experience. Good advice moves you along faster, but making mistakes yourself is an important and unavoidable way to learn. This course is intended to do both—teach you what works and give you a chance to make mistakes without costing you anything. You'll find traditional instruction alternating with "words of wisdom," a series of trading games that I encourage you to play, and comments on what is likely to go wrong when you trade. Those comments are the result of reviewing the trading of other ambitious students. We can learn from their mistakes in order to make fewer mistakes of our own.

I've been developing trading systems for 30 years, traded them myself, and directed others while they were being traded. I've profited from their successes and lost when they failed. By now I have a good understanding of what works and what doesn't work, and why. This course is an effort to pass on that knowledge to you.

In case you're thinking that this is a magical method for profitable trading, you're wrong. There are no secrets in this course, just sensible methods and hard work. You should be able to take what you learn and use it as a solid foundation for moving forward, or you can trade successfully using only what you learned in this course.

OTHER READING

This course is based on experience; however, there are other books that can be used to expand each lesson. John Murphy's *Technical Analysis of the Financial Markets* (New York Institute of Finance, 2000) is always a good place to start. Jack Schwager's *Schwager on Futures: Technical Analysis* (Wiley, 1996) covers charting step-by-step and adds another level of understanding. Perry Kaufman's *Trading Systems and Methods*, 3rd edition (Wiley 1998), my own book, has much more extensive coverage and evaluation of trading techniques. The last lesson in this course is based on a fine article by Ralph Acampora and Rosemarie Pavlick, "A Dow Theory Update," originally published in the *MTA Journal*, January 1978, reprinted in the *MTA Journal*, Fall-Winter 2001.

PERRY J. KAUFMAN

Redding, Connecticut
May 2003

Acknowledgments

My thanks to the students of Baruch College Graduate Course in Finance, FIN 9790, Spring 2002, for their enthusiastic participation, and to Bill Abrams, the best student of all, who never stops learning. Bill has been a constant supporter of my efforts and an invaluable aid in reviewing the manuscript. My appreciation to David Krell, who motivated this effort and continues to help facilitate education and knowledge in the financial industry.

I would like to acknowledge the gracious help of *TradeStation Technologies, Inc.*, and Janette Perez for providing their systems. Since their inception, I have found their programmable platform an indispensable tool for implementing many of my strategies. The charts in this book were all produced using the *TradeStation Platform*.

My warmest thanks to my mother for, besides other things that mothers do to make things work, her very astute comments when reviewing the manuscript.

Of course, the most important and extensive help came from my wife, Barbara, who worked along with me every weekday and every weekend reviewing the constant flow of hundreds of orders in the Trading Game. It was an effort far beyond the call of duty.

And, to all the dedicated teachers who give so much to future generations.

P. J. K.

CHAPTER 1

Timing Is Everything

This course is about how to trade, not how to hold a position. It's about being on the right side of the hill. It will teach you when to buy, when to sell, and how to take losses before they affect your net worth.

There are some basic market truths that everyone needs to know before trading. One of the most important things to learn is that *things change*. Because things change, you need to ground yourself with trading facts. After all, you are going to be immersed in stock prices, interest rates, and the barrage of information that floods the news. You will need to know some of the terms used in trading and in analyzing price patterns. You'll also want to know what works and what doesn't work—mostly what works—and why. For the answer to this last question, you will need to work your way through the lessons. By the end of this course, you will understand why a technical approach to trading makes sense.

THE MARKET CHANGES

The stock market is evolving. It is not the same as it was 10 years ago, or even 5 years ago. That's good news for those of you starting now because you won't be burdened by unnecessary and incorrect ideas about the way the market should act. Consider the obvious things that have changed:

- The equipment is faster.
- The people who are trading are more knowledgeable.
- More people are using the markets—there is more competition.
- Exchanges are becoming electronic.

SP_REV CSV-Weekly 09/20/2002 C=872.50 -18 70 -2 10% O=887 70 H=905 50 L=871.70 V=361714

FIGURE 1.1 *a*   Unprecedented trends. S&P 500 trends 1993–1997. The mid-1990s had an unprecedented bull market. Nearly any purchase was highly profitable. From 1995 through 1997 the S&P gained 50 percent.

- A lot of the order entry is computerized.
- Commissions are so low that they no longer force you to hold a trade for a long time just to break even.
- Improved communications technology has caused globalization.
- New trading vehicles, such as trusts, Fed funds rates, single stock futures, and derivatives have changed the way institutions and individuals use the markets
- Everyone reacts to news faster than ever before.
- We've discovered recently that the recommendations of stock analysts often were biased.

How could prices move in the same way now, when the basic structure of the market is in constant change?

The importance of these changes is that what was successful trading in the past is unlikely to work as well today—if at all. During the 1990s we saw an unprecedented bull market trend in stocks that stretched around most of the world. That was followed by an equally dramatic, highly volatile drop in prices and an erratic sideways price period. In Figure 1.1*a*, we see the S&P

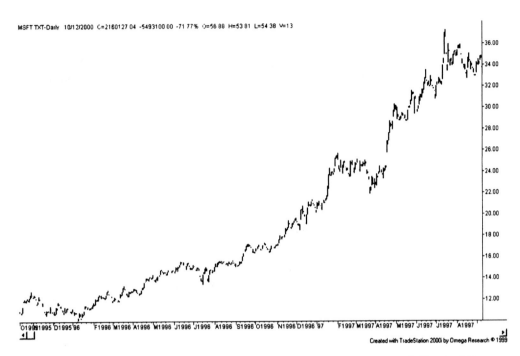

MSFT TXT-Daily 10/12/2000 C=2160127 04 -5493100 00 -71 77% O=56 88 H=53 81 L=54 38 V=13

Created with TradeStation 2000i by Omega Research © 1999

FIGURE 1.1*b* **Unprecedented trends.** Microsoft trends 1995–1997. Much like the S&P, Microsoft moved steadily higher from 1995 through 1997, gaining 260 percent, a remarkable 86 percent per year.

500 index from 1993 through 1997, and in Figure 1.1*b*, Microsoft from late 1995 through 1997. The trends are remarkable. During the last three years of that period, the S&P 500 gained 50 percent, and Microsoft gained 260 percent.

We see how quickly these markets can change in Figure 1.2. The S&P (Figure 2.1*a*) loses 50 percent of its value during 2000 and 2001, with very sharp drops and mild rallies. Microsoft (Figure 1-2*b*) loses half of its value, changing to an erratic, volatile sideways pattern before dropping half its value in one month. As if global warming affected the markets, we are seeing one extreme after another.

HOLDING ON FOR THE BIG PROFIT

Of course, you can still profit from a buy-and-hold approach, given enough time. You also can profit from a sustained policy of the Federal Reserve to lower interest rates and stimulate growth—a plan that can last two years or more and create trends in everything from stocks to real estate and art. But when you hold a position for a long time, you are exposed to more price fluctuations and more risk. With the exception of the mid-1990s, there haven't been many periods of high profitability for investors and long-term traders.

Beginning in 1999 anyone holding equity positions found out that the stock market doesn't just keep going up. It's been three years of downward, sideways, and volatile price movement; trying to keep losses to a minimum isn't easy. Investors are now looking at the market with the eye of the trader, trying to hold a position when it's doing the right thing and getting out when it's not. There's nothing wrong with that approach. In fact, there's a lot that's right with it.

EXTRA BENEFITS OF TRADING

When you actively trade a stock or a futures contract, you are not holding a position all of the time. That's very important because stocks spend a lot of time doing nothing, or doing the wrong thing. To offset these sometimes prolonged periods of aggravation or boredom, we get an occasional price shock, such as September 11, 2001, the U.S. invasion of Kuwait, a presidential

FIGURE 1.2a   Changing markets. 2001 and 2002 show a completely different picture for the S&P, dominated by volatile downward price moves and erratic sideways periods. Trading techniques that worked for the strong trends in the mid-1990s do not work from 2000 to 2002.

election, or a surprise interest rate increase by the Federal Reserve. *A price shock causes an unpredictable, large jump in prices.*

Note that the term *unpredictable* means that you can't plan to make a profit, no matter how clever you are. When you are always in the market, you will always be tossed around by price shocks, most of them small, a few of them very big. We're going to spend some time throughout this course looking back at price shocks. They are the rare random events that cause the greatest losses among traders. The longer you trade, the more you'll see price shocks. *You don't ever want to make the mistake of thinking that it was skill that netted a big profit from a price shock. It was luck. Next time, or the time after, you won't be lucky. It's a 50-50 chance.*

WHAT IS TECHNICAL TRADING?

Technical trading is the process of making trading decisions based on clear, objective, predetermined rules. Those rules apply only to price data, volume, and for futures markets, open interest. You could include other economic

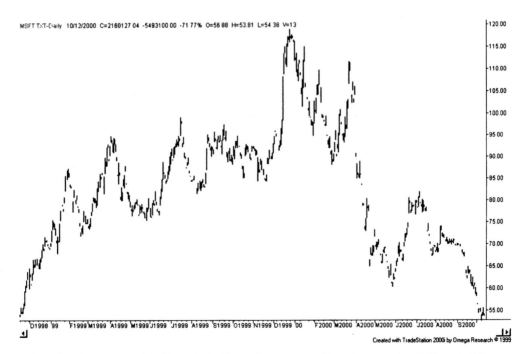

MSFT TXT-Daily 10/12/2000 C=2160127 04 -5493100 00 -71 77% O=56 88 H=53.81 L=54 38 V=13

Created with TradeStation 2000i by Omega Research © 1999

FIGURE 1.2b **After its historic bull market,** Microsoft's price turned volatile and sideways before dropping half its value in April 2000.

data, such as unemployment and the Consumer Price Index (CPI), but that's not necessary and we won't do it here. Besides, it's not clear that using all these facts will improve our profits.

The techniques used in technical trading include trendlines, moving averages, chart patterns, and a few indicators based on simple mathematical formulas. None of it is complicated, but it takes practice to do it right.

Some people call this *systematic trading*. The way to be sure that the indicators are done correctly is to enter them into a spreadsheet, or program them into a software trading program that helps us get results quickly. Charting and pattern recognition remain special skills, but ones that are not very difficult to master.

CHOOSING THE SYSTEMATIC WAY

It is not a choice between "which is better," investing based on fundamentals or technical trading. They are two very different methods chosen for completely different reasons.

The *fundamental investor* may be looking for a cheap price or good value on a piece of merchandise with the idea of holding it until it returns to value, or appreciates in value. You don't want to overpay for real estate or stocks because it cuts into your returns.

The *systematic trader* is foremost a trader. A trader doesn't hold a position based on value, but decides whether the price is *relatively* too high or too low, whether it is in a long-term or short-term trend, extremely volatile or quiet. For each of these technical qualities, the systematic trader has a clear rule to follow. The rules are based on common sense and then tested using historical data to be sure they actually work. We will learn how a spreadsheet or special computer program may be used to validate the rules. You will find that many of the rules that are based on charting methods have been handed down from one generation to another.

TECHNICAL TRADING AND VALUE

A technical trader may also be influenced by fundamentals. A long-term trend follower—one who buys a stock when the trend is rising—is really tracking the increase in the value of the stock in an objective way. If Mrs. Hathaway was long Cinergy (a public utility) in 1997 based on a 100-day trend, she would be taking advantage of the Fed policy of lowering rates even though the reason for rising prices might not be important to her, and she may not have seen the close relationship between Cinergy's stock price and interest rates.

The fast systematic trader could even profit if the stock or futures market were above value. He or she could be in a trade for a few hours or a few days. The value of a stock isn't very important for a fast trader, only its volatility and short-term direction. Even when stocks were trending higher, as they were in 1997, the impact of the long-term trend on a one-day trade was very small. You could buy or sell and still return a profit. Value, or fundamental information, is of minor importance for short-term traders.

We choose systematic trading because

- It provides discipline.
- We can backtest (check the rules using historic prices) to see if the trades would have been profitable.
- We have confidence by knowing what results to expect both risk and return.
- We can monitor current performance to decide if the method is still working as we expected.

USING A METHOD WE UNDERSTAND

By using trading rules based on prices, we are going to avoid some important problems. For example,

- We don't know how to find out if a stock is undervalued. In fact, we're not sure that the experts can find the right value. We've found out the hard way that those who try to assess value may not have all the facts.
- We don't need to watch a stock price drop by 90 percent before being told by an expert that its value has changed.
- We are concerned that news, opinions of others, or just a bad day can change the opinion of a fundamental or value trader.
- We don't know if using fundamentals can produce consistent profits.

We will let the market tell us that prices are rising or falling and not rely on the advice of broker. A trend follower needs a Yogi Berra type of philosophy: "It's not going up until it's going up!"

> ### Basic Questions You Must Always Ask
>
> Whether you're managing your own personal money or you're a professional money manager, you need to ask the same questions: Which method of trading is more consistent? Which one has more integrity? Which one can be influenced by outside factors? Which one can give you a fair assessment of expected returns and risks? Which one is most likely to make money?

What's the Downside to Technical Trading?

Every method has its problems. To use systematic trading, you also need to know what can go wrong.

- You can't find a method that works.
- You may take a position opposite to what is being said on CNBC.
- It may seem stupid to take another long position after just posting two losses in a row.
- It started working great, but now something's gone wrong.
- The risk is too high.

Each one of these problems has a reasonable solution. The purpose of this course is to show you some of the methods that are most likely to work, and

> ### Why Technical Trading Works
>
> Let's be realistic. Not all trading systems work, but many systems do work. Those are the ones based on a sound premise. Once you understand how to follow the rules, systematic trading works because
>
> - It identifies price trends and patterns objectively and applies clear rules.
> - It will profit from a fundamental or seasonal trend—if one exists.
> - It controls losses using stops.
> - It takes profits, based on predefined values.
> - It easily allows diversification.
> - It can be adjusted to personalized risk levels.
> - It is not affected by news or opinion.
> - It generates profits when continuously applied over time.

help you get comfortable with their good and bad parts. *If you can't find a simple method that works, you won't find a complicated one.*

WHAT ARE THE OTHER GUYS DOING?

Let's take a few minutes to look at how man.y fundamental traders decide on what stock to buy, and when they will enter and exit the position.

How Do We Normally Decide to Buy a Stock?

- We make a qualitative decision: Is it a good company?
- Is it profitable? Has it paid dividends regularly? Is the stock rising? Does it have a lot of debt? Is the P/E ratio high or low? In other words, is the company a *good value*?
- Is the company healthy? Is it in good strong hands? Is the management competent? Is there a large employee turnover? Are salaries reasonable?
- Is the company likely to be competitive in the future?
- Add to these concerns some new questions, such as: Does the CEO have a sensible exit package? Are there any accounting irregularities?

All of these questions and answers are important. They try to reach the vital areas that determine whether a company is sound and likely to remain that way. The problem is whether you can get answers to these questions, and whether those answers are reliable. Even when they appear to be answered, what is your level of confidence in a decision based on so many complex issues?

Reliability of Information

Let's look at the most outrageous event of the past 10 years—the collapse of Enron. Briefly, Enron was a powerhouse in energy trading. It had assets in the form of a pipeline, and a large trading "book" in electricity. It was thought of as innovative and highly successful, a business model for the future. It was a substantial component of the S&P.

We see now that much of that was done with mirrors. It appears that Enron had off-balance-sheet deals that were not reflected in their numbers, and the company was said to have generated artificial trades to make it appear that their trading volume was higher. Enron closed out trades before producing its monthly risk report, and then reset them the next day. The company did everything it could to inflate the Enron stock price and with the apparent blessing of their accountants. With the full benefit of hindsight, how reliable is the information that we use to base our value decisions?

Pro Forma Results—What Are They?

Amazon.com has made an art of publishing *pro forma* company performance. What is that? It's not the net earnings of the company, or its profitability. It's a statement of "what company earnings would be if . . . ," where "if" can be

- *If* we didn't need to write off a one-time loss due to a mistake in starting a new product
- *If* we didn't need to pay out debt that was obligated when we began the company
- *If* we didn't have to pay our employees a salary

The problem is that *pro forma* results can be anything, as long as you explain what you've done. As remarkable as it seems, the stock price will rally after good *pro form* results—why would a *pro forma* report be anything but good?

What Happens When Public Confidence Changes?

Returning to Enron, we need to remember how fast public confidence eroded. In Figure 1.3 we see the stock quickly drop from $30 to nothing in the final days, but Enron prices had peaked a year earlier. Even before the off-balance-sheet transactions became public and problems became obvious, prices had declined from $90 to $60. What is most upsetting is that the major brokerage firms did not issue a sell signal until Enron was in the throws of death, a decline of nearly 90 percent of the stock price.

How Would You Have Done?

Look at Figure 1.3 again. During all of 2000 and the first part of 2001, Enron held above $60, peaking at $90. In early 2001 it dropped from about $70 to $60, then to $50 within a few weeks. That was an unprecedented decline, leaving prices well off the highs by 40 percent. Traditional thinking declares a bear market when prices decline 20 percent. At least we need to recognize that something has changed. Why would the price drop 40 percent unless there was a problem?

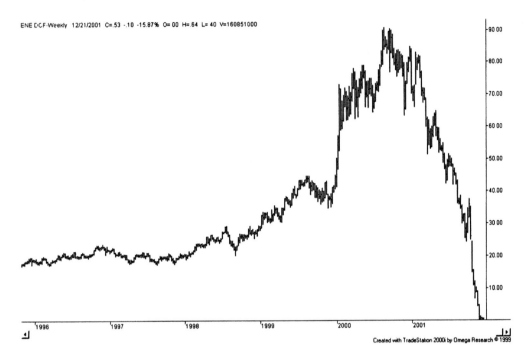

ENE DCF-Weekly 12/21/2001 C=.53 -.10 -15.87% O= 00 H=.64 L= 40 V=160851000

Created with TradeStation 2000i by Omega Research © 1999

FIGURE 1.3 **Was the fast collapse of Enron (ENE)** the result of a sudden lack of confidence by the public or insider selling in excess of $1 billion? Did you care about the insider selling before the collapse? Did you think about it when accounting irregularities were announced?

HOW DO YOU DECIDE THAT YOU SHOULD NO LONGER OWN THE STOCK?

The decision to sell a stock is at least as important as the one to buy. Ask yourself

- What is the opposite of a buy decision when using only fundamental information?
- How long does it take to realize that the quality is no longer there?
- How far down does a stock price need to fall from the highs before you sell?
- One major retail broker waited until Cisco had declined 75 percent before taking it off their hold list. What would you have done?

Do you remember that the public was told (on CNBC) that the major houses had shifted from a buy recommendation to a neutral when Enron hit $10? Let's look at other examples to get an idea of some of the recent price

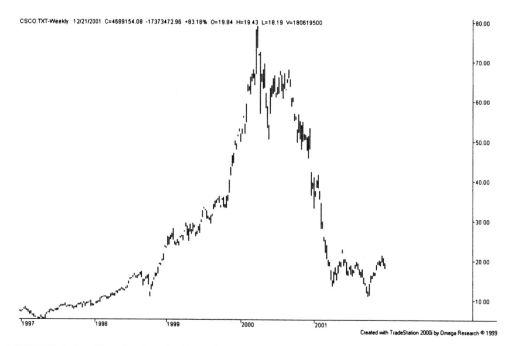

CSCO.TXT-Weekly 12/21/2001 C=4689154.08 -17373472.96 +83.18% O=19.84 H=19.43 L=18.19 V=180619500

Created with TradeStation 2000i by Omega Research © 1999

FIGURE 1.4 **Cisco's clear bull market** and subsequent dramatic drop is easy to see in hindsight, but would you have closed out your long position at 60 when you still had a 300 percent profit in your original position?

patterns. If you were holding these stocks from 1997, consider whether you could have made an objective decision to sell them before the major price drop. If you did not actually get out while you still had profits, then you need to learn some things about technical trading.

Cisco

Cisco (Figure 1.4) moved higher for three years, along with all of technology, with very little retracement. At the beginning of 2000 it dropped more than one-third in two weeks, a sign that something had dramatically changed. Prices tried to rally, but by the third quarter of that year they began falling to new lows. There was still a 300 percent profit in the original position. Would you have gotten out?

General Electric

General Electric (GE), the flagship of the Dow, had a steadier rise and a less volatile fall than Cisco (see Figure 1.5). You may have exited at $40, or even $45, as prices fell, and then regretted that decision when prices moved back over $50. General Electric certainly doesn't look like Cisco, but a decline from $60 to $30 is an unnecessarily large loss to absorb when you easily could have done better.

American Airlines

It was not possible to be prepared for the price shock in American Airlines that came in mid-1998 (see Figure 1.6), when price turned from a perfect bull market to fall 35 percent in a few days. You might have been lucky when the second shock hit, at the beginning of 2000, because prices were already heading lower. You might even have escaped the third shock on September 11, 2001, because prices were still looking weak. The first shock should have been a lesson in itself.

Amazon.com

Amazon is a remarkable investment story. We all believe in the future of the Internet, and Amazon was up front taking advantage of that promise. However, expectations and profits are different, and Amazon has not been able to deliver quarterly profits. Instead, it feeds the hopes of the investors by releas-

FIGURE 1.5   General Electric (GE), the flagship of the Dow, is down one-third from it's highs. Would you still be holding it? Would you have gotten out at $40 and then gotten back in at $50 because it looked as though it was heading back up? If not, where would you get in again?

FIGURE 1.6   American Airlines is different from the other examples because of a series of price shocks. Would you have been on the correct side of the market? Would you be correct next time?

FIGURE 1.7   Amazon.com lost $50 million each quarter yet continued higher through 1999. It was the product of dreams. Fortunes were made and lost. Does the extreme volatility in 1999 tell you anything?

ing *pro forma* financial statements showing that profits are likely if everything goes according to projections. So far, that hasn't happened. We are still hoping.

The volatility of Amazon (see Figure 1.7), much greater than many other stocks, is based on overspeculation, constant promotion by the company, and a lack of any basis for valuing the stock price. How do you price the stock when the company posts a loss every quarter since inception?

IF YOU CAN'T HELP LOOKING AT THE CHART PATTERNS THEN YOU'RE GOING TO BE A GOOD TECHNICAL TRADER

It's fun to look at chart patterns and trends and imagine what trades you could have made. In technical trading we're going to learn rules about price patterns and apply them in the same way to all of the stock and futures markets. Before you move on to the next lesson and see these rules, think about what you already know about price patterns.

Can You Apply the Same Buy-Sell Principles to All Stocks?

- Can you write down the rules you've used to buy and sell a stock, any stock? Can you write down the rules for when you would have exited the long positions in the previous stock charts? If so, you're a systematic trader.
- When you look at a chart, do you see it in terms of continuous price moves? Do you look at the highs and lows of price swings? Do you draw conclusions, make up rules, and imagine that you can capture large profits?

Looking at a historic chart is frustrating and deceiving. It makes you think that you could have profited from the price moves. It's much harder when you can't see the future. However, high-tech display equipment lets you see the past price movement of any stock. It has brought many new traders to the table who think they can profit from future price moves because they can see the past.

THE IMPORTANCE OF TIMING

A few thoughts about timing are important before we move forward. We would like to think that we can profit from the news if we act faster than others. It's not true.

- The market moves on anticipation. "Buy the rumor, sell the fact." If you bought on every piece of good news published in the *Wall Street Journal,* you would be broke.
- The market responds to the difference between the actual news and what was expected. The unemployment rate could have dropped 0.2 percent, and the market falls because it expected a drop of 0.4 percent.
- *Action* does not always mean immediate *reaction.* When did the Fed start lowering interest rates? When did the market start to respond? In the case of interest rates, it always takes more than one move by the Fed before you see a reaction in the economy.

EVOLVING MARKETS

The market is dynamic. It is not the same as it was, yet it is driven by the same underlying economic forces.

What Has Changed?

- The equipment has changed, allowing instantaneous analysis, program trading, electronic orders (smart order entry), high-momentum trading, and unreasonable expectations.
- Methods have changed, with far more systematic traders, especially professional fund managers.
- Participants have changed, with a larger influence from pensions, designer funds, and institutional investors. Day traders are common because commissions are low.
- Electronic exchanges and side-by-side trading are new. You can beat your competition by creating an electronic order the instant a system "signal" is triggered.
- Globalization has changed the way world markets move, with alternating leaders and followers.
- There are more trading vehicles, including ETFs for index and sector investing, and single stock futures.
- Markets are noisier because of more participation. Sometimes they have irrational swings because of piggy-backed orders. The frequency of extreme moves is increasing, causing greater volatility.

Will a system that worked in 1990 work in 2002? *Probably not.*

Will the people who made money in the 1990s make money now? *If they change, too.*

WORDS OF ADVICE

Throughout this course there will be trading tips, trading insights, and some old-fashioned advice. Take some time to think about all of it.

Don't Confuse Luck for Skill

In a prolonged bull market, all buyers are eventually right. They buy all dips, regardless of size, because it has always worked. As they gain confidence, they may add leverage by buying on margin. At the end of the bull market they are usually wiped out.

- It's a business, not a casino.
- It's all about risk.
- Learn how to take a loss.
- Don't turn a profit into a loss.
- Anticipation is the key to success.

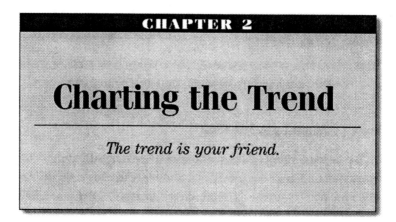

CHAPTER 2

Charting the Trend

The trend is your friend.

In this chapter you will learn about the trend. The trend is simply the direction of prices over some time period. No matter how much you learn, you will always want to know the trend of the market.

TRENDS

Trends are very easy to see on a chart. They are seen best over a long time period—weeks, months, and years. If prices are going up, the trend is up; if prices are going down, the trend is down. Here we get to the first problem. If prices go up and then down, is the trend up or down? Look at Figure 2.1, the S&P weekly chart. Is the price going up or down? The answer is "yes." It's going up in the long term, over the period of the entire chart, but down in the shorter term, the last two years.

The Trend Depends on Your Time Frame

If you're a very, very long-term investor, the trend will always be up because inflation and economic growth eventually will cause the stock index to make new highs. If you've been holding Merck from 1994 through 2002, you've watched the price rise from $5 to $60, a gain of 1,100 percent. If you bought Merck at the beginning of 2001 and held it through 2002, you watched the price go from $90 down to $60, a loss of 33 percent.

The trend is always a matter of time interval. Even over a few days, two traders may see the same market as going in different directions. Each one can make money or lose money within the same period by correctly or incorrectly deciding where to buy and where to sell.

> ### What Creates Trends?
>
> - *Government policy.* When economic policy is to target a growth rate of 3 percent, then the Federal Reserve (the Fed) raises and lowers interest rates to accomplish this. Lowering rates encourages business activity. Raising rates controls inflation by dampening activity.
> - *International trade.* When the United States imports goods, it pays for it in dollars. That is the same as *selling* the dollar. It weakens the currency. A country that increases its exports strengthens its currency.
> - *Expectations.* If investors think that stock prices will rise, they buy, causing prices to rise. *Consumer confidence* is a good measure of how the public feels about buying.
> - *Supply and demand.* A shortage, or anticipated shortage, of any product will cause its price to rise. Too much of a product results in declining prices. These trends develop as news makes the public aware of the situation.

The Trend Is Always Easier to See Afterward

Look again at the S&P chart in Figure 2.1. You can easily see the upward trend. But after an uptrend, how far down do prices need to fall before you say that the trend is down? That's a difficult question, and we'll answer it in

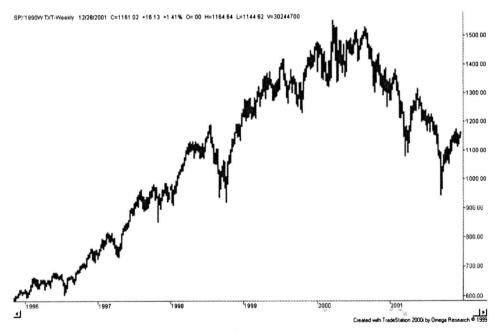

FIGURE 2.1   S&P weekly 1996–2001. Is it going up or down? Yes. It was going up, and it's now going down. If you're a long-term trader, then you can still say that it's going up.

this chapter. Part of the answer depends on your time frame, but most of it depends on the market itself.

What It Means to Be a Trend Follower

A trend follower buys when the price trend is up and sells when the price trend is down. A trend follower believes that, if the trend is up then it will continue to go up; therefore, trend followers make the assumption that *trends persist*. If everything works as expected, the trend continues long enough to yield a profitable trade.

Why Should the Trend Continue?

There's a good reason why the trend persists. Most trends are the result of government economic policy. In the U.S. the Federal Reserve (Fed) targets an economic growth of 3 percent. In order to accomplish that in a bad economy, they will lower interest rates. First they lower rates by 0.5 percent to see how the economy reacts. Then they lower rates by another 0.5 percent and watch (see Figures 2.2 and 2.3). This process of ratcheting down interest

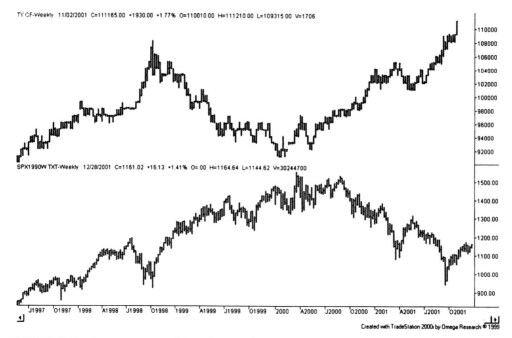

FIGURE 2.2   Interest rates drive the stock market. Top: 10-year notes continuation series. Bottom: S&P 500 Index. There's a clear relationship between interest rates and the stock market but it's not always the same. Interest rates always lead, but the market doesn't always respond. T-note prices begin going up in January 2000 (interest rates declining), but the stock market has not yet reacted.

rates causes a trend in all of the markets that depend on rates and all companies that have debt—which is pretty nearly all of them.

The biggest trends usually begin with a change in interest rates. Sometimes, the beginning can be a change in the value of the U.S. dollar. The dollar can drop when the U.S. imports much more than it exports. When you buy foreign products, you buy their currency as well.

Expectation also drives prices. Will a hot summer cause a shortage of electricity, or a shortage of water? Will a weakening economy reduce the number of airline passengers and shorten hotel stays? Will the economy strengthen or weaken? These events don't occur overnight; they evolve gradually. Prices rise and fall in anticipation.

The Reason for Shorter Trends

There are other trends besides long-term interest rates and currency. You'll find seasonal trends in many businesses that focus on travel and leisure, such as airlines or hotels. The agricultural products are seasonal because they have a clear growing and harvest period. Heating oil is used during the winter

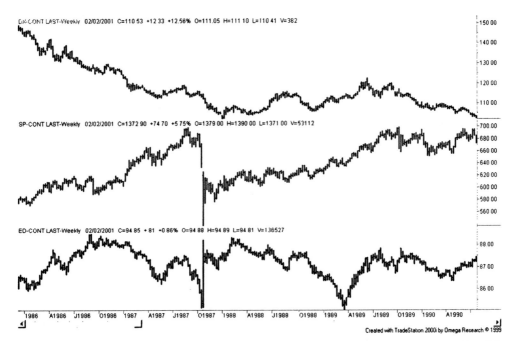

FIGURE 2.3 Cause and effect: good news versus bad news. When the stock market falls (S&P, center panel), short-term interest rates (Eurodollars, bottom panel) are lowered to start a recovery. When the stock market moves higher too quickly, rates rise to slow it down. The Fed manages growth using interest rates; policy lasts for 6 months to 2 years. At the same time, a cheaper dollar (Dollar index, top panel) stimulates trade and encourages foreign investment into stocks.

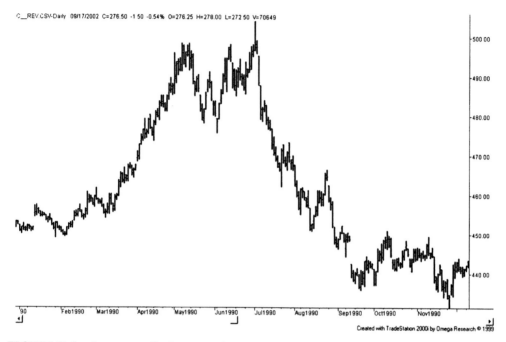

C__REV.CSV-Daily 09/17/2002 C=276.50 -1 50 -0.54% O=276.25 H=278.00 L=272 50 V=70649

Created with TradeStation 2000i by Omega Research © 1999

FIGURE 2.4   Summer rally in corn. The summer growing season provides more than one opportunity to expect a problem with the corn crop. In 1990 prices began to rise before the crop was planted and continued through the middle of the summer based on lack of rainfall and news reports of devastation to land in some states. But technology won in the end, and the crop was much larger than expected. Price fell to levels lower than the previous year. (Prices shown are an adjusted continuous series of futures contracts.)

and gasoline is consumed in larger amounts during the summer. These patterns can cause extreme trends that last about three months.

There are always unexpected events that cause a surge in prices: a cold spell that could affect the orange juice crop in Florida or a good chance that a new cancer drug will be approved for a medical research company.

Shorter trends can also be caused by expectation. The public expects earnings to improve because interest rates are dropping. The public expects the cost of wheat to be higher because there's been very little rain in the Midwest. As the news confirms their opinion, prices move steadily higher. You really don't know how the corn crop is affected by rain until it is harvested in October. Any rise in prices over the summer is expectation, not fact (see Figure 2.4).

FINDING THE TREND ON A CHART

What is the trend in Figure 2.5? It's down because prices at the end of the chart are lower than prices at the beginning. Simple enough. There are periods when prices are rising, but the overall picture is a downward trend.

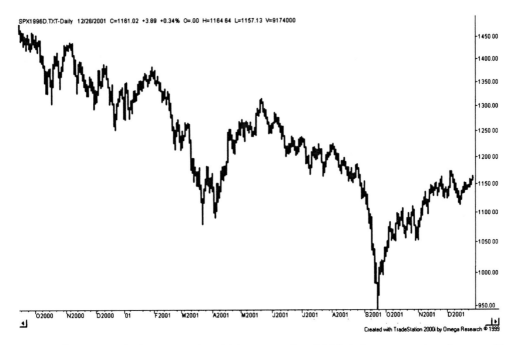

SPX1996D.TXT-Daily 12/28/2001 C=1161.02 +3.89 +0.34% O=.00 H=1164 64 L=1157.13 V=9174000

Created with TradeStation 2000i by Omega Research © 1999

FIGURE 2.5   S&P daily, September 2000–December 2001. Is it an uptrend or downtrend? Are you influenced by how much of the chart is visible? Try to keep your long-term perspective.

The Trend Is Seen Best Using Weekly or Monthly Charts

Everything looks smoother when you see it at a distance. You can't see the details. That's especially true with price charts. A monthly chart looks smoother than a weekly chart, a weekly chart is smoother than a daily chart, and a daily chart is smoother than an hourly chart.

You can see the trend best on a weekly or monthly chart. You see more market "noise" on a daily or intraday chart. *Market noise* is the erratic up and down movement that occurs over a period of a few days.

CHARTING THE TREND

It's time to draw classic trendlines on a chart in order to get a relatively objective assessment of the trend direction. It's relative because you can change the trend by choosing a longer or shorter trendline, or a daily, weekly, or monthly chart. There's usually a way to make the chart say what you want if you're determined to force your opinion on your analysis. We'll try to avoid that approach. To begin, you'll need to know that:

- An *uptrend* (a *support* line) is formed by connecting the lowest rising prices.
- A *downtrend* (a *resistance* line) is formed by connecting the highest declining prices

Where Do You Start?

You can start a major upward trendline at a low price and then draw the trendline up and to the right, touching the lowest price or prices. Using Cisco as an example (see Figure 2.6) the upward trendline, *A*, starts at the low in October 1998 and touches the two lows in the third and fourth quarters of 1999. After that, prices move quickly away from the trendline and only cross it on the way down.

The major downward trendline, *B*, was started at the high of the move. Of course, you don't know the high until after prices have dropped significantly. At that point we can draw the line *B* from the peak, touching the high of the right shoulder where a second rally ended.

FIGURE 2.6   Trendlines drawn on the Cisco weekly chart. This company shows a clear major upward trend and a major downward trend. Lines can be redrawn to keep current with the price move.

Redrawing the Trendlines

Price patterns change and so should the trendlines. They need to be redrawn from time to time in order to stay current with the price move. When Cisco prices begin to drop quickly in late 2000, we can redraw the downward trendline, *C*, at a sharper angle. Later, we might find that both lines, the original one and the new one, are both helpful for trading. After a while, your chart will look like a "work in progress" with redrawn lines everywhere.

How Many Points Should the Trendline Touch?

You can draw a trendline with two points, but three or four are even better. The more points that lie on the same line, the more confidence we have that we've drawn the correct trendline. However, you can't expect the lows to fall exactly on the same line—the market is just not that precise. If you can see a clear trend, even though the bottom is a little ragged, then draw the trendline anyway.

In Figure 2.6, a shorter, intermediate trendline (the broken line) was drawn across the six bottoms during 1999. The first two low prices and the last low price fall right on the line but the middle three go through the trendline by small amounts. You should still see it as a trend. A price that penetrates a trendline and then corrects itself is considered a strong confirmation of that trendline.

More on Redrawing Trendlines

Redrawing the trendline is a normal part of tracking the direction of prices. In the S&P chart shown in Figure 2.7 the first trendline is drawn from the October 1998 low to the October 1999 low (line *A*), then redrawn to touch the lows of February after a new high is made in March 2000 (line *B*), and redrawn a third time along the lows of April, May, and June (line *C*). We can stop redrawing the upward trendline after the downward trend begins.

Which Trendlines Are More Important?

If an upward trendline is drawn from one long-term low to another, it is more important than a line connecting two intermediate lows. If a trendline can be drawn across three or more lows (even though one point might poke through the line by a small amount), it is more important than a line through two lows. If a trendline is not violated, it gains in importance.

FIGURE 2.7   Weekly S&P futures continuation chart. Upward trendlines are redrawn after new highs and then stop after the downtrend begins.

Charting the Trend on Daily Prices

Up to now the charts used in the examples have been weekly and monthly because they show the trend more clearly, but daily charts will be used for our trading. We need to learn what to expect. In Figure 2.8 trendlines are drawn on an S&P daily chart. The first downward trendline, *A*, is perfect. It touches three points and crosses the final upward move as prices gap through the trendline. However, trendlines on daily charts can be confused by market noise.

The upward move in October and November does not provide a third point for the trendline. You can redraw the upward trendline a number of times, and none of them will look as good as the downtrend line. Because of the increased noise, daily prices won't line up as clearly as weekly prices and the trends won't be as easy to draw. When you're trading, be prepared for frustrating periods where you get in and out of the market because of noise. You need to hang on through those periods until the clear trends return.

The Evolving Trend of Enron

One of the best recent examples of the benefits of charting is the demise of Enron. As the news tells it, a well-paid analyst continued to recommend the

SP_REV.CSV-Daily 09/17/2002 C=872.50 -20.50 -2.30% O=903.00 H=905.50 L=871.70 V=180857

FIGURE 2.8 Trendlines on a daily S&P chart. The downtrend is very clear, but the initial uptrend doesn't fit very well. The redrawn uptrend seems to be better, but market noise that shows up on a daily chart makes it difficult to find a clear pattern.

purchase of Enron while prices were falling to $10 (see Figure 2.9). Was it a conflict of interest or simply bargain hunting? Now that you've been introduced to charting trendlines, when would you have sold your Enron shares?

For certain, there is a major upward trendline that connects the lows during the summer of 1998 with the lows of December 2000. If that line is continued, it crosses the price decline in May 2001 at about $55. The fast break in March 2001 that took prices from just under $70 to the low $50s gives us

---

Tip: Real Market Conditions

Real market conditions are never perfect for the technical trader. Each stock or futures market has its own personality. Instead of a bull market correction stopping at the trendline, it will stop a little above or below the trendline before starting back up. It's smart to give a little room for a *false break* of the trendline. After all, this isn't an exact science—prices are moved by news, emotion, and occasionally facts that create a public opinion.

Exactly How Much Do You Let Prices Penetrate the Trendline?
About 10 percent of the current price volatility. Let's say that IBM has been moving in swings of $5. Allow an extra 50¢ for excessive movement.

ENE.TXT-Weekly 12/21/2001 C=.53 -.10 -15.87% O= 00 H=.64 L=.40 V=160851000

Created with TradeStation 2000i by Omega Research © 1999

FIGURE 2.9   Enron during its best and worst times. How would you have traded it using classic trendline charting?

the idea that there was an intermediate trendline across the lows of the topping formation from the first quarter of 2000 until the break in May 2001.

Whenever you question why you've decided to trade technically, think of Enron. Any chartist or technician would have been safely out before the worst of the news caused the final collapse of the stock price. How could any rational person recommend holding Enron down to $10?

TREND TRADING RULES FOR TRENDLINES

It may seem clear from the charting examples that the trendlines show where to buy to enter a trade and sell to exit; however, traders place their orders in a few different ways:

Entry Rules

- *Buy* when the price closes above the downtrend line (conservative).
- *Buy* when the intraday price penetrates the downtrend line (aggressive).
- *Buy* in an upward trend when prices decline to near the upward trendline.

Exit Rules

- *Sell* when the price closes below the upward trendline (conservative).
- *Sell* when the intraday price penetrates the upward trendline (aggressive).

Notice that the aggressive trader buys during the day when prices cross through the trendline. A more conservative trader will wait to see if the closing price is going to be above the trendline. Price action during the day can be very volatile and the direction of prices can change, and often does, from midday to the close. On the other hand, if important news reaches the market during the earlier trading hours, the first one that buys gains the most profit. You can only decide your style from practice. Start with the closing price as a measure of direction until you are confident that another way is better.

Getting Out of the Trade

When the upward trend is finished, prices will move down through the trendline. At that point you *sell*, closing out your trade, hopefully with a profit. However, not all trades are profitable. About two-thirds of all trend trades lose money, and yet trend trading is still a reliable, profitable way to trade.

Profits Through Persistence. The majority of times, a change of direction *does not* turn into a trend; however, when prices do continue in one direction, they produce good profits. Success is a matter of numbers. You can expect 6 to 7 out of 10 trend trades to be losses, some small, some a little larger. Of the 3 or 4 good trades you can expect one small profit, two medium-size profits, and one large profit. On average, a profitable trend trade should be about 2.5 times the size of a loss. With enough trades, that should result in a net profit in your trading account.

As an example, say we lose $100 on each of the 6 losing trades, for a total loss of $600. On the four profitable trades we get an average of $250 per trade for a total profit of $1,000. The individual profits are most likely $100, $200, $200, and $500. That's a $400 gross profit less some slippage for entering and exiting and commissions on 10 trades. If instead of 6 losses there were 7 losses and 3 profits, we would net only $50. Expect the real results to be somewhere in between $50 and $400.

As a trend trader, you should expect mostly small losses, some small profits, and a few large profits.

What Can You Expect Your Trading Results to Look Like?

- Most trades will be small losses
- About 25 percent of the trades will be small or medium-size profits.
- About 10 percent of the trades will be larger profits.
- A small number of trades will be very large profits.

Trend trading is successful because of the occasional very large profit.

The Fat Tail

Trend trading is successful because losses are kept small and profits are allowed to grow. That technique is called *conservation of capital.* What makes trend trading profitable in the long run is the unusually large number of big profits compared to what is expected in a normal distribution. For example, in a normal distribution of 1000 coin tosses, half of them would be single runs of heads or tails. Half of those, 25 percent, would be a sequence of either two heads or two tails. Half of the remaining, 12.5 percent, would be sequences of three in a row, and so on. Therefore, in 1,000 coin tosses you can expect only one run of 10 heads or tails in a row.

Apply that to prices. In 1,000 days of trading (about four years) you would expect only one time that prices would go up or down 10 days in a row. However, that happens much more often than once; therefore, price movement is not normally distributed, and not random. It has a *fat tail* distribution. There are fewer days where prices turn from up to down, or down to up, and more longer runs. That's what makes trend trading profitable.

IMPACT OF THE TIME HORIZON

Before leaving trendlines, think about the importance of the length of the trendline and the use of daily, weekly, or monthly data:

- Using major tops and bottoms to draw a trendline identifies the most important trends; monthly and weekly charts will show these points clearly.
- Longer time horizons put the points where the trend changes farther away, causing a longer delay, or larger lag, in your decisions.
- Longer time horizons allow larger price swings; therefore those trades have larger risk.

- Longer time horizons are more reliable because they allow prices more freedom of movement. Even in a trending market, prices do not go straight up or straight down.

These features show a trade-off between reliability and risk. You need to accept more risk to have better results. All trading has choices between risk and return. You can never have both large profits and low risk.

A Computerized Approach: Finding the Points Automatically for Drawing Trendlines

Most analysts will look at a chart and pick the low prices that will be used to draw an uptrend line. However, you also can find those points automatically. Anyone who enjoys working with a spreadsheet or writing a computer program might find the rules for finding those points a good first step toward automating a trading method.

In Figure 2.10 the dots above the price peaks mark the *swing highs*, and the dots below the bottoms are the *swing lows*. They are called swing highs

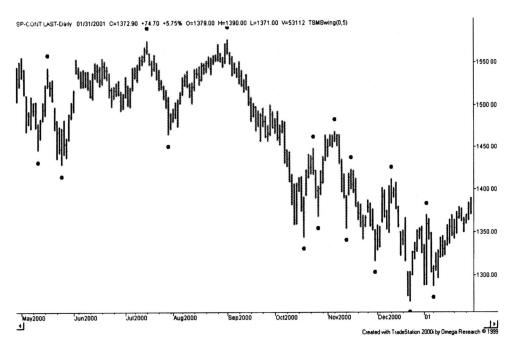

FIGURE 2.10 **Finding the tops and bottoms automatically.** The points showing the tops and bottoms of this S&P chart are separated by price swings of at least 5 percent.

For Computer Mavens:
Finding the Swing Points Automatically Using a Spreadsheet

Set up your columns with the following data:
A   Date
B   High price
C   Low price
D   Closing price
C3 Put the minimum swing percentage value in cell C3 (for example, 5% = .05)

Put the following formulas in the corresponding cells. Row 6 initializes the process.
E6 = B6 (the current swing high)
F6 = C6 (the current swing low)
G6 = IF (D6 > (E6 + F6)/2,–1,1) (where –1 is a downswing and +1 is an upswing)

Row 7 is the beginning of the repeated process. Row 7 can be copied down.

E7 = IF($G6 = –1#AND#B7 > E6,B7,IF($G6 = 1,B7,E6))	(the new current low)
F7 = IF($G6 = 1#AND#C7 < F6,C7,IF($G6 = –1,C7,F6))	(the new current high)
G7 = IF($G6 = –1,IF(C7 < E7 – C3× D7,1,$G6),IF(B7 > F7 + C3× D7,–1,$G6))	
	(test high or low)
H7 = IF($G7 = 1#AND#G6 = –1,E7,H6)	(the new swing high)
I7 = IF($67 = –1#AND#G6 = 1,F7,I6))	(the new swing low)

and lows because they are separated by at least a 5 percent price move in this example. You can choose any percentage. A larger percentage identifies major points, while smaller percentages show minor points. Major points are more reliable.

When we use the dots in Figure 2.10, we draw an upward trendline only when the bottom dots are rising and a downward trendline when the top dots are falling. The trendlines do not need to be formed by connecting consecutive dots.

EVOLUTION OF A TREND

The trend is constantly being redrawn based on new highs and lows. In Figure 2.11, only the automatically calculated swing highs and lows are used to give you an idea of how your chart will look as time creates new patterns. Some of the main features of this Amazon chart are:

* The highest point, 1, on the left remains the highest throughout this period.

FIGURE 2.11   Evolution of a trend. In this Amazon chart we see how trendlines need to be redrawn as price patterns develop. This chart used only swing highs and lows computed automatically. The result shows that these trendlines clearly mark the changes in price direction.

- The downward trendline, *A*, beginning at point 1, is redrawn each time prices move above the existing downward trendline (*B*, *C*, *D*, and *E*), creating a new swing high.
- An intermediate downward trendline, *E*, may be drawn beginning from another high (see mid-April 2001).
- Other downtrend lines (*G* and *H*) begin in July 2001 at point 4 after prices drop.
- Good lines are confirmed by the market, often with a price gap.
- The major downward trendline, *E*, formed by connecting points 1 and 4, seems to hold after the rally to point 5 at the far right.

MAKING THE TREND WORK

It is easier to see a trend using a weekly chart instead of a daily chart, but trading using a weekly chart is very slow and exposes you to larger price swings and larger risk. Many professional traders will use the weekly chart to draw the major trend, but a daily chart to decide where to get in and out. It is easier to find the trend on a weekly chart, and this assures us that we don't loose sight of the correct trend.

Questions

1. What is the reason for drawing a trendline?
2. What is the intended relationship between interest rate changes and stock market changes?
3. If you wanted to see the trend on a chart more clearly, would you use a daily, weekly, or monthly chart? Why?
4. How could you have a chart where the trend was both up and down?
5. In the S&P monthly chart shown in Figure 2.12, draw the major uptrend lines as they develop. Is there a point (or points) at which you would have gone short?

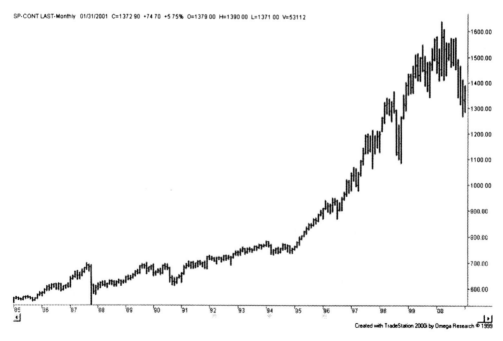

FIGURE 2.12   The S&P futures monthly continuation series shows the sustained bull market of the 1990s and the peak in 2000.

6. Using the chart of Cisco during 1998 shown in Figure 2.13, draw the trendlines and outline the (ideal) trades you would have made based on the price penetration of the trend.

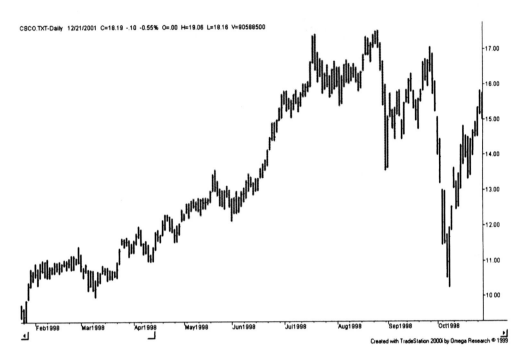

FIGURE 2.13 Daily Cisco prices from February through October 1998. A strong uptrend followed by a difficult, volatile period makes finding the trendlines more challenging but makes trading more exciting.

CHAPTER 3

Breakout Trends

U pward and downward trendlines, or *angled* trendlines, are not the only way of finding the trend. Although they are the classic method, there is a simpler way of identifying the trend that many think is more practical for trading. It's called a breakout.

BREAKOUTS

The start of a trend can be recognized by a price *breakout*. A breakout is simply a new high price or new low price after a sideways pattern. The longer the sideways pattern, the more important is the breakout.

In Figure 3.1 we see a sideways pattern in General Electric (GE) from November 1996 through April 1997. The breakout occurs near the end of April when prices move over the previous highs of $18. They move quickly higher before stabilizing.

Not all sideways breakouts are as clear as GE. The AOL chart in Figure 3.2 has three different sideways patterns, all overlapping. The shortest period from October to November 1996 is broken by a sharply higher move that begins at $1.75 and ends at $2.80 in 7 days. A larger sideways pattern from July to November 1996 is ended with the same breakout. Following that move, we see another sideways period from December 1996 ending at the beginning of March 1997 with a break above $2.75.

Notice that the support line for the first two sideways patterns did not include the two lows in October. They can be considered *false breakouts*. When you ignore them, the support line for the sideways pattern is very clear.

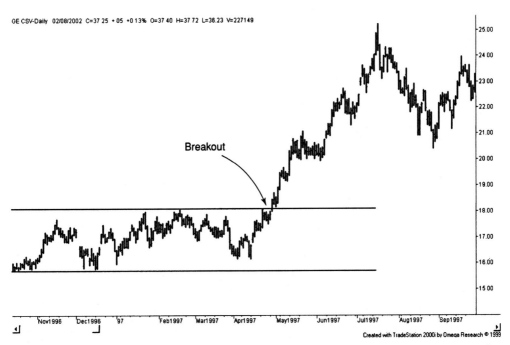

GE CSV-Daily 02/08/2002 C=37 25 + 05 +0 13% O=37 40 H=37 72 L=36.23 V=227149

Breakout

FIGURE 3.1   An upward breakout from a sideways pattern in GE. After six months of sideways price movement, GE prices break out to the upside in April 1997.

It is an advantage to smooth out the patterns with your eyes. Very few patterns are perfect.

Why Do Breakouts Look So Good?

A breakout is a sure sign that something has changed. If GE has been trading between $45 and $55 for 3 months and then makes a new low, something has changed. There are expectations of bad news.

When you draw a classic upward trendline, as we did in Chapter 2, you are imposing the expectation that prices should continue higher at the same rate, or faster, in order to keep above the trendline. That may not be realistic. As long as prices go higher rather than lower, it doesn't matter how long they take between new highs. By looking only at new highs and new lows, we can recognize the trend without placing as many conditions on price movement.

Pinpointing the Breakout with Horizontal Support and Resistance Lines

In order to recognize a breakout we draw two horizontal lines on a chart, one beginning at the highest high of the most recent sideways period and the

FIGURE 3.2   Multiple breakouts from sideways patterns in AOL. Three clear sideways patterns can be found in AOL. The fast price move through the resistance line, especially in pattern 1, is a confirmation that traders recognized this pattern.

other from the lowest low of the same period. If today's high price crosses the resistance line, we have a new upward trend breakout; if the low crosses the support line, we have a new downward trend. In Figure 3.2 the horizontal lines cross through some of the highs and lows. That's good if it makes the sideways pattern clearer.

The trend remains the same until prices cross the support or resistance lines going in the other direction (see Figure 3.3). Cisco is an interesting example. It breaks above a sideways pattern in July 1998. It drifts sideways for three months and then starts up, and it doesn't consolidate and move sideways until it forms a broad top in 2000. To show that support is a real phenomenon, look at the number of times the price bars had a low of $50. Someone must have been buying large quantities at that price in order to have stopped prices from going lower. Finally, at the end of 2000 the market wins (as it always does), and prices break through support. Whoever was buying has been stopped out or is very unhappy.

CSCO.TXT-Weekly 12/21/2001 C=18 19 -1.20 -6.19% O=.00 H=19 85 L=18 08 V=369671000

FIGURE 3.3   Breakouts can be used to identify major trends. In this chart of Cisco, a break-out to the upside at the beginning of 1998 is followed by a downside breakout at the end of 2000. Note the number of times the price touches $50 during all of 2000 before finally breaking down.

Trading Rules for Breakouts

Breakouts are the easiest of all methods to trade.

- You *buy* when prices make a new high above the previous resistance level.
- You *sell* when prices make a new low below the previous support level.
- You do nothing in between.

Placing Your Sell Order after Buying a Breakout

When there is an upward breakout from a sideways pattern, the sell order goes below the bottom of the sideways pattern. Prices must be allowed to flop around before they continue their upward pattern. We would like them to go straight up after we buy, but it usually doesn't happen that way. The beginning of a trend can be sloppy, and prices usually fall before moving higher. By placing your initial sell order below the original sideways pattern, you are saying that you'll only exit the trade if the breakout was false. That is, if prices now make a new low, then something was wrong and the market wants to go lower.

Later, we'll show how to use support levels to set a stop-loss order. We don't want to turn a profitable trade into a loss.

Enron is another good example of breakouts (see Figure 3.4). At the beginning of 1998 it moves above its previous high. Something new has happened. It gets more volatile but moves steadily higher until the summer of 1999 when it takes a setback before surging above $70. Now prices seem to form a sideways market with clear lows between $63 and $64. If you were watching for a change of direction based on breakouts, you would be short on a break of $60. It would seem clear that something had changed.

False Breakouts

A *false breakout* occurs when the resistance level (previous high) is penetrated during the day but prices close back inside the range. There are volatile days in which prices are pushed to new highs on expectations that fail to develop. By the end of the day those higher prices could not be reinforced by fact and so prices return to previously lower levels inside the range. Although we can now redraw the top of the range to include the new higher high, it is best not to consider a breakout unless the closing price confirms the direction by staying above the high of the sideways range.

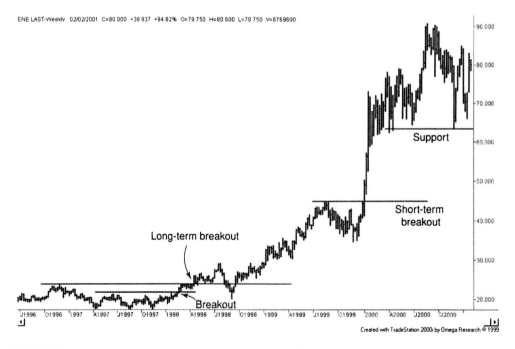

FIGURE 3.4   Enron upward breakouts and impending downward break.

The Risk of Using the Breakout Method

If a new upward trend occurs with a new high and a downward trend with a new low, then the risk of trading using the breakout method is the difference between the high price and the low price. Looking back at Figure 3.2, we can see the risk in the sideways pattern 1 is about one-third of the risk of pattern 2.

During volatile periods the risk significantly increases; while during quiet times the risk is small. The strongest feature of the breakout method is that the risks and the trends adjust to market conditions. You also may think of the larger risk as a problem, but it can be corrected simply by trading a smaller position.

THE ROLLING BREAKOUT

We normally find a sideways period and the corresponding breakout levels by looking at the chart. However, computerized programs have taken a different approach by always looking backward by the same number of days. If we always use the highest high and lowest low over the past 20 days, we call that a *20-day rolling breakout* or simply a *20-day breakout system*. For each new day we drop off the oldest day and find the highest high and lowest low of the new 20-day period.

Is the "Rolling Breakout" Better Than the Old-Fashioned Method?

No, but it can be very profitable, and it can be tested on a computer. It has the same profit and risk characteristics as the handdrawn lines but sometimes gets fooled into using the wrong highs and lows. It's a lot more practical than drawing lines on each of a large number of charts each day. A computer can calculate the breakout trends of all the markets in a few seconds. If you like the diversification of trading a number of markets, the rolling breakout is a good method to use.

Example of Trading Results of a 30-Week Breakout.   Table 3.1 shows the Enron trades using a 30-week rolling breakout system. This calculation period gives results similar to those in Figure 3.4. The trades can be seen in Figure 3.5 with the words *buy* and *sell* below and above with an arrow pointing to the day of the trade. Figure 3.6 gives the Excel code and a small piece of an Excel worksheet that can calculate the breakout trends, including buy and sell signals. Using a spreadsheet greatly simplifies the problem.

TABLE 3.1		Enron Trades Using a 30-Week Breakout System					
Trade No.	Date	Type	Units	Price	Signal Name	Trade P/L	Cumulative P/L
1	6/17/1994	Buy	1	17.313	Buy		
	11/25/1994	Exit	1	14.438	Sell	−2.875	−2.875
2	11/25/1994	Sell	1	14.438	Sell		
	2/24/1995	Exit	1	16.438	Buy	−2.000	−4.875
3	2/24/1995	Buy	1	16.438	Buy		
	4/4/1997	Exit	1	18.500	Sell	2.062	−2.813
4	4/4/1997	Sell	1	18.500	Sell		
	1/23/1998	Exit	1	20.813	Buy	−2.313	−5.126
5	1/23/1998	Buy	1	20.813	Buy		
	9/4/1998	Exit	1	21.719	Sell	.906	−4.220
6	9/4/1998	Sell	1	21.719	Sell		
	12/25/1998	Exit	1	29.156	Buy	−7.437	−11.657
7	12/25/1998	Buy	1	29.156	Buy		
	12/1/2000	Exit	1	65.500	Sell	36.344	24.687
8	12/1/2000	Sell	1	65.500	Sell		

There were a lot of breakout systems that would have made money on both the rise and fall of Enron. This one went short on December 1, 2000, and would still be short.

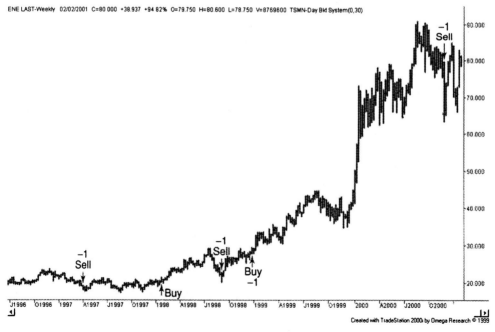

ENE LAST-Weekly 02/02/2001 C=80.000 +38.937 +94.82% O=79.750 H=80.600 L=78.750 V=8769600 TSMN-Day Bkt System(0,30)

Created with TradeStation 2000i by Omega Research © 1999

FIGURE 3.5   Enron rolling breakout trades. Buy and sell signals for a 30-week rolling breakout system are shown at the point of the breakout.

Calculating the Rolling 10-Day Breakout System Using a Spreadsheet

Set up your columns with the following data:
A   Date
B   High price
C   Low price
D   Closing price

Repeat (copy down) the following lines. There are no constants and no initialization. For a 10-day calculation the data begins in row 1 and the calculations begin in row 11.
E11 = MAX(B1:B10)   the 10-day high through the previous day
F11 = MIN(C1:C10)   the 10-day low through the previous day
G11 = IF(B11>E11#AND#D11>D10,1,IF(C11<F11#AND#D11<D10,-1,G10))
      trend direction
H11 = IF(G11 = -1#AND#G10^ = -1,"Sell",IF(G11 = 1#AND#G10^ = 1,"Buy"," "))

You'll need to change your calculations if you want something other than 10 days. To generalize this to any calculation period, use the Excel function "OFFSET".

FIGURE 3.6   **An Excel spreadsheet that creates breakout trends and trade signals.**

COMPARING SIDEWAYS AND ROLLING BREAKOUT METHODS

There is no doubt that an intelligent technical trader could identify the sideways patterns better than the computer, but the computer can do it faster and give you the chance to trade a more diversified group of stocks and futures. That's important and we'll discuss that as we move forward. Let's now try to follow the weekly S&P 500 prices during the strong upward move from 1994 to 1997 (see Figure 3.7) by drawing sideways ranges manually and comparing the results to a rolling breakout. It's difficult to be objective when looking back at the entire picture, but let's try:

1. The sideways period from April 1994 through February 1995 is very clear. The lows form a support line and the highs in March, September, and October (*A*, *B*, *C*) form resistance. The resistance line is drawn across the highest high, point *B*, but we could have lowered that to cross *A* and *C*, cutting the top off at *B*. Cutting the tops off is the better way.

2. We get a breakout to the upside in mid-February. The rolling 30-week breakout also gets a buy signal because prices move over point *B*, which is within the past 30 weeks.

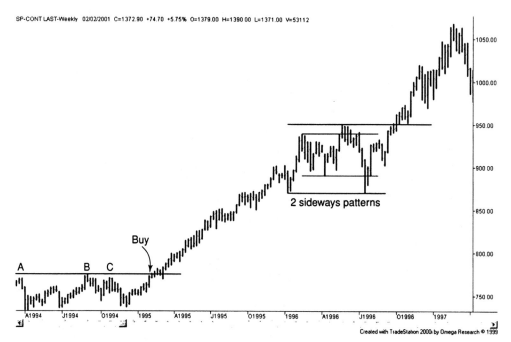

FIGURE 3.7   Stepping through the process of finding breakouts. The S&P 500 weekly chart shows a clear sideways range and breakout in 1994, a smooth upward trend, another sideways period, and a renewal of the uptrend. It took two tries to find the correct sideways range in the middle.

3. The steady move up doesn't require any decisions until the sideways period, beginning in July 1995, has a sharply lower move in October. We don't see the sideways pattern until prices start to fall to point *H*, the lowest level of the pattern.

4. The decline to *H* stops at exactly the same level as *D*, but we may have sold when prices first broke through the line formed by *F*. We may have drawn a support line connecting the two lows on both sides of *F*. If we sold at the first line, we take a profit of about 115 points and then sell short.

5. If we're fast, we sell at the thin support line crossing at *F*, and then see prices stop at the major support line drawn from *D* to *H*. Prices rebound higher, and we realized that support held and we need to get net long again. The new high is at 950, at which point we would be sure the uptrend has resumed but take a 60-point loss in the S&P.

6. You may have waited for the major support line at *H* to be broken and remained long. Prices would have dropped from 950 to about 870, a loss of 8.4 percent. Would you have been able to wait that long? Not likely.

7. The rolling breakout also closed out the long position and sold short on July 19 at 902. Not a bad spot, but not clear from a chartist view. It reversed from short to long on October 4 at 961 following the same breakout above the major resistance line.

In this example, the 30-week rolling breakout captured a little more profit than the classic charting method because it didn't need to interpret the support lines in the middle of the chart. Figure 3.8 shows the breakout signals posted on the S&P weekly chart.

The Benefits of Hindsight

It's always possible to find a rolling breakout of some calculation period that would do better than manual charting, but it's not clear that you could have found the right one to use *before* seeing the chart. Then again, it's not clear that we would have drawn the same support and resistance breakout lines before seeing the whole chart. This is an important problem that we will discuss throughout this course. For now, we can say that we applied both methods using hindsight and they came out about the same.

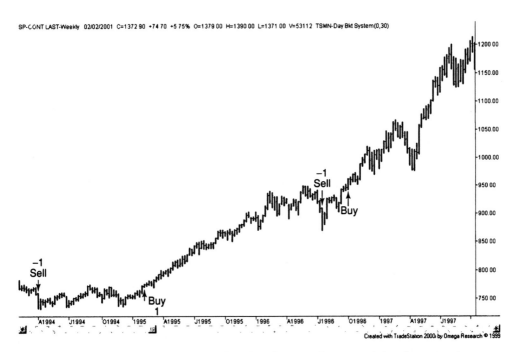

FIGURE 3.8 S&P with 30-week rolling breakouts. The 30-week breakout signals are very similar to those breakouts resulting from manually drawing support and resistance lines. There is a false breakout in the middle of the trend where the 30-week breakout uses the smaller trading range. It gets a long signal when prices reverse and the trend starts up again.

THE IMPORTANCE OF A SIDEWAYS BREAKOUT

A sideways trading range occurs when there is no compelling news in the market. The range between the support and resistance lines actually shows the underlying market noise (volatility) caused by normal trading in and out of that stock or futures contract.

When prices move out of a sideways range, there must be news, or anticipation of news, to cause enough buying or selling to drive prices to a new level. This might be expectations of higher earnings, a possible acquisition, lower interest rates, or pending bad weather for crops.

A breakout of horizontal support or resistance will work successfully using daily closing prices (a conservative choice), daily highs and lows (an active choice), or even intraday prices (an aggressive choice). The risk of the trade is always measured by the distance between the support and resistance lines. This varies with the volatility of prices. Breakout systems are extremely popular because they:

- Are highly reliable even though they have high risk.
- Do not have a lag because signals come at the moment of breakout.
- Allow prices to move freely within the support-resistance band, imposing few restrictions.

Which Is Better, Using the Trendline or Breakout?

The breakout is more dependable because it recognizes an obvious change in the market at the time it occurs. The trendline shows the direction of prices based on their rate of increase or decrease. The breakout usually corresponds to a special event.

The breakout is reliable, partly because it has more risk. Remember that price moves are fickle. Prices may move up, but they do it in a very erratic way. It's best to give prices room to flop around. Prices may break out of the trading range, make a new high, and then fall back into the sideways pattern for a while. The only thing we really know is that if we bought on a new high and prices then make a new low, something is wrong. Prices shouldn't make a new low after making a new high. There is good, simple logic in a breakout system.

ADVANCED TECHNIQUES

There are always special rules for improving trading signals. They are a bit more complex but can add profits.

Improving the Buy Signal from a Downtrend Line

If you prefer using trendlines, you can combine the trendline and breakout to create a more reliable buy signal. When prices move above a downward trendline after a long move lower, it rarely goes straight up. This is true particularly if volatility has dropped, indicating a truly low price. At that point the price will go sideways before it finally begins an uptrend. It is best to wait until there is a breakout of the sideways pattern before buying so you can avoid being too early in a trade that goes nowhere. A break of the downtrend line may indicate that the downtrend is over, but an upward trend may still be sometime off.

A New Downtrend is Different. It's not the same when going from an uptrend to a downtrend. Prices that are too high can turn and drop quickly. You don't need a confirmation, only quick action.

Anticipating a Breakout

Breakouts are so popular that there can be a large number of buy and sell orders placed at a new high or low price. This is true particularly for a major support or resistance line that is clear to everyone. A clear breakout is usually seen as a gap on a chart. You can be sure that you've drawn your lines correctly if they cross at the point where prices jump higher or lower.

If you place your order at the same point as everyone else, right at the previous highs or lows, you'll be unhappy with your execution price. Price will gap across the resistance level (see the breakout from pattern 1 in Figure 3.2), and you may get the high price. Instead, place your order slightly ahead of the breakout. If the prices jump up at the break, you will gain the *free exposure* profits. Chances are, once prices get close to the breakout point, they will go through. If not, close out your position and, if you're an active trader, wait for another chance. When trading, it's always better to be ahead of the crowd even if you're sometimes wrong.

Other Breakout Trading Rules

Whenever you find a successful set of trading rules, it is always good to look at other situations that are related. In the case of sideways patterns and breakouts, we should ask ourselves, "What can be done if prices remain sideways?" If we're a buyer, then we can write another set of rules for trading inside the range (longs only):

- If the ranges is sufficiently developed, then buy when prices approach the support line.
- Close out longs when prices approach the resistance line.
- Close out longs when prices close below the support line.

So, You Really Want to Know More About the Fat Tail and Why the Trend Works?

Price patterns are a mixture of short-, medium-, and long-term trends. These can be thought of as similar to runs of heads and tails when tossing a coin. We all know that these runs are random. The frequency of these runs is shown in Figure 3.9.

In a random distribution of 100 coin tosses:

- 50 will be a head or a tail followed by the opposite head or tail.
- 25 will be 2 heads or 2 tails in a row.
- 12½ (if we could have ½) will be 3 heads or 3 tails in a row.
- About 6 will be 4 heads or 4 tails in a row.
- About 3 will be 5 in a row.
- About 1 will be 6 in a row of either heads or tails.

You should have recognized that we keep halving the number of runs to get the frequency of the next longer run. That's a random distribution. Therefore, in 100 coin tosses we only expect 1 run of either 6 heads or 6 tails.

If these were prices, think of heads as a move up and tails as a move down. If the pattern of up and down price moves follows the distribution in Figure 3.9 (of course, they would have to go up and down by the same amount), then we could say they were random—but they're not. Price runs

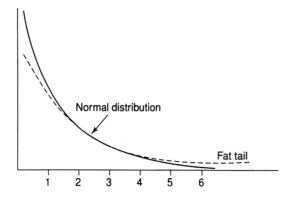

FIGURE 3.9 Distribution of runs. The solid line shows the normal distribution of random runs. The broken line represents the distribution when there is a fat tail. In the fat tail distribution there are fewer short runs and an unusually large number of longer runs.

have a fat tail. That means there are price runs that are much longer than expected. Instead of one run of 6 out of 100 days of trading, we may see a run of 12, or 3 runs of 6. That's not random and it's enough to make trend trading profitable. Figure 3.9 shows the fat tail distribution as a broken line. Compared to the normal distribution there are fewer short runs and an exceptionally large number of longer runs.

FINAL COMMENTS

Recognizing the trend is the most important technical tool for the trader. When trading the trend, it is easiest to profit from long-term trends, and more difficult as trends get shorter.

A Warning to Computer Experts

A valid trading technique must have a sound premise. It must simulate a real market situation. You cannot discover it by crunching numbers on a computer. Although a fast trend may be profitable during a computerized test, it is unlikely that it will put money in your pocket in real trading. It may not be possible to get your expected execution price.

Don't let short bursts of price movement fool you into thinking that they're trends. Although it may appear as though you could have made money in the past, you won't in the future. Stay with the longer trends that are based on economic activity, interest rates and political policy.

Don't Fall in Love with Your Trade

Get used to taking losses, it is an important part of trading. Don't take a loss personally—there are too many of them. We all want to be right. We want most of our trades to be profitable, and we want the losses to be very small. However, that's not the way it works, and a successful trader understands and accepts the way it works. Technical trading is a numbers game. You need to play for a while in order to make the numbers come out on your side. The discipline is not easy; you may find it the hardest part of trading.

What to Expect

Trend trading has a lot of false starts. It looks as though we're seeing the beginning of a trend, but prices don't follow through. So we get out and wait for the next chance. We take a small loss at least twice, maybe three or four times, before the trend really takes hold. Once the trend starts, we stay with it as long as possible. We finally get out with a large profit that is more than all the losses we took waiting for the trend.

If you don't accept a lot of small losses, you can't be a trend trader. There are a lot of small losses and a few big profits. There may also be a small profit instead of a loss, or a small loss instead of a profit, but in the long run the pattern of a few big profits will be seen. Trend trading is called *conservation of capital.* When prices go the wrong way, you get out with a small loss. You can afford to take small losses if you eventually get a big profit. Most important, it protects your trading capital.

QUESTIONS

1. What is a breakout?

2. Why does a breakout occur after a sideways price pattern?

3. If you buy when an upward breakout occurs, what is your initial risk in the trade?

4. What is a false breakout?

5. Explain when you would get a sell signal from a 20-day rolling breakout.

6. Explain why a technical trader might choose to use an *N*-day breakout instead of drawing classic trendlines on a chart.

7. How would you combine a penetration of a classic downward trendline with a breakout method?

8. Is the distribution of the length of trends random?

CHAPTER 4

Calculating the Trend

In the previous two chapters we've found the trend by charting. Now we'll look at different ways to calculate the trend. While we're doing this, remember that the purpose of fiddling with all these numbers is to uncover the correct direction of prices. In the same way that a chartist can be fooled by a false breakout, a calculated trend can give you the wrong answer because of the same false move. There is no perfect method; however, we're going to look for the one that has the best features for our type of trading.

There are four different and important trend calculations: moving averages, exponential (percentage) smoothing, regression slopes, and breakouts. Each appears to be different, but they all are searching for the correct trend direction.

MOVING AVERAGES

Of all the trend calculations, the moving average is by far the most popular. You see it on many of the charts shown on CNBC as a smoothed line running in a wavy pattern across the chart. The 200-day moving average seems to have become a benchmark for deciding that a particular stock or index is going up or down. If the price of the stock is above the 200-day moving average, then the trend is up.

A 10-day moving average is simply the average price over the past 10 days. Each moving average value is plotted on a chart under the most recent day used in the calculation. That's easy; everyone knows how to calculate an average. To do it faster, use the *average* function in your spreadsheet.

If t is today, and $t - 1$ is yesterday, then a five-day moving average is calculated as:

$$MA(t) = \frac{close(t) + close(t - 1) + close(t - 2) + close(t - 3) + close(t - 4)}{5}$$

In Excel, if the prices are in column A, rows 1 through 5, and the answer goes into cell B5. This calculation becomes:

$$B5 = average(A1:A5)$$

When you add a new day of data, it is easiest if you continue in A6 and calculate the new average (from A2 to A6) in cell B6.

Because today's value $MA(t)$ is plotted in the column t on a bar chart, it is below the current price when prices are rising (the most recent price will be above the average), and above the price when they are falling. Figure 4.1 shows three moving average trendlines plotted on an Enron chart. The line that stays closest to the prices is the fastest moving average (using the fewest number of days in the calculation), and the line that is farthest away (*lags* the most) is the slowest moving average. In this chart the fastest is a 20-week average, the middle is a 40-week, and the slowest is an 80-week. That's the same as 100-, 200-, and 400-day moving averages. (For ambitious Excel users, insert a block using *offset* if you want to try different moving average speeds without entering all new formulas.)

Trend Direction

Now that you've gone through the trouble of calculating the moving average, what's the trend? The easiest rule, and probably the best, is that an upward trend is in force when today's moving average value is above yesterday's value. The trend is down when today's moving average is below yesterday's. We use the direction of the trendline to decide the trend. We *do not* decide based on whether the price is above or below the trendline.

Longer Is Smoother

If you look at the difference between the 20-week and 80-week averages, you'll see that the 80-week is smoother. Naturally, when you use 80 weeks in the calculation, the effect of one or two odd weeks will be very small; therefore, the 80-week line has fewer irregularities and shows the smoothest trend.

Longer Is Less Responsive

The good news is that *longer is smoother*. The bad news is that *longer is later* in telling you that the trend has changed direction. In Figure 4.1 you can see the the turning points at the top of the trendlines move farther to the right as the trend gets slower. In the case of Enron, the faster 20-week average shows a few downturns as prices rise. The 40- and 80-day averages are both consistent in their direction, turning once at the top. The 80-day average is unnecessarily slow for this chart because it signals a price turn when prices fall below 50; the 40-week average turns down when prices fall below 70.

Choosing the trend that works best is always a compromise. You'll need to find the most acceptable balance between smoothness and speed. You'll need to learn more before you can make that choice.

Trading Rules for Trends

The best rules for trading the trend is to *buy* when the moving average turns up and *sell* when the moving average turns down. However, there are many

FIGURE 4.1   Enron with 20-, 40-, and 80-week moving averages. The 20-day average stays closest to prices and the 80-day lags the most. Although the 80-day is smoothest, it also is slowest to tell you that the trend has changed.

traders who find that method too slow. Instead they *buy* when prices move above the moving average and *sell* when they move below.

The problem with using a price penetration for buy and sell signals is that price can move back and forth through the moving average for a number of days before taking off in one direction. In Figure 4.1, both the slowest and medium trends have this problem. There are some added rules that can be used to avoid this, but those rules also have problems. Why go through the trouble of more complicated rules when you end up at the same place?

Two Microsoft Examples.   If we take a similar period for Microsoft (MSFT), 1995–2001 (see Figure 4.2), we see much the same pattern as Enron. The 20-, 40-, and 80-week averages have one primary upward trend and one downward trend. Neither the 40- or 80-week averages has any false trend signals, while the 20-week is much more erratic than in the Enron example. Longer is smoother.

The daily chart of Microsoft shown in Figure 4.3 uses days rather than weeks for the moving average calculations. The 20-, 40-, and 80-day moving

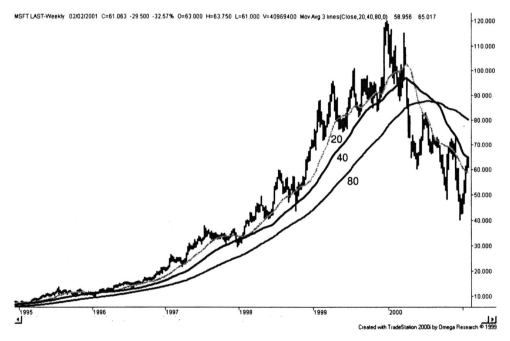

FIGURE 4.2   Microsoft weekly chart, 1995–2001. The 20-, 40-, and 80-week averages show a pattern similar to Enron.

MSFT LAST-Daily 01/31/2001 C=61 063 -29 500 -32 57% O=63 000 H=63.750 L=61.000 V=40969400 Mov Avg 3 lines(Close,20,40,80,0) 56.400 53.389 58.592

Created with TradeStation 2000i by Omega Research © 1999

FIGURE 4.3 Microsoft with 20-, 40-, and 80-day moving averages. Because daily data is much noisier than weekly data, none of the moving averages are as smooth as the weekly ones in Figure 4.2.

averages are all much faster than the fastest weekly average (20 weeks is equivalent to 100 days); therefore, the trendlines track the prices closely and have frequent changes in direction.

In the daily chart, all of the moving averages seem to catch a good part of each trend. The 20-day average has a series of shorter trades, while the 80-day average has fewer, larger, and longer trades. The 80-day seems to do the best, holding the downtrend for the entire move lower. However, how do we know that the results of the 80-day average are better than the 20-day? Even though the 20-day has a few bad trades, the total of all buys and sells using the faster trend might be greater than the 80-day result.

To find out which trend is the best, you'll need to add up all the trades. In addition, you'll want to know which trend has the largest loss. Both the amount of profit and the size of the risk decide the best trend.

Conservation of Capital.   Before showing the actual trades generated by a moving average system, you should know that a trend system is a *conservation of capital* approach. It takes many small losses and has a few large

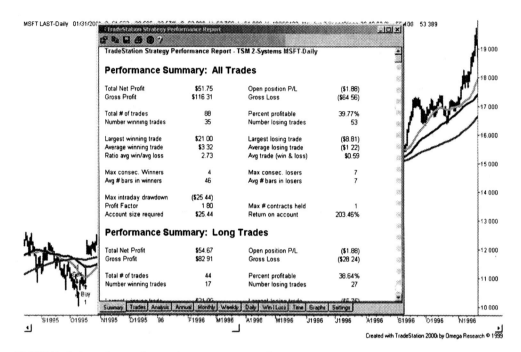

FIGURE 4.4   Microsoft moving average performance statistics.

profits. The small losses occur when we enter a new trade and prices turn and go the wrong way. The moving average trend changes within one or two days, and we close out the trade with a small loss. Taking a small loss is called conservation of capital.

Results of an 80-Day Moving Average Applied to Microsoft.   Figure 4.4 shows a summary of the trades for Microsoft using an 80-day moving average for the 10 years ending January 2001. This system traded both the long and short side There were a total of 88 trades, of which 36 were profitable, only about 40 percent. That's actually good for a trend system which often has closer to 35 percent good trades. Total profits were $51.75, which means an average trade made $0.59 before commissions.

An interesting result in this trend system is that there are 7 bars (in this case "bars" mean "days") in the losing trades and 46 bars in the winning trades. That shows the system is holding onto profits and cutting losses short. Also, the average winning trade yielded $3.32, and the average loss was $1.22. The losses are smaller and the losing trades are exited faster than the profitable trades—it must be a trend system. Study the trades in Figure 4.5 to see a typical trend performance.

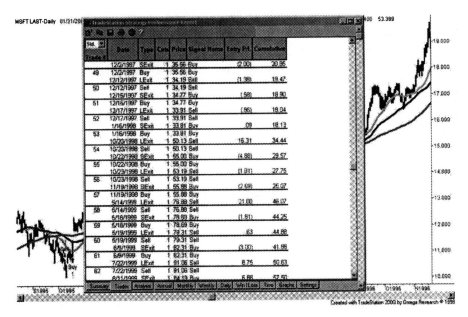

FIGURE 4.5   **Microsoft moving average sample trades.**

EXPONENTIAL (PERCENTAGE) SMOOTHING

Moving averages are not the only way to smooth prices. *Exponential smoothing* is another simple technique that came out of the aerospace industry. It was a way of calculating the trajectory of a missile. The name is the most complicated part of it. If we had called it *percentage smoothing*, it would not sound as intimidating. Never let the mathematicians name something.

If you want a trendline smoothed by 20 percent, then each day you bring the last trendline value closer to the last closing price by 20 percent of the distance between the two values. For example, if yesterday's trendline value was $50, today's price is $60, and your smoothing is 20 percent, then the new trendline value is:

New exponential value = old exponential value

$$+ 0.20 \times (\text{today's price} - \text{old exponential value})$$
$$= 50 + 0.20 \times (60 - 50)$$
$$= 50 + 2$$
$$= 52$$

A 20 percent smoothing causes the trendline to move closer by $2 when the new closing price is $10 away from the previous trendline value. That's 20 percent of $10, the difference between $60 and $50. One of the good points

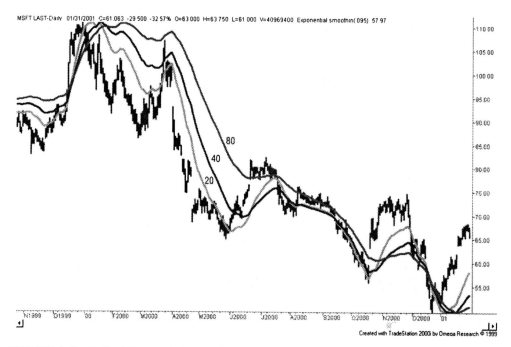

FIGURE 4.6   Daily Microsoft chart with percentage smoothing equivalent to 20-, 40-, and 80-day moving averages. The trendlines seem a bit more sensitive than the moving average equivalent because the smoothing is a front-weighted method; moving average is equally weighted.

of exponential smoothing is that it only needs the value of the previous trend-line, the new price, and a smoothing (percentage) value (see Figure 4.6). A moving average needs as many prices as the length of the average. The rules for trading a smoothed trendline are the same as those for a moving average. You trade in the direction of the trendline.

Finding a Moving Average and Smoothing Percentage That Gives the Same Trendline

Although the calculations seem very different, we can come close to finding a moving average trendline and a smoothed trendline that are very similar. Beginning with the number of days in the moving average calculation, we can find the equivalent smoothing value using the formula:

$$\text{Exponential smoothing percentage} = \frac{2}{(\text{moving average calculation period} + 1)}$$

Then a 20-day moving average has an equivalent smoothing percentage of $2/21$ = 0.095, a 40-day moving average is $2/41$ = 0.049, and an 80-day moving average is $2/81$ = 0.0247.

An advantage of smoothing is that you can select values that represent a 2.5-day moving average while it is impossible to actually average 2.5 days using daily data. If we want to go from smoothing to a moving average, we can reverse the formula:

$$\text{Moving average calculation period} = \frac{2}{\text{exponential smoothing percentage} - 1}$$

Smoothing Gives More Importance to Recent Price Moves

The important difference between a moving average and smoothing is that smoothing gives greater importance to the most recent data. Think of a 10 percent smoothing as the same as a company continually diluting itself by giving 10 percent of the total company to each new shareholder. If there are 20 original shareholders, each with 5 percent of the company, and a new shareholder gets 10 percent, then each of the 20 original shareholders ends up with 4.5 percent (10 percent less) and the new shareholder has 10 percent.

If another shareholder is now issued 10 percent, the original shareholders are diluted to 4.05 percent, the previous 10 percent owner now has 9 percent, and the new shareholder has 10 percent. Each time a new shareholder is added at 10 percent, all previous shareholders are diluted by 10 percent. The most recent addition will always have 10 percent, the previous one 9 percent, the one before that 8.1 percent, then 7.29 percent, and so on. This type of trend is also called *front-weighted*.

REGRESSION SLOPES

A *regression line* is the "best" straight line drawn through the prices to show the direction. The angle up or down is the *slope* of the line. It is the method used by economists and is similar to our charting trendlines except that it is drawn through the center of the price move rather than across the highs and lows. The calculation of the slope takes more time than we would like; therefore, it's best to use the function *slope* on a spreadsheet and follow the example at end of this chapter.

When you draw a trendline on a daily chart, *the slope of that line is the amount that it rises or falls each day.* For example, if we draw a rising line for IBM that goes from $50 to $70 over 20 days, the slope of that line is 1 ($1 increase per day). If it falls to $60 over the next 20 days, then the slope during that period was –0.50 (50¢ decline per day).

MSFT LAST-Daily 01/31/2001 C=61.063 -29.500 -32.57% O=63.000 H=63.750 L=61.000 V=40969400

Created with TradeStation 2000i by Omega Research © 1999

FIGURE 4.7 Microsoft daily chart with regression lines of about 6 months. Each line shows the direction of prices during the period and runs through the middle of the price movement.

Figure 4.7 gives an example of regression lines drawn at different points in time. Each line includes about six months and runs through the middle of the price pattern.

When we use the slope for trading, we are only interested in the most recent slope value. If the slope is rising, then the trend is up; if it is falling, then the trend is down. We use it in the same way as the previous trends. A chart of the slope is shown in Figure 4.8 along the bottom of the chart and also in the top part of the chart. Because each point of the slope is measured over the previous six months, the daily increase or decrease in price is very small. When MSFT declines from $120 to $60 (December 1999–June 2000), the daily slope was –0.40 (an average of 40¢ per day).

The slope has small values that the can be both positive and negative based on whether the regression line is angling up or down; therefore, it is very different from prices and cannot be plotted on the same chart scale. The trendline on the price chart is drawn to give you an idea of what the slope would be at different points. The slope value that we want is the angle of the line as it changes each day. The line plotted along the bottom shows the true slope. The angle of the line is rising when the slope value is above zero and

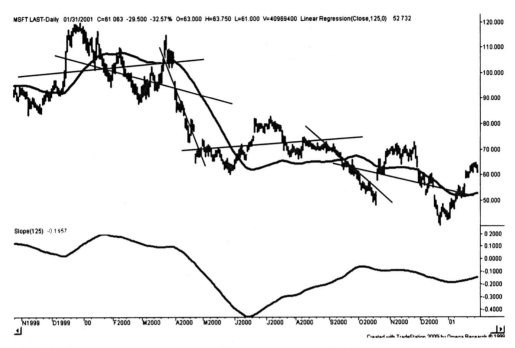

FIGURE 4.8 Microsoft with slope. The last point of the 125-day regression line is plotted on the price chart, and the slope value is plotted along the bottom.

falling when it is below zero. The larger the value, the stronger the upward price move.

Although the slope seems to be falling from January to June of 2000, *it is actually rising at a slower rate* from January to May. Any slope value above zero means that prices are rising. When it crosses the zero line, it then indicates that prices are falling.

BREAKOUTS

We have already discussed the *N*-day breakout in Chapter 3. It is both a very popular and very reliable way of identifying the trend. To review the trading rules:

Breakout Rule 1

> *Buy* on an upward penetration of the highest high of the past *N* days
> *Sell* on a downward penetration of the lowest low of the past *N* days

There are alternative rules that are considered more conservative and avoid entering on days when there is a higher high but prices close back inside the trading range. This situation is potentially a false breakout, and can be avoided with Rule 2.

Breakout Rule 2

> *Buy* when prices *close* above the highest high of the past *N* days.
> *Sell* when prices *close* below the lowest low of the past *N* days.

The drawback of Rule 2 is that it may keep you out while prices are moving steadily higher or lower. That leads to Rule 3.

Breakout Rule 3

> *Buy* if there is an *N*-day high and today's close is higher than yesterday's close.
> *Sell* if there is an *N*-day low and today's close is lower than yesterday's close.

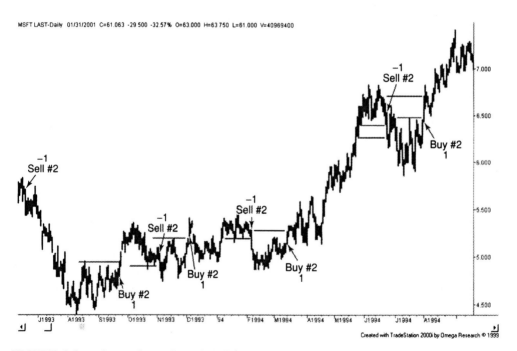

FIGURE 4.9   Microsoft trading signals using a 20-day breakout. Lines have been drawn at the points where the breakouts occur. As with other trend methods, it takes more small losses and a few large profits.

Of the three rules, Rule 3 may be the best compromise. It avoids false breakouts and gets a confirmation from the higher closing price.

Figure 4.9 shows the Microsoft buy and sell signals using a 20-day breakout. Lines have been drawn across the chart at the point where a trading signals occurs.

WHICH OF THE FOUR TRENDING METHODS IS BEST?

Now that we've looked at the four most important trending techniques, we naturally want to know which is best. To get that answer, we need to use special testing software that will give us the results of trading the trends for calculation periods from 5 to 200 days. This way we can see which methods work best for faster or slower trading, and which work best in general over the entire range of tests.

Table 4.1 gives the results of testing Microsoft for five years ending January 2002. This period has a strong bull market at the beginning, changing to a volatile sideways pattern and then lower prices towards the end of the period. Some of the important features to notice are:

- Except for the calculation periods from $20 to $55, all tests were profitable. It is interesting to note that the range $20 to $55 is the most popular for trend followers.
- Profits all were made with long positions rather than shorts. Long positions had the largest losses using averages in the range of 45 to 50 days; the shorts were only profitable in the range of 10 to 15 days. That's because price drops are shorter and more volatile than price rises. In order to profit on the short side, you need to trade quickly and get out. Because the market has a long-term history of reaching new highs, slower trends work better for long positions.
- The average profit from a trade gets larger as the trend gets slower. Fast trading in the range from 10 to 15 days may look attractive, but an average return of 29¢ to 38¢ per trade can be eaten up quickly with commissions and a few bad executions in a fast market.
- The profit factor (gross profits divided by gross losses) get much higher as the trend gets slower. The profit factor measures the smoothness of the returns, although this measure only looks at the returns after the trade is closed. Still, it argues that *slower is better*, as do many of the other values.

| | TABLE 4.1 | | Results of Backtesting a Moving Average for Microsoft over the Five Years Ending January 2002 | | | | | | |

Period	NetPrft	L:NetPrft	S:NetPrft	#Trds	%Prft	Avg W/L	AvgTrd	MaxDD	PFact
5	1.16	29.69	−28.53	535	30	2.29	0.00	−47.92	1.00
10	97.08	71.11	25.97	338	28	4.12	0.29	−20.45	1.63
15	102.90	75.96	26.94	274	31	4.02	0.38	−22.50	1.84
20	−25.78	12.18	−37.96	246	23	2.78	−0.11	−67.12	0.86
25	−16.95	20.63	−37.58	192	28	2.22	−0.09	−42.37	0.89
30	−67.26	−4.53	−62.73	212	24	1.90	−0.32	−75.24	0.62
35	−1.39	28.19	−29.58	212	25	2.90	−0.01	−36.50	0.99
40	−61.31	−0.36	−60.94	182	24	2.05	−0.34	−86.32	0.65
45	−73.87	−10.61	−63.26	185	23	1.88	−0.40	−99.83	0.59
50	−73.79	−13.73	−60.07	151	21	2.06	−0.49	−124.12	0.55
55	−39.50	12.33	−51.83	149	23	2.30	−0.27	−83.89	0.71
60	14.23	32.16	−17.93	145	26	3.05	0.10	−76.68	1.12
65	2.50	30.36	−27.86	147	27	2.72	0.02	−93.41	1.02
70	75.46	66.84	8.62	103	32	4.69	0.73	−21.92	2.21
75	42.33	50.27	−7.94	116	25	4.29	0.37	−28.99	1.50
80	47.72	53.93	−6.21	102	34	3.24	0.47	−26.01	1.69
85	59.10	58.66	0.44	97	37	3.29	0.61	−18.14	1.94
90	44.15	52.90	−8.76	79	35	3.23	0.56	−32.78	1.77
95	50.46	57.87	−7.41	79	24	6.39	0.64	−38.01	2.02
100	-9.71	27.85	−37.56	89	15	4.89	−0.11	−80.03	0.91
105	27.48	46.00	−18.53	89	25	3.68	0.31	−66.50	1.28
110	76.18	71.20	4.98	61	18	13.05	1.25	−24.70	2.87
115	78.90	71.53	7.37	51	23	11.98	1.55	−16.81	3.69
120	56.83	60.49	−3.66	63	20	8.75	0.90	−20.21	2.27
125	59.64	60.93	−1.29	65	27	5.61	0.92	−31.16	2.15
130	53.61	54.07	−0.46	79	30	4.20	0.68	−30.38	1.83
135	76.42	70.29	6.13	65	30	7.36	1.18	−11.38	3.27
140	65.05	63.63	1.42	63	26	7.80	1.03	−15.20	2.88
145	85.15	74.65	10.50	55	29	9.85	1.55	−11.71	4.04
150	116.95	90.55	26.40	41	43	11.99	2.85	−7.05	9.38
155	81.13	83.42	−2.30	35	45	7.84	2.32	−14.46	6.60
160	62.10	72.66	−10.56	31	25	10.90	2.00	−17.94	3.79
165	42.80	61.91	−19.12	37	27	5.51	1.16	−29.23	2.04
170	52.98	55.60	−2.62	37	27	5.61	1.43	−38.25	2.08
175	71.75	76.39	−4.64	27	25	13.75	2.66	−17.03	4.81
180	84.24	86.14	−1.90	31	29	63.21	2.72	−2.73	25.86
185	84.26	86.15	−1.88	19	26	73.48	4.44	−3.43	26.24
190	84.31	86.17	−1.86	17	29	64.87	4.96	−2.89	27.03
195	80.65	82.09	−1.44	19	21	113.17	4.25	−3.00	30.18
200	77.35	79.19	−1.84	13	23	36.38	5.95	−6.11	10.91

Explanation of columns: (1) calculation period, (2) net profit, (3) profits from long trades, (4) profits from short trades, (5) number of trades, (6) percentage of profitable trades, (7) average win/loss ratio, (8) average profits per trade, (9) maximum drawdown, and (10) profit factor (gross profits divided by gross losses).

Comparing the Results of the Four Trends

The same tests that are shown in Table 4.1 for the moving average were performed on the other three trending methods, smoothing, regression slope, and breakouts. The net profits of the four methods are shown together in Figure 4.10. The left scale is the net profit and the bottom scale is the calculation periods from 5 through 200 days.

Let's not look at the chart too closely. You should see that the overall pattern of profitability is very similar for all four trend methods. All the lines move together. Sometimes one is a little better, sometimes another, but all of them peak at 15 days, drop to lows at about 35 days, and then move steadily higher.

The Importance of Similar Results

Let's look at the big picture for a moment. Figure 4.10 says that, if a market has price trends, then any of the trending methods should make money. That's important. Each of these four methods is technically very different, as we'll see in the next section; nevertheless, the final picture is the same.

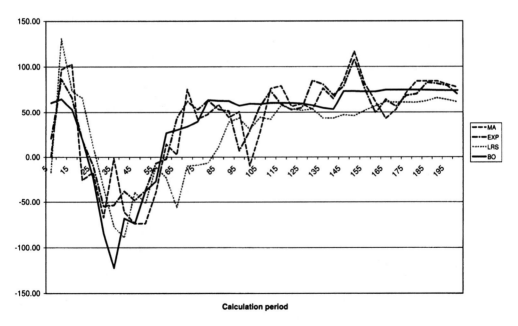

FIGURE 4.10 Net profits of four trending methods. When viewing the big picture, all four methods have very similar results over all calculation periods.

When you're searching for the best trend for the market that you want to trade and you find that the breakout method gives reasonable profits but the moving average and smoothing methods lose money, then don't trade the trend. You need a market with clear trends, not subtle ones, to have confidence that trend following will work. Don't think you've discovered a secret because only one method works. It was just an odd combination of price patterns that is not likely to be repeated in the future.

The Differences between Trending Methods

Now we can look at the features that make one trending method different from another.

Profits per Trade.   Both the *N*-day breakout and the regression slope have noticeably larger profits per trade than the moving average or smoothing methods (see Figure 4.11). Larger profits per trade are safer for trading, but it is necessary to take larger risks in order to have larger profits. We've seen that the moving average and smoothing techniques cut losses short, while the

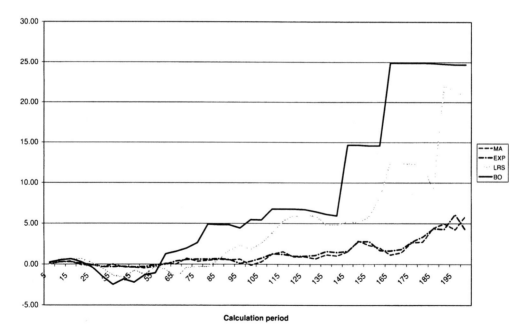

FIGURE 4.11   Comparison of profits per trade. The breakout and slope methods show much larger profits per trade than the moving average and smoothing techniques. In order to get the same result, the breakout and slope techniques must take more risk.

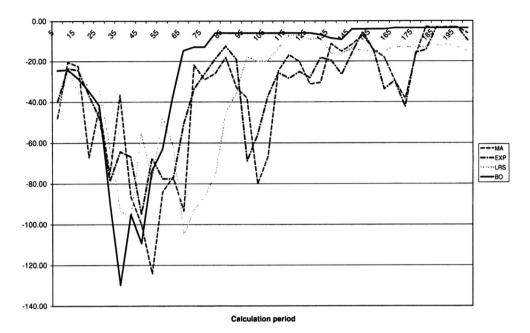

FIGURE 4.12   Comparison of maximum drawdowns. There is an overall similar pattern, but the *N*-day breakout shows slightly larger losses in the short term and smaller losses in the long term.

breakout and slope techniques allow prices to flop around in a wide range in order to hold onto the trend. This difference in style can be seen in the larger profits per trade for the breakout and slope methods.

Drawdowns.   The *maximum drawdown* is the peak-to-valley drop in equity, measured from day to day, rather than only when the trades are closed out. In Figure 4.12 we again see a similar overall pattern of drawdowns in the four systems, although the *N*-day breakout has a slightly larger loss than the others when trading faster.

Number of Trades.   The frequency of trading is another significant difference in the style of the four techniques. When there are fewer trades, each trade must be held for a longer time, resulting in net larger profits and losses and larger equity swings. In Figure 4.13 we can see that the moving average and smoothing methods are similar in the way the number of trades decline as the calculation periods get larger (the trend gets slower). The moving average and smoothing techniques have many more trades than either the breakout or slope methods because no matter what speed is used, the moving

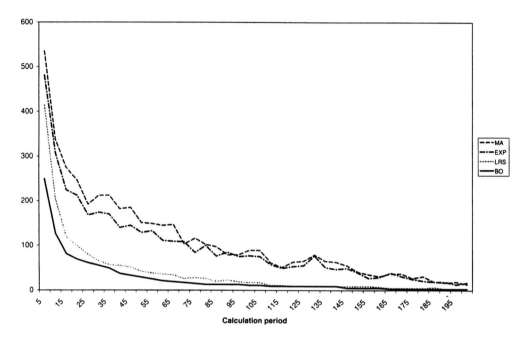

FIGURE 4.13 **Number of trades comparison.** The moving average and smoothing methods always have more trades than either the breakout or slope techniques because moving averages will give a series of false signals during many of the trend changes.

average will get caught in a trend change that moves back and forth across the trendline, causing a series of false signals. False signals are a fundamental part of the moving average approach and can't be eliminated.

Percentage of Profitable Trades. The last important quality of the systems is the percentage of profitable trades. We can see the similarity of the moving average and smoothing methods in Figure 4.14, each posting slightly above 30 percent at best, and falling to lower reliability as the number of trades decline for slower trends. Even when the moving average is calculated over a long time period in order to capture the major trend, it still produces a series of false signals at the trend change. When there are only a few good trends, these false signals become a larger percentage of the total number of trades. As discussed earlier, this pattern is called *conservation of capital.*

The breakout system is just the opposite. When a long time period is used, the highest high and lowest low are very far apart. It is unlikely that there will be more than one or two trades, and each trade will be held through a wide range of price movements, most often yielding a net profit.

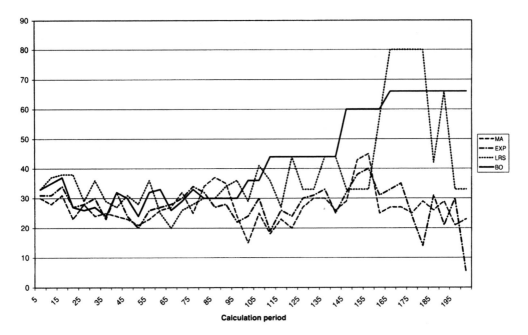

FIGURE 4.14 **Percentage of profitable trades comparison.** The breakout system gets more reliable for long-term trends, while the moving average and smoothing methods continue to generate false signals at trend turns.

The percentage of profitable trades goes up for the breakout system when you hold the trade longer, but the risk also goes up.

Summary of Trend Characteristics

Net profits	All systems have very similar net profits.
Profits per trade	All increase, but the *N*-day breakout is 5 times larger than the moving average or smoothing methods.
Maximum drawdown	Similar for all methods, but more uniform for the slope and *N*-day breakout.
Number of trades	*N*-day breakout and slope have less than half the number of trades of the moving average or smoothing methods.
Percentage of profitable trades	Both moving average and smoothing decline, the slope method is erratic, and the *N*-day breakout is uniformly higher.

Which is best? It's the one with the *highest ratio of returns to risk.* The best trading method is always the one that gives the largest return for the smallest amount of risk.

What You Need to Remember

Identifying the trend is the most important single element of technical analysis, no matter how you choose to use it. If you're going to be profitable trading the trend, then any one of the four methods will work. The choice of method should not turn a loss into a profit.

The *N*-day breakout has the best overall characteristics although it has the higher risk on individual trades. The moving average method is the best choice if small losses are important to you.

Remember that the trend works because it capitalizes on the distribution of price movement called the *fat tail.* Price patterns have fewer short runs (one day up or down followed by the opposite price move) and more longer runs (more than 10 ups or downs in a row). Price movement is not distributed randomly.

Calculating the Methods on a Spreadsheet

All four trending methods can be easily calculated on a spreadsheet. You can use the trend direction to create a long or short trading signal. Figure 4.15 is an Excel spreadsheet that uses Microsoft prices for calculating the four trends over a 10-day period (columns F, G, H, and M) and shows the market positions that should be held for each system (columns J, K, L, and M). The formulas are shown so that you can do your own comparison.

TRADE ON THE CLOSE, NOT ON THE NEXT OPEN

You'll find it very convenient to do all your calculations after the market closes, and then have your orders ready for the next morning. Don't do that.

Placing your orders on the close by calculating the trendlines just before the close of trading puts you ahead of almost everyone else. You always need to be ahead, not behind. If prices have crossed an important resistance line on the close, then you'll see prices jump higher on the next open. Entering your trade before that jump gives you *free exposure.* Take advantage of it.

(A)	(B)	(C)	(D)	(E)	(F)	(G)	(H)	(I)	(J)	(K)	(L)	(M)
		Microsoft prices and volume			10	10	10			Trading signals		
Date	High	Low	Close	Volume	MA	EXP	LRS		MA	EXP	LRS	NDB
19990201	87.969	85.406	86.469	40864600				1				
19990202	86.281	83.125	83.813	45982800				2				Short
19990203	84.938	83.000	83.406	36874600				3				Short
19990204	84.188	79.438	79.531	44575800				4				Short
19990205	80.813	77.438	80.000	63972600				5				Short
19990208	82.781	80.813	82.625	54933400				6				Short
19990209	83.375	79.875	80.031	38646800				7				Short
19990210	82.188	79.313	80.313	36847000				8				Short
19990211	81.938	80.188	81.375	30183000		81.38		9				Short
19990212	81.844	78.563	78.875	31465200	81.64	80.92	-0.942	10	Short	Short	Short	Short
19990216	79.938	77.281	78.125	36833400	80.81	80.41	-1.126	11	Short	Short	Short	Short
19990217	77.063	74.250	75.000	50607800	79.93	79.43	-0.938	12	Short	Short	Short	Short
19990218	75.688	71.992	72.875	58517600	78.88	78.24	-0.778	13	Short	Short	Short	Short
19990219	74.625	72.875	73.875	36542800	78.31	77.44	-0.801	14	Short	Short	Short	Short
19990222	74.500	72.375	74.406	46257200	77.75	76.89	-0.809	15	Short	Short	Short	Short
19990223	77.813	75.250	77.719	47553400	77.26	77.04	-0.742	16	Long	Long	Short	Short
19990224	79.688	76.375	76.438	33848400	76.90	76.93	-0.668	17	Short	Short	Short	Short
19990225	76.875	74.813	76.750	35408600	76.54	76.90	-0.510	18	Long	Short	Short	Short
19990226	76.250	74.750	75.063	29636600	75.91	76.57	-0.309	19	Short	Short	Short	Short
19990301	76.281	74.750	75.875	29166000	75.61	76.44	0.208	20	Long	Short	Long	Short
19990302	77.063	73.813	74.281	29284800	75.23	76.05	0.675	21	Short	Short	Long	Short
19990303	75.344	73.531	74.813	38399200	75.21	75.82	0.511	22	Short	Short	Long	Short
19990304	76.750	74.063	76.125	30848200	75.53	75.88	0.091	23	Long	Long	Long	Short
19990305	77.688	76.563	77.469	23651400	75.89	76.17	0.062	24	Long	Long	Long	Short
19990308	79.617	77.500	79.500	23363000	76.40	76.77	0.408	25	Long	Long	Long	Short
19990309	82.375	79.875	80.906	45064800	76.72	77.52	0.926	26	Long	Long	Long	Long
19990310	81.250	79.594	80.688	26557400	77.15	78.10	0.991	27	Long	Long	Long	Long
19990311	82.281	79.656	80.719	31474200	77.54	78.58	1.037	28	Long	Long	Long	Long
19990312	81.375	78.406	80.094	36697600	78.05	78.85	1.039	29	Long	Long	Long	Long
19990315	83.000	78.938	82.938	30304800	78.75	79.59	0.977	30	Long	Long	Long	Long

Price/average formulas:

"MA=@average(D3:D12)"
"EXP=G11+(2/(G1+1))*(D12-G11)"
"LRS=@slope(I3:I12,D3:D12)"

Signal formulas:

"MA=if(D13>F13,"L","S")"
"EXP=if(D13>F13,"L","S")"
"LRS=if(H13>0,"L","S")"
"NDB=if(B13>max(B3:B12),"L","
" if(C13<min(C13:c12),"S",M12)

FIGURE 4.15 Excel spreadsheet showing the calculations for the four trend methods.

Can We Figure Out, in Advance, When the Moving Average Will Change Direction?

Of course, and it's a surprisingly simple calculation. If you're using a 10-day moving average, simply calculate the value of the 9-day moving average (leaving off the oldest day). That value is the turning point. If today's prices are higher, the trendline will turn up; if today's price is lower, the trendline will turn down. For any moving average, just remove the oldest day and take the average of the remaining days to get the critical turning point. That will help anticipate where you will go long or short just before the close. Remember:

Moving average turning point = average of closing prices over $N - 1$ days

where N is the calculation period you are using for your moving average.

What if You're Wrong?

Sometimes it looks as though the trend will definitely turn up 10 minutes before the close and then *wham!*, big selling on the close forces prices down and the trend doesn't turn up. You've already bought. Just close out your trade on the next open. It sounds awful, but prices don't usually make a severe move in the last 10 minutes of trading. More often they just languish and drift lower, just missing your trend signal. You can get out in the morning with little price change.

Over time you'll find that anticipating the trend change is much more profitable, even when you're wrong a few times. Always move ahead of the other traders.

WHICH TREND SPEEDS WORK AND WHY THEY WORK

Choosing a trend speed is not a random event. There is a big picture that must be understood in order to be successful in the long run.

We first need to be aware of *market noise*. Noise is the erratic up and down movement that results from the high volume of trading by investors, all whom have different objectives. Not all buying and selling is done by high-tech traders and bank dealing rooms, each trying to get the most profit out of each position. Much of the stock market activity reflects movement of pension money by big funds. As money flows in and out, these funds must adjust their positions within a few days. Other activity may be the result of investors liquidating part of their portfolio to have cash for a new house, or some other unrelated market event. In futures markets, many of the transactions are for hedging financial commitments, that is, reducing risk exposure, rather than for profitable returns.

This buying and selling, not focused on making a killing in the market, causes *noise*. When there is a lot of noise you can get false trend signals. Prices move quickly higher, causing the moving average to turn up. Prices then fall back to their original level, and the moving average turns back down.

The Relationship Between the Moving Average Speed and Market Noise

The slower the moving average, the less it is going to be fooled by noise. The longer calculation period makes a single day less important and the average more able to hold onto the longer-term direction.

Some markets have more noise that others. The high-volume index markets have the most noise and, if you're going to find the trend, you'll need to take a very long view of those price moves. Foreign exchange markets and stock sectors have less noise and can be traded with a somewhat faster trend (medium speed is considered to be 25 to 60 days).

If you use a very fast trend, then you'll want to take profits as often as possible since noise causes prices to change direction unexpectedly, as seen in Figure 4.10. If you can't expect prices to trend, then you must take profits often.

To summarize the way you need to look at a trading method based on long-term and short-term trends, remember that the short term is strongly influenced by noise, while the long term makes noise appear less important:

Short-Term Trend	**Long-Term Trend**
Noise dominates short-term price movement.	Noise is small compared to the length of the trend.
Take profits often because noise causes sudden changes of direction.	Stay with the trend, and don't take profits. Take advantage of the fat tail.
Expect many small profits and a few large losses.	Expect many small losses and a few large profits.
Use daily or intraday data.	Use daily or weekly data.

TREND PROFITS USING DIFFERENT TREND SPEEDS

To see that trend trading works best for slower trends—longer calculation periods—we can look at a summary of trading results for Eurodollar futures

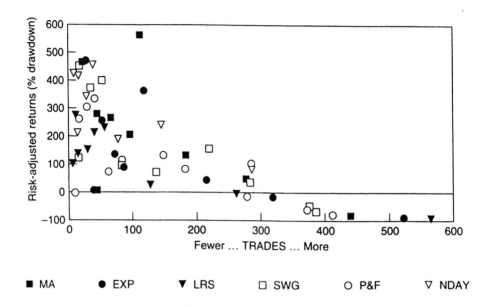

FIGURE 4.16 Eurodollar results using six trending methods. Faster trends have more trades and their results are farther to the right. Regardless of the trend method, profits are consistent with slower trends. As trends become faster, none of the systems are profitable.

in Figure 4.16. The risk-adjusted returns, return divided by risk, are shown on the left, and the number of trades for a 10-year period are shown along the bottom. The more trades, moving from left to right, the faster the trend.

Six trending methods are used in Figure 4.16: moving average (MA), exponential smoothing (EXP), linear regression slope (LRS), swing (SWG), point-and-figure (P&F), and *N*-day breakout (NDAY). The results clearly show that as any system trades faster (more trades), the results turn to losses. It is not a matter of selecting the best method—there is no best method for trading fast with a trend. It just doesn't work.

HOW MANY DAYS OF PRICE HISTORY DO YOU USE TO TEST A TREND?

If you're using a computer, use as much data as possible to test your trend system—or any trading method. When there is more data, there are more price patterns and more chance that the trend will see good times and bad times.

Even when you use 10 or 20 years of daily price history, you still may not have all the patterns. Be sure you include the market crash in 1987. You need to see how your trend would have fared during as many bad scenarios as possible.

Be sure your data includes a bull market, a bear market, and a sideways market. That might be a problem for U.S. Treasury bonds, because they've only gone up for the past 20 years (that is, rates have dropped).

Do the best you can. Just remember that *more data is better.*

A COMPARISON OF FAST AND SLOW TRENDING METHODS

Think about how fast or slow trading interacts with price movement:

Slow Trading	Fast Trading
Emphasizes the trend	Sees mostly market noise
Must let profits run	Needs to take profits often
Has large profits	Takes larger losses than profits
Has frequent losses	Has frequent profits
Best with weekly-monthly data	Best with hourly-daily data

Price noise prevents you from seeing the trend; you need to view the bigger picture of longer-term prices to overcome market noise.

LEARNING FROM THE PAST

Moving averages were used before computers and before electronic calculators. Because it took time to calculate longer averages by hand, the 10-day average was the most popular. All you needed to do was add 10 numbers and move the decimal point one place to the left. Besides the 10-day average, the 5-day and 20-day averages were the most common. Traders believed that the average of the week and month were most important. They were probably right.

Rather than use a computer to test every possible moving average speed looking for the most profitable, why not decide which calculation period makes the most sense? Weekly is good, monthly is good, and perhaps quarterly is even better. For stocks, most of the reporting is quarterly.

Perhaps the market simply flops around in between but must come true to its direction each quarter. Monthly might also be good because many of the government economic reports are issued monthly and pension funds must add and withdraw by the end of a month. Why not use something logical? By the way, for calculation purposes, a trading month has 21 days.

Questions

1. Using the following S&P index prices from November 2002:

   908.35, 915.36, 923.76, 902.57, 894.73, 876.19, 882.95, 882.53, 904.27, 909.81, 900.36, 896.74, 914.15, 933.79, 930.55, 932.87, 913.31, 938.87, 936.31, 934.53

   a. What are the last three values of a 10-day moving average?
   b. Is the trend going up or down?
   c. What would be the next price in order to change the direction of the trend?

2. Which trend will change direction first—a 10-day moving average or a 20-day moving average?

3. With percentage smoothing, the most recent price changes are given (a) less importance, (b) the same importance, or (c) more importance than previous price changes?

4. If today's closing price is $50, yesterday's trendline value was $40, and you are using a percentage smoothing of 10 percent, what is today's trendline value?

5. When the slope of a regression line is greater than zero, are prices rising or falling?

6. What is the daily slope of a regression line that rises 10 points in five days?

7. When the slope values today and yesterday are both 1.5, are prices rising, unchanged, or falling?

8. If yesterday's slope value was 1.5 and today's slope value is 1.0, are prices rising, unchanged, or falling?

9. Using a moving average to trade, when do you get a buy signal? A sell signal?

10. Using a breakout system, the previous 10-day high was $30.50 and the previous 10-day low was $28.50. Prices break out to the upside and you buy 100 shares at $31.00. What is the risk of your trade in dollars?

11. Which of the four trending methods, moving average, smoothing, breakout, or slope,
    a. Is usually most reliable?
    b. Has the smallest losses?
    c. Has the largest losses?

12. If the moving average method produced good profits when you checked its performance on the history of IBM, but none of the other trending methods were profitable, would you trade IBM using the moving average? Why?

13. You've just read an advertisement for a trend system that has 80 percent profitable trades and very low risk. What's wrong with that statement?

CHAPTER 5

The Trading Game

A Brief Review and a Little Extra

- The reason for using a trendline or moving average is to get an objective assessment of the price direction.
- Disciplined trading is most important because it clearly tells you when to get out of your trade and take your loss.
- You can't follow the trend and take profits at the same time. Profit-taking works with short-term trading, but *profit-taking fights with the long-term trend.* You can't hold onto a trend trade to get a big profit and at the same time take a small profit when things go your way for a few days. You'll need the big profits to offset lots of small losses.
- Trend analysis says (à la Yogi Berra) *the market is going up when it is going up.* There's no hocus pocus. Fundamentals, or value investing, may say that the company is in great shape while prices are falling. You'll do much better trading technically.

Y ou now know enough to start trading—that is, paper trading. You can't learn everything from reading; you need to make trading decisions and see what works best for you. Everyone must develop their own trading style—fast, slow, conservative, or aggressive. This experience is as important as anything else you might get out of this course. Although we've only learned about trendlines and calculated trends, they are the most important techniques for trading, and for now, that's what we'll use.

During this course there will be three trading games, each one loosening the rules to allow more natural trading. At all times you can apply any trading techniques that you've learned, whether in this course or from others, but don't go outside the other rules for each game. The object is to learn how to make these tools work for you.

From now on, at the end of each chapter, we'll review the trading problems that you might have encountered. You'll see that you're not the only one that makes mistakes. Remember that you can't learn to trade without taking losses, and it's best to learn from those losses now, before you try it with your own money.

OBJECT OF THE GAME

We have some ambitious goals for the trading game:

1. Apply technical analysis correctly.
2. Achieve the highest returns with the lowest risk.
3. Learn how to be disciplined and objective about your trading decisions.
4. Learn how to place orders correctly.
5. Get used to taking a loss.

TO BEGIN GAME 1

1. You have $100,000 cash available for trading.
2. You have a portfolio of six stocks and three futures contracts. I suggest you start with a sample of interesting stocks from different sectors. You might choose from:

Amazon (AMZN)	AOL Time Warner (AOL)	General Electric (GE)
IBM (IBM)	Microsoft (MSFT)	Nokia (NOK)
Tyco (TYC)	American Airlines (AMR)	Raytheon (RTN)
Barrick Gold (ABX)	Exxon Mobile (XOM)	Merck (MRK)
Wal-Mart (WMT)	Procter & Gamble (PG)	

Try to pick stocks that have had good movement during the past three months. We don't want to get bored; we're trading, not investing. In addition, you need to watch the futures markets that have the greatest impact on the economy:

10-year Treasury notes (TY)

Euro FX (EU, European currency unit)

S&P 500 index (SP)

Treasury notes are traded on the Chicago Board of Trade from 7:20 A.M. to 2:00 P.M. Central Time), and the Euro and the S&P are traded on the Chicago Mercantile Exchange (International Monetary Market and Index & Options divisions). The Euro trades from 7:20 A.M. to 2:00 P.M., and the S&P 500 from 8:30 A.M. to 3:15 P.M., both Central Time. The *emini* S&P 500 trades 24 hours.

For futures markets you'll need to watch the nearest contract for delivery. If you're trading in the month of February, it will be the March contract. These three markets have four delivery months each year: March, June, September, and December (months are coded as H, M, U, and Z, so that Treasury notes to be delivered in December 2003 are usually seen as TYZ3 on your screen). Remember that the trading hours for futures are not the same as those for the stock exchange.

3. You can track these stocks on the Internet at a wide variety of websites. Try looking at BigCharts.com, MoneyCentral.msn.com (where you can also download the prices), or Bloomberg.com. Futures prices are not as easy to find, but INO.com has both intraday and daily prices for all active domestic futures markets. European quotes can be found on Eurexchange.com. You can also go directly to the exchange websites, CME.com and CBOT.com, to get prices. All of the websites deliver *delayed* quotes that are 15 minutes late. That's why they're free. On some of these websites you can enter and display your own moving average and other indicators. If you don't have access to a computer on any particular day, you can use the old standby, the *Wall Street Journal*, or *Investors Business Daily*.

TRADING RULES

1. Begin trading on Monday. Orders must be placed at least five minutes before the close for execution on the close. Orders must be placed at least five minutes before the open for execution on the open. There are no *market* orders (orders executed immediately) in this game. You need to plan in advance.

2. All positions will be liquidated on the close of Friday in four weeks.

3. Send all orders by e-mail to an address set up for just this. There are many free e-mail vendors where you can set up a new account.

4. The only orders that are allowed are *market on open* (MOO), *market on close* (MOC), *stop* (STOP), and *limit* (written as limit, OB, or nothing). No *market* orders are allowed. An explanation of how to place orders appears later in this chapter.

5. All equity orders are for 100 shares. All futures orders are for 1 contract. You won't be using much of your $100,000 in this game.

6. You must be in at least three positions at any one time. They can be a combination of stocks and futures.

7. You can only go long in stocks. You can go long or short in futures. To sell futures short, you simply place a *sell* order. To exit, you place a *buy* order for the same quantity. There are no extra costs or complications. The Clearing House keeps track of everything.

8. There will be no commissions and no slippage. We'll trade for free. It's unrealistic but not important at this point. You need to make the right trading decisions and not spend too much time on your accounting.

9. Along with your e-mail order, include a one sentence explanation of why you're making this trade. Be sure it's technical.

10. After you've entered the trade, you must place an order to exit if prices go the wrong way. It's a bad habit to have an open trade without risk protection.

11. You will need to keep a record of all your trades, *marked to the market*. *Marked-to-market* means that you calculate the accumulated profits and losses each day. You must see whether you a making or losing money on the trades. It's best that you do this each day, but no later than Friday of each week. You can use the spreadsheet in Figure 5.1 to record your positions, profits, losses, and capital used.

A Little Advice Before Starting

1. Diversification reduces risk. Avoid holding positions in only one or two markets.

2. Trading too quickly incurs large transaction costs. The price you get in real trading will usually be worse than the one you expect, and commission costs add up. Don't try to get in and out each day.

3. A small loss is better than a big loss; don't fall in love with your trade.

4. Don't trade unless you have a plan and the timing is right; otherwise, you can be earning interest in a money market account on the unused funds.

5. Review your positions at the end of each week. Look at the major trend. Look at your risk. Look at your profit potential. If you would not get into the same position today, then you should get out.

HOW TO PLACE AN ORDER

You need to be very careful and very precise when placing an order. This is true especially if you place the order by telephone. In the heat of trading, even experienced traders can make the mistake of buying when they wanted to sell. With electronic order entry you should not press the *send* button before you've checked and rechecked that you've entered everything correctly.

Terminology

You'll need to get familiar with using the right words to enter an order. Long descriptions don't work. The order clerk doesn't care why you're making this trade. Learn the following terms:

1. When you have no position and you *buy*, you are *initiating (entering) a long position*.

2. When you are holding a long position and you *sell*, you are *liquidating (exiting) a long position*.

3. When you have no position and you *sell*, you are *initiating (entering) a short position*.

4. When you are *selling short*, you are *initiating (entering) a short position*.

5. When you are holding a short position and you *buy*, you are *liquidating (exiting) the short position*.

In futures:

- If you are long 1 contract and you sell 2 contracts, you have *closed out* your long and you are now *short* 1 contract.
- If you are short 1 contract and you buy 2 contracts, you have *covered* your short and are *long* 1 contract.
- When you go from long to short, or short to long, you can say that you've *reversed* your position.

TABLE 5.1	Types of Orders
Notation	**Description**
MARKET	*Market order* (at the market). You want your order filled immediately, at whatever price is being traded (the *asking* price when you're buying and the *bid* price when you're selling).
MOO	*Market on open.* You want your order executed at the opening of the next session. The opening session is about the first 60 seconds of trading. You may get any price within that 60-second period.
MOC	*Market on close.* You want your order executed at the close of the trading session. The closing session is usually the last 60 seconds of trading. You do not get the closing price, but any price within the last 60 seconds.
PRICE	*Price order* (the word "price" is not actually used). You want you order executed at a specific price or better. If you are *buying at $15*, then you must get a price of $15 or better; otherwise, you are not filled. A price order is placed *below* the currently traded price when buying and *above* when selling.
STOP	*Stop order.* You want your order executed if the price is reached. A stop order is placed *above* the current market price when you are buying. If the price moves up and reaches your price, your order becomes a *market order.*
OCO	*One cancels the other.* You place two orders and if one is filled, then the other is automatically cancelled.
CANCEL	*Cancel order.* You want to remove the order from the system.
CR	*Cancel replace.* You want to change your previous order. If you do not cancel it, then the new order will be placed *in addition* to the original order.
GTC	*Good 'til cancelled.* Your order remains active until you cancel it. Unless specified, all orders are *day* orders; that is, they are automatically cancelled at the end of the trading day.

The type of order must be one of those shown in Table 5.1. You can combine these orders in a variety of ways, as shown in Table 5.2.

There are other types of orders, and more complex combinations, but you'll be able to trade for a long time without knowing them. These orders are all that's needed. Be sure you practice writing the orders in the correct form. It's always:

Buy or Sell	Quantity	Stock or Futures	Price	Type of Order
Buy	100	MSFT	65.00	STOP

TABLE 5.2   Combinations of Orders

Notation	Order	Description
MOO MOC	SELL 100 IBM MOO BUY 1 TYH4 MOC	Sell 100 shares of IBM on the next open. Buy 1 contract of March 2004 Treasury note futures on the close.
Price	BUY 100 IBM 51.00	Buy 100 shares of IBM no higher than $51.00 When you enter a price with no other notation, it is automatically an "or better" (*price* or *limit*) order.
STOP	SELL 100 IBM 45.00 STOP	Sell 100 shares of my long position if IBM drops to $45.00 (it is now trading higher at $47.00).
STOP-MOC	BUY 1 SPZ3 950 STOP MOC	Buy 1 contract of December 2003 S&P 500 futures if the price is above 950 at the close of trading (the price was below 950 when you placed the order).
OCO	BUY 100 MSFT 53.00 OCO SELL 100 MSFT 65.00	Microsoft is trading at $57.00 and you are already long 100 shares. Buy 100 more if the price drops to $53.00 *or* liquidate your 100 if the price rises to $65.00, whichever comes first.

CALCULATING PROFITS, LOSSES, AND MARGIN

Stocks and futures are quite different. Keeping a record of your profits and losses can be tricky for futures but very straightforward for stocks.

Stock Profit and Loss

You pay face value when you buy stocks. Your cash balance is reduced by the number of shares times the share value, plus the commission you pay. For stocks you pay a commission each time you buy or sell.

For example, in a normal stock trade you might buy 100 shares of GE at $40. It costs you $4,000 plus a $10 commission. If you sell those shares at $45 you get $4,500 less another $10 commission. You net $4,490 – $4,010 or $480. You may find it easier to leave the commissions for last, doing the calculation as $4,500 – $4,000 – $20 = $480. Your return is 12 percent.

Futures

Futures trading is very different from stocks because it always uses leverage and you trade in larger size. If you buy the June 2004 S&P futures (SPM4) at

950, you are buying the dollar equivalent of 250 times the price, $250 \times 950 = \$237{,}500$. You put up margin of $20,000, which is a *good-faith deposit*, not the purchase price. You can actually receive interest on your deposit.

If you buy SPM4 at 950 and sell it at 960 you have gained 10 points less commission. Each point is worth $250; therefore, you have a profit of $2,500 less $10 commission, for a net of $2,490. If you think of the margin as your investment, your return is 12.4 percent. You could calculate your profit using the total value of your purchase. You bought ($950 \times 250 = 237{,}500$) at 950 and sold when the value was 960 ($960 \times 250 = 240{,}000$) for a gain of $2,500, less commissions.

Returns on Stocks and Futures

A $5 move in GE (12 percent) and a 10-point move (1.05 percent of the S&P price) in the S&P 500 index futures both yielded a return on investment of 12 percent. Yet the S&P made only a small move, while GE moved much further. It looks much easier to get a profit from futures. However, there are no hidden risks trading GE, while the S&P trade has lurking disaster. It's the same *leverage* that gave you the "easy" profit.

For stock trades you put up the full value of the share price. No one will ever ask you to invest more. Not so in futures. Your margin is not the full price of what you've purchased, only 5 percent to 10 percent of the face value. For the S&P trade in the previous example, the margin was 8.4 percent of the contract value. That was a $20,000 margin for the purchase of $237,500 in stocks.

If the S&P price dropped to 925 from your purchase price of 950, you would be losing $6,250 ($250 \times 25$). The rule in futures trading is that, if your deposit falls below 75 percent of its initial value, you must replenish the full margin. Therefore, your loss of $6,250 brought the $20,000 deposit to $13,750 (68 percent) and you now need to deposit another $6,250. Your investment is now $26,250. If you were to now take a profit of 10 points, your return would be $(10 \times 250) / 26{,}250 = 9.5$ percent. With futures you gain valuable leverage, but at the risk of having to deposit more if the price goes the wrong way. That can be a big risk.

Some additional examples and facts:

1. In the trading game, the futures margin for the S&P 500 (SP) will be $20,000. The margin for Treasury notes (TY) is $2,500 (about 2.5 percent), and the margin for the Euro (EC) is $2,500 (also about 2.5 percent).

2. The minimum move for a stock is $.01, or 1 cent. Stocks are no longer traded in 8ths.

3. The minimum move for the S&P is .05, equal to $12.50.

4. The minimum move for the Euro is .01, equal to $12.50. Each purchase is for $125,000 worth of Euros.

5. Treasury bonds trade in 32nds. Each purchase is for $100,000. When the price is quoted as 102-08, it means 102 and 8/32nds, or 102.25 (in decimal); therefore, a price move from 102.00 to 103.00 is worth $1,000. A quarter-point change from 102.00 to 102.25 is worth $250.

Selling Short Futures

One of the advantages of futures is that no one cares if you're long or short. If you decide that the price is going up, you buy; if you think it's going down, you sell. In either case you put up the same margin and pay the same commissions. You can profit from a move in either direction.

For example, you think the dollar is weakening; therefore, you *buy* 1 contract (worth $125,000) of Euros at .9850 (98½ cents in U.S. dollars). If the price of the Euro rises to .9900, you have a ½ cent profit, equal to $625 less commissions. If you think the dollar will strengthen, you *sell* Euros at .9850. If the price rises to .9900, you have a loss of $625 plus commissions. If the Euro dropped to .9750, you would have had a profit of $1,250 less commissions. There is no penalty and no added cost for selling.

KEEPING A RUNNING RECORD OF RESULTS

You must keep a record of all your trades in a ledger, or *trade blotter*. At the beginning of each day you need to see all of your open positions at a glance. You will also want to know your

1. Total profit or loss on all closed-out trades

2. Average profit or loss per share on closed-out trades

3. Profits and losses on open trades

4. Total profits and losses on open and closed trades in each stock or futures market.

You must show all profits and losses each day, both closed-out and open positions. The open positions are marked-to-market at the closing price of the previous day, as though they were closed out. For tax purposes it is not necessary to post profits or losses on stocks that you are currently holding, but you must know the success or failure of your current trades when making trading decisions. You can't wait until you file your tax return to know how much you gained or lost. Futures positions have always been marked-to-market for tax purposes.

Write the Reason for Each Order

In addition to posting each trade that is filled, write the reason for each order on the trade blotter (Figure 5.1) at the time it is placed. Briefly explain why you're entering the trade and write your objective on the trade blotter when you are filled. When you look back after the trade is over, these reasons will form a pattern.

Examples of Reasons for Entering a Trade

1. SELL (close out) MICROSOFT 40.00 STOP. Break of most recent low.
2. BUY MSFT 73 STOP OCO BUY MSFT 40.00 LIMIT. Buy on breakout of recent high or buy on a pullback to the downtrend line formed by the three lows in late May, mid-October, and mid-December.
3. SELL (close out) MSFT 68.00 LIMIT. Taking profits below resistance at 70.
4. BUY MSFT MOO. 20-day moving average turned up on previous close. Stay with the trend.

A Look at the Trade Blotter

After a week, your trade blotter should look like the spreadsheet in Figure 5.1. Trades are entered in the order in which they occur. Profits and losses are marked-to-market each Friday after the close. There is a running total of profits and losses as well as the cost of each position and the total capital invested.

In this spreadsheet there are six losing trades and six winning ones, but the winners are bigger than the losers for a net open profit of $3,260 on invested capital of $51,206. It's a good start for the week, but it's only an example.

IT'S TIME TO GET STARTED

Now you'll need to pick your stocks and print out the charts from one of the Internet services. Print out both a long-term chart (at least five years) and a shorter-term period (probably six-months). You may want to download those prices into a spreadsheet using MoneyCentral.msn.com or another provider.

Name Trader

Week ending 2/15/02

	Entry	Date	Position	Price	Close	Stops	Condition	PL	CumPL	Capital	Cash	P/L	Equity
AMR	Buy	01/30/02	100	25.070	24.500	21.900		(67.00)	(67.00)	2507			
AMZN	Buy	01/30/02	100	14.220	13.410	10.500		(91.00)	(158.00)	1422			
AOL	Buy	01/30/02	100	26.700	26.050	24.500		(75.00)	(233.00)	2670			
GE	Buy	01/30/02	100	36.460	37.110	34.900		55.00	(178.00)	3646			
IBM	Buy	01/30/02	100	103.000	102.890	99.900		(21.00)	(199.00)	10300			
MSFT	Buy	01/30/02	100	62.320	60.230	58.900		(219.00)	(418.00)	6232			
NOK	Buy	01/30/02	100	22.690	21.640	20.500		(115.00)	(533.00)	2269			
TYC	Buy	01/30/02	100	33.650	27.900	27.500		(585.00)	(1118.00)	3365			
XOM	Buy	01/30/02	100	37.950	38.900	37.800		85.00	(1033.00)	3795			
SPH2	Sell	02/13/02	-1	1115.500	1104.800	1108.000	MOO	2690.00	1657.00	10000			
TYH2	Buy	01/30/02	1	106.297	107.066	103.280	stop	754.13	2411.13	2500			
ECH2	Sell	01/30/02	-1	0.8599	0.8717	0.8825	trend	(1460.00)	951.13	2500			
										51206	48,794	4,960	$105,911.13

FIGURE 5.1 Trade blotter.

First, draw your traditional major trendlines on the long-term chart to get the big picture of price direction. If the trendline is clearly up, then you'll be looking at the shorter-term chart to find an entry point to buy. If the trend is down, you might not want to enter any position at all.

You can also display different moving averages on your charts. Try looking at more than one length; for example, show the 50-, 100-, and 200-day moving averages on the same chart. Look to see which of them fits the pattern of the market best.

Compare the moving average trends with your own hand-drawn trendlines. Are they both indicating that prices are moving higher? Consider trading only those stocks and futures whose trendlines *and* moving averages are saying the same thing.

Paper-Trading Websites

Some Internet websites offer the ability to track your orders without actually trading. It prevents you from entering an order too late, entering an incorrect order, or making an error in your accounting. It gives you practice using the system. Try looking at the websites for Lind-Waldock and StockTrak.com. Figure 5.2 shows an order entry screen for Tradestation. It's all intended to be very simple and fast.

Enjoy the game. It's not real money now, but it will be soon!

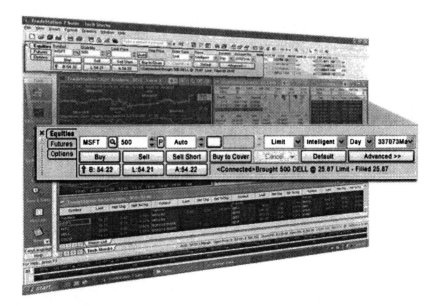

FIGURE 5.2 TradeStation order entry screen. They try to make it simple and fast. Image created with TradeStation® 7 by TradeStation Technologies, Inc.

Questions

1. Why do you want to choose at least three stocks from three different market sectors?

2. In the price shock of 9/11, which way did GM move and which way did Raytheon move? Why?

3. If the price of Amazon.com is $10 and you wanted to go long 100 shares at $12, what order would you place?

4. IBM is trading at $38. You own 500 shares at $40 and want to buy an equal amount if it drops to $36. What order do you place?

5. You want to buy 250 shares of GE if it rises to $45 and closes above that level. What order do you place?

6. The December S&P futures contract has been in a narrow, sideways range for three weeks, trading from 950 to 990; therefore, you want to go long above 990 or short below 950 to take advantage of any new direction. What order do you place?

7. You bought 200 GE at $30 and the price is now $28. What is your profit or loss?

8. You sold 1 contract of TYZ at 108-16 and the price is now 108-00. What is your profit or loss?

CHAPTER 6

Channels and Bands

W e're now going to return to charting and expand the single trendline into a *trend channel*. Channels are useful because they identify
the volatility of price moves. Wider channels show greater price
volatility. Because price channels add more information to your analysis, you
will be able to add a few more rules to your trading plan.

CHARTING CHANNELS

1. An upward channel is formed by drawing a line parallel to the upward
   trendline, touching the highest high of the same period.
2. A downward channel is formed by drawing a line parallel to the downward trendline touching the lowest low of that period.
3. You may draw the channel line by cutting off a few extreme high and low
   prices, if the new line seems to fit the price pattern best.

In Figure 6.1 there are three channels drawn as prices move higher. Trendline
A shows a very uniform rise with slightly increasing daily volatility (the size
of the daily bar increases as prices increase). A thin channel line is drawn
above prices touching three points, 1, 2, and 3. Near the end of the channel
the price breaks through the top of the channel.

The second channel, drawn above the upward trendline *B*, touches the
highest prices at the beginning and middle of *B* (points 4 and 5), but is penetrated toward the end of the channel. Volatility is increasing.

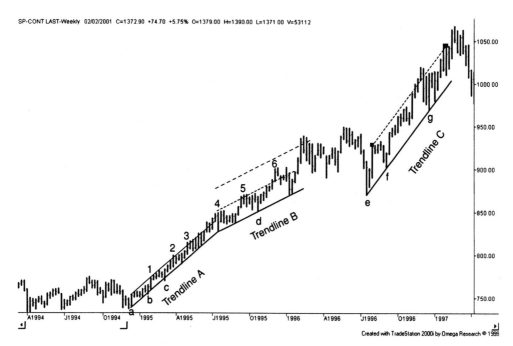

FIGURE 6.1   Drawing channels. Channels are drawn only after the trendline is determined. Trendline *A* can be drawn across points *a*, *b*, and *c*. You can immediately draw a parallel channel line using the highest point (1) between *a* and *c*.

The third trendline, *C*, is very steep, and the channel line cuts through most of the upward price moves near the top of the channel. The channel could be expanded to allow for the higher volatility at the top of the move, or you could accept the situation in which you get frequent penetrations of the channel, yet the channel still represents the price direction and volatility.

These charting techniques aren't perfect. No matter how carefully you plot your trendlines or channels, the market will violate them and then reverse, as though it knew where you had placed your lines and wanted to show you that the lines mean nothing. By drawing trendlines that already have a few penetrations, you prove that you are ready for a few more.

Trading Rules for Channels

The ideal channel trade is to *buy* near the bottom of the channel and *sell* near the top of the channel. That method would have worked well in the first channel in Figure 6.1.

The first channel could have been drawn safely when the three bottom points, *a*, *b*, and *c*, fell in a straight line, about one-third of the channel length. You could have bought at the time you drew the upward trendline *A*, have bought at the time you drew the upward trendline *A*, sold at the top of the channel three days later, and again bought after another three days when prices touched the trendline again. More buys and sells followed, all profitable.

The second channel offered only one or two chances to trade. If you buy when the trendline *B* is formed at point *d*, you can sell when prices move through the top of the channel at $6. Prices retrace to the bottom of the channel once more, giving you another chance to enter, and then move up through the top of the channel. This last move is so large that we must consider the channel no longer intact.

The third channel is more of a problem. The first two bottoms, *e* and *f*, are very close together and you may wait until the third low in order to draw trendline *C*. If you bought at *g* and took your profit at the top of the channel, you've made the only trade possible.

Trading Not Quite at the Top and Bottom of the Channel. It's unrealistic to think that you can buy right at the bottom trendline, or that you would want to buy there. When prices are dropping to the point where the trendline would be drawn, you need to wait to see if prices stop. If they keep dropping through the trendline, you won't buy.

To be sure prices have stopped declining, they need to reverse and begin to go higher. It's only after you see that they've stopped that you can comfortably buy. It is normal practice to think of dividing the channel into zones of 25 percent, or even a lower and upper zone of 20 percent. Anything smaller is too narrow.

Your new channel rules become *buy* in the lower zone of the channel and *sell* in the upper zone of the channel.

An Important Word on Taking Profits

Profit-taking should only be used if you are trading quickly. It fights with the ability to hold the trend and take advantage of the big profits. In Chapters 2, 3, and 4 it was stressed that, as a trend follower, you must have a few very large profits to offset the many smaller losses. These large profits are part of the *fat tail* of the distribution—they don't happen very often. If you take profits on a trade, you cut short the extremely large profits that will be needed for success—you turn a profitable strategy into a losing one.

Channel trading is fast; therefore, you can enter on a pullback to a trendline or a breakout, and then take profits based on volatility in the top zone of a range or channel. A long-term trader will follow the trend, taking profits and losses only when the trend finally changes direction.

Redrawing Channels

Channels will be redrawn in just the same way that trendlines were redrawn in Chapter 2. If the trend changes direction, the channel must also change.

Channels are also redrawn when the price breaks through and stays above the channel top for a few days. Remember that you have a choice of leaving the channel line untouched and viewing a price breakout penetration as a *false breakout* or redrawing the channel to include the top of the penetrating move, representing increased volatility. The channels become clearer as price patterns develop.

Figure 6.2 shows AMR, American Airlines' parent company, in a strong, uniform upward trend. The trendline A drawn along the lows of the move, beginning with the mid-April 1997 and July 1997 points (a, b, and c), is confirmed in September (d), October (e), January 1998 (f), and February 1998 (g) lows.

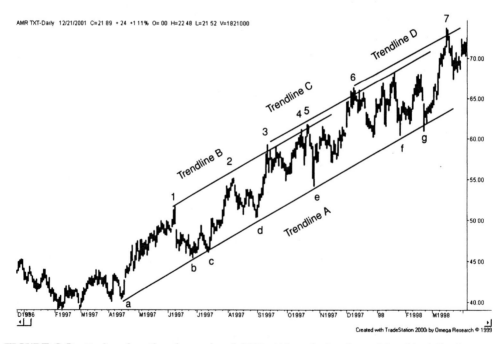

FIGURE 6.2 Redrawing the channels of AMR. Although the channel for this daily chart of AMR is very uniform, it must be redrawn from time to time to account for the increase in volatility.

The first channel line is drawn from the high (1) that came between points *a* and *b*, parallel to the trendline. It does quite well defining the upward move. Although it is above the high of April (2) and cuts off the highs of September (3) and October (4, 5), it should be considered intact until December.

The penetration of the channel line in December (6) exceeded the previous false breakouts 3 and 4. You might still continue with the original channel line, but you should see this as a continued, natural increase in volatility as prices move higher. After the December penetration, go back to the previous highs and redraw the channel *C* to show December as a false breakout but the earlier price moves as part of the channel.

The same situation occurs in March 1998. Higher prices result in higher volatility, and prices again push through the top of the channel (7). This time it is too much of a penetration to ignore, and you would redraw the channel line *D* from the high of December (6), allowing the March high (7) to be treated as a false breakout.

Channels as They Develop for Trading

We'll take one more look at AMR in the way you would see it if you were actually trading. This time we'll take a more recent period, July 2000 through September 2001, including September 11, just to keep a note of reality (see Figure 6.3).

1. The first upward trendline *A* is drawn connecting the obvious major low points *a* and *b*. The upper channel line *B* is drawn parallel to *A* beginning at the high in between, point 1.

2. The channel top is broken on the next move up and peaks at 2 near the traditional price objective of the channel width measured from the old channel top (the distance from *A* to *B* added to *B*).

3. We can only watch now until the low at *c* is made, which is clear after prices stop and reverse about $3 to $4.

4. A new trendline *C* can be draw slightly higher than the original line touching the two lows *a* and *c*, treating *b* as a minor false breakout to the downside.

5. A new channel line *D* is drawn from the highs (2) parallel to the new trendline.

6. The next highs (3 and 4) actual fall on the original channel top, making the peak at 2 look like a false breakout. Time will tell.

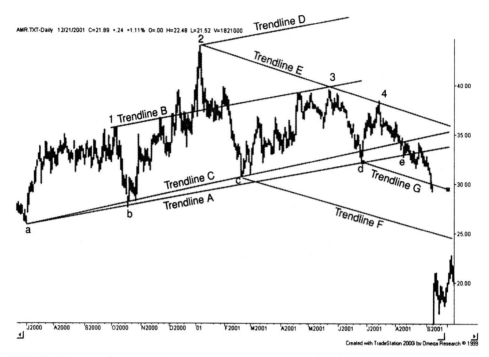

FIGURE 6.3   Trading the channels as they change. It is normal that trendlines and channels change with price patterns. In this chart there is a classic change of trend from up to down and sell signal—just in time.

7. A price drop to the low *d* makes everything more complicated. We might have a downside breakout, moving below trendline *C*. We can now draw a new downward trendline *E* from the highest high 2 across the next high 3. We draw a downward channel line *F* parallel to *E* starting at the low *c*.

8. Prices move higher after *d*, and we can now choose whether we want to use the first or second upward trendline. Either one could work.

9. Prices fail at point *e*, right on the new downtrend line, and start declining again. The next breakout becomes important because the price pattern is narrowing and it must break out either up or down.

10. In August prices break below both uptrend lines *A* and *C*, rally briefly above the newer line, and then start falling. You should be short.

11. Persistence and good analysis are rewarded. September 11 causes prices to drop 25 percent and you're short. Although prices were heading down, September 11 could have come when the trend was still up. The charting was good but the last profit was luck, not skill. Never mistake luck for skill.

ENVELOPES AND BANDS

While a channel is formed by two rigid parallel lines, an envelope or band will follow the shape of a moving average trendline, or some other calculated line. It can be very flexible and quickly adjust to volatility changes.

Percentage Bands

A common way to form a band is to use a percentage of the moving average value. For example, to get the values of a 5 percent band, one way to do this is:

1. Create a 20-day moving average (MA) that will be the center of the band.
2. Multiply the current value of the moving average by 1.05 to get the upper band. If the moving average value is $30, then the upper band value is $31.5.
3. Divide the current value of the moving average by 1.05 to get the lower band. For a moving average value of $30, the lower band is $28.57. You may also multiple by .95 to get the lower band of $28.50.

$$MA20 = \text{current value of a 20-day moving average}$$
$$\text{Upper band} = MA20 \times 1.05$$
$$\text{Lower band} = MA20 / 1.05$$

In Figure 6.4, the 5 percent bands get slightly wider as AMR prices rise, reflecting the normal increase in volatility. Prices stay above and below the bands for only a few days at a time.

Trading Rules for Percentage Bands. We trade a percentage band the same way as a channel, buying at the bottom, selling at the top, and exiting in the middle. It's a little easier to wait for a penetration of the band using this type of mechanical approach. We can make the bands narrower or wider so that prices move through the extremes as often as we choose. If we make the bands a little wider than those we see in Figure 6.4, the number of opportunities decreases, but the timing and profits per trade increase.

Volatile Patterns. Percentage bands work best with slow trends and sideways markets where the volatility remains steady. The best example is Figure 6.4. Stocks also have periods where volatility increases quickly, and times when prices drop sharply and continue to drop. In Figure 6.5, AMR falls

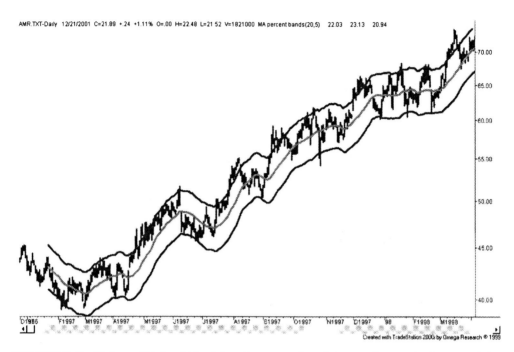

AMR.TXT-Daily 12/21/2001 C=21.89 +.24 +1.11% O=.00 H=22.48 L=21 52 V=1821000 MA percent bands(20,5)   22.03   23.13   20.94

FIGURE 6.4   Using a 20-day MA with a 5 percent band. We can buy at the bottom of the band, sell at the top, and produce quite a few profitable trades. However, the pattern doesn't always look this good.

sharply in July and August 1999, remaining below the lower band for two one-month periods (with a small reprieve in the middle). If we had bought when prices fell through the lower band at $80 (point *a*), we wouldn't get out of the trade until the middle of the band is touched in August at $67. We would have taken a large loss.

This all means that every method has good periods and bad periods. Nothing is foolproof. Bands still seem to be a good idea. What can we do to improve the way we use bands?

One possibility is to change the percentage value of the band when the prices get more volatile. In Figure 6.5 a wider band would allow fewer prices to break through, but still does not solve the steady drop in July and August. Once prices break through the bottom, we're forced to hold the trade until August.

Bollinger Bands

Bollinger bands offer an alternative to using a fixed percentage. A Bollinger band varies in width as price volatility increases and decreases. It makes the

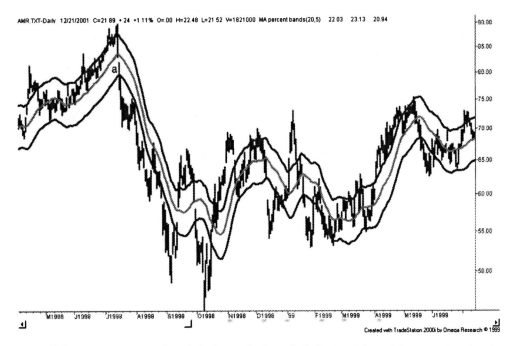

FIGURE 6.5 A 5 percent band during a bad period. During July and August prices break below the lower band and don't cross above the center of the band until August. Is it just a bad period for the band, or can we do better?

band fluctuate in a pattern that seems natural to price changes. Bollinger bands try to answer the question, "Are prices high or low in relative terms?"

As with the previous bands, a traditional Bollinger band has a 20-day moving average at its center. The half-width of the band is found by:

1. Calculating the standard deviation of the closing price changes over the past 20 days.
2. Multiplying the standard deviation by 2.
3. Adding and subtracting the value from the 20-day moving average.

In Excel, the instructions for calculating today's Bollinger bands around a 20-day average, where the closing price data is in column A and the price changes (A100 – A99) are in column B, are:

Upper Bollinger band = average(A81:A100) + 2 × stdev(A81:A100)
Lower Bollinger band = average(A81:A100) − 2 × stdev(A81:A100)

Using the standard deviation gives us a measure of confidence. Because of the non-normal distribution of prices, two standard deviations means that 87% of all prices will close inside the Bollinger bands, or 13 prices out of 100 will be outside either the upper or lower band.

Bollinger bands do a better job isolating the highs and lows of the upward move of AMR, shown in Figure 6.6, compared to the percentage bands in Figure 6.4. As the standard deviation promises, the peaks and valleys penetrate the bands in fewer cases, and their occurrence seems to be spread out over the entire upward move. In Figure 6.4 many of the penetrations through the top band remained above the band for many more days than they did in Figure 6.6.

If we now look at the AMR problem period from mid-1998 to mid-1999 (see Figure 6.7), the Bollinger bands are penetrated on the downward move at the same point in July 1998; however, prices do not stay below the lower band. Bollinger bands do a better job of isolating the extreme moves. It doesn't help our trading profits because prices do not return to the

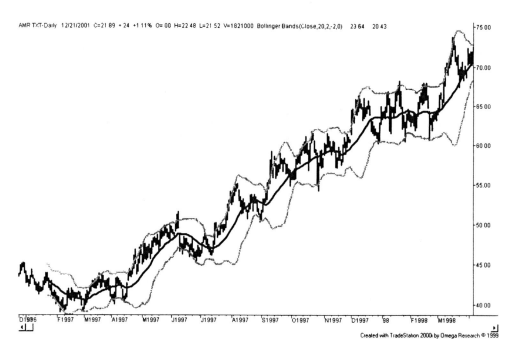

AMR TXT-Daily 12/21/2001 C=21 89 + 24 +1 11% O= 00 H=22 48 L=21 52 V=1821000 Bollinger Bands(Close,20,2,-2,0) 23 64 20 43

Created with TradeStation 2000i by Omega Research © 1999

FIGURE 6.6 Bollinger bands. Bollinger's 2 standard deviation bands on either side of a 20-day moving average seem to adjust to the shape of price movement. The bands contain 87 out of every 100 prices.

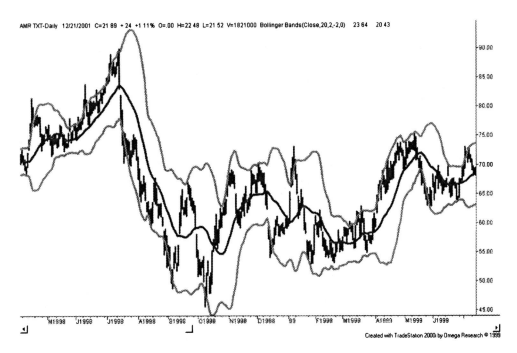

FIGURE 6.7   Bollinger bands during a more volatile period. Even though Bollinger bands are an improvement over the percentage band, buying on the break during July 1998 results in the same loss.

the center of the band until August, giving us the same result as the percentage band.

Overall, Bollinger bands are more responsive to price movement. They can be very helpful identifying overbought and oversold conditions used in combinations with chart patterns such as tops and bottoms; they can improve your entry timing in a trend. You can learn more about Bollinger bands by going to the website www.BollingerBands.com.

Finding a Calculation Period That Works.   There is always a solution if you look in the right place. When prices are as volatile as they are in July and August of 1998, we can simply extend our calculation period. The 2 standard deviation bands will then show the 5 percent highs and lows that penetrated the bands during the longer period.

In Figure 6.8 we apply a classic 200-day moving average with Bollinger bands. In this case we greatly improve the results, but have fewer trades and more risk. By the nature of the standard deviation, prices will only

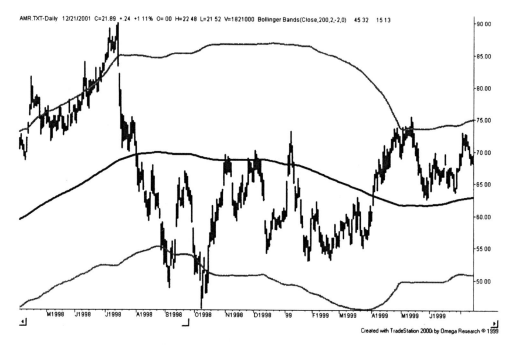

AMR.TXT-Daily 12/21/2001 C=21.89 +.24 +1 11% O= 00 H=22 48 L=21 52 V=1821000 Bollinger Bands(Close,200,2,-2,0) 45 32 15 13

Created with TradeStation 2000i by Omega Research © 1999

FIGURE 6.8   200-day Bollinger bands. A longer calculation period can reduce the initial risk for volatile markets, but provides fewer opportunities. Once you are in the trade, prices can fluctuate widely before they reach the price objective at the center of the band.

penetrate the bands 5 percent of the time, or 10 days during the past 200. Of those 10 penetrations, 5 should be highs and 5 lows, although that is not guaranteed.

Using a 20-day calculation period, the band width was about $15 (see Figure 6.7), but when a 200-day period is used, the band width increases to about $30. Once the lower band is penetrated and you get a buy signal, it can be a long time and a lot of price fluctuations before you finally see prices reach your objective at the center of the band.

Regression Bands: The Economist's Approach

Although the methods used by economists often do not apply to trading, the regression line is very appealing for constructing bands. When we think of the trend of prices, we instinctively draw a straight line through the price pattern and observe whether that line is angling up or down.

The classic way of creating confidence bands is to draw the regression line through the center of the price pattern, and then find the standard devi-

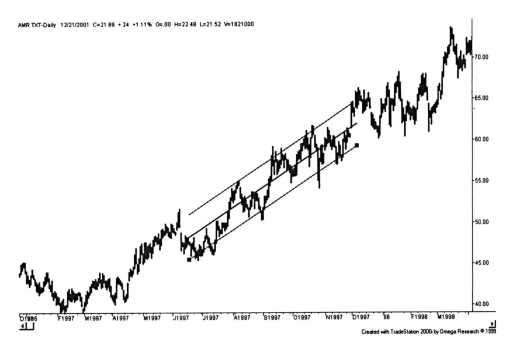

AMR TXT-Daily 12/21/2001 C=21 89 + 24 +1 11% O=.00 H=22.48 L=21 52 V=1821000

Created with TradeStation 2000i by Omega Research © 1999

FIGURE 6.9   Classic bands formed around a regression line. This economist approach requires the use of a spreadsheet for calculations, but gives the most intuitively satisfying results.

ation of the price changes in the same manner as Bollinger bands. If you continue to use 2 standard deviations for the bands, you would get the channel shown in Figure 6.9. For this six-month period, the channel is a perfect fit. Unfortunately, as with the percentage band and Bollinger band methods, the only period we can use for trading is the last day of the calculation. The other days are considered "in sample"; that is, they were used to construct the bands.

If you calculate a new 60-day regression every day and look only at the last point on the regression bands, you'll see that the bands can bend with price changes in the same way that Bollinger bands change direction. In Figure 6.10 the center line is the last point of a straight line drawn through the last 60 days. It tends to be in the middle of prices more that the moving average. The bands around the regression points get narrower and wider, reflecting price volatility, but they are penetrated by highs and lows at good points less often than in the other charts because of the longer 60-day calculation.

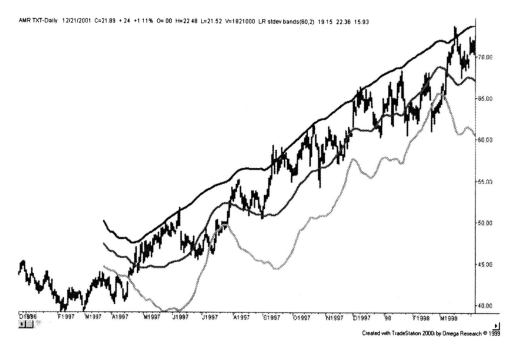

AMR TXT-Daily 12/21/2001 C=21.89 + 24 +1 11% O= 00 H=22 48 L=21.52 V=1821000 LR stdev.bands(60,2) 19 15 22.36 15.93

Created with TradeStation 2000i by Omega Research © 1999

FIGURE 6.10   Rolling linear regression bands. Plotting the end points of the linear regression and 2 standard deviation bands shows a different pattern.

THE REALITY OF USING CHANNELS AND BANDS

Channels and bands both have the same objective—to put a framework around price movement. They tell us when prices are unusually high or low. We can turn that into trading by buying at the low end of the channel, or when prices penetrate the bottom band, and selling at the high end. It works most of the time. It is best when prices aren't moving too fast.

By expanding the channel or band width and slowing down the trendline used to form the bands, we can identify more extreme price moves and be more selective about our buy and sell signals. This helps eliminate some bad situations, but it reduces the number of trades and increases the time you are in a trade. We know by now that the longer you hold a trade, the larger the price swing you will endure.

There is no perfect channel or band. They all have the same basic problem. When price begin moving quickly higher, selling is a mistake; when prices drop sharply, buying is a mistake. All trading methods will have situations in which they lose.

As we develop our trading skill further, we will find ways to reduce the risk of a large loss. We may use a protective stop-loss order, or a rule that says that the trend direction requires that we exit or reverse our position. We can be more conservative by only buying in an uptrend and being net short in a downtrend.

TRADING GAME TIPS

1. *You should have lost money the first week.* In the first few days of trading it is most important to chart the trends correctly and place your orders where the price breaks the trendline. Alternatively, you can follow your moving average trend. Making money is important, but don't expect much the first week. Losses teach you more than profits.

2. *Problems when buying on a pullback.* It seems sensible to buy when prices drop to a support level, but it doesn't seem to work in practice. *Major* support levels are good points to buy, after prices have stopped dropping and the support level has still not been penetrated. *Minor* support and resistance levels are not reliable, and the opposite seems to work more often. When prices drop to a minor support level, they are most likely to continue lower. When you're starting out, wait for a confirmation that prices are stopping. That may be a small upward movement after the decline.

3. *Overusing moving averages.* Moving averages are good indications of the long-term trend, but they are not very good at telling you the best place to get in or out of a trade. Combine the moving average with a support or resistance level. If you a looking for a buy signal, you'll want the moving average to be trending up and want to buy when prices move up and through the next resistance level. That will help your timing.

Questions

1. Once you've drawn an upward trendline, how do you draw the upward channel line?

2. When would you redraw the upward channel line? What point would you use to redraw it?

3. If you are trading a channel, where would you buy and where would you sell?

4. If you've bought near the bottom of the channel, where are the two places you would exit the trade?

5. If prices move above the channel line for only one day and then fall back below the channel line, explain why you would or would not redraw the channel line.

6. How do you construct a 3 percent band around a 10-day moving average?

7. How would you trade a percentage band?

8. What are two advantages of Bollinger bands over percentage bands?

9. If prices penetrate through a 5 percent band too often, what can you do?

10. What are two disadvantages of a larger band?

11. When does profit-taking work best? Anytime you have more than a 10 percent profit, in a noisy market, or as a long-term trend follower?

CHAPTER 7

Event-Driven Trends

There are two distinct types of trends, one based on how prices move over time and the other triggered by events. The two methods have very different trading signals and different performance profiles. The moving average represents a time-driven trend and a breakout is the event-driven approach. There are an equal number of traders in each camp. In this chapter we'll look at breakouts.

TIME-DRIVEN OR EVENT-DRIVEN?

A moving average system is *time-driven;* that is, the moving average closes in on current prices when the price movement slows. In Figure 7.1 Exxon (XOM) prices move sideways from January through mid-April 1997, before the sideways period. The moving average tracks rising prices smoothly, and then turns down at the beginning of March although prices only show a slight decline. Using the trendline for the buy and sell signals forces us to close out our trade at the March lows, although prices are $1 higher one month later.

This characteristic of the moving average can't be removed. It is a benefit when prices turn slowly from up to down, and a problem when prices slow down and then continue in the same direction as in Figure 7.1.

A clear example of an *event-driven* trend is the breakout. We learned in Chapter 3 that a breakout that creates an upward trend begins with a new high and ends with a new low. The trend doesn't change unless prices move to new highs or new lows. You can consider a new high price as being caused by an event: a news release, an earnings report, or a change in government

XOM.CSV-Daily 02/08/2002 C=38 29 - 01 -0 03% O=38.05 H=38.36 L=37.99 V=87311 Mov Avg 1 line(Close,40,0) 38.70

Sideways price movement

Moving average
turns down

Created with TradeStation 2000i by Omega Research © 1999

FIGURE 7.1   A moving average is time-driven. It has an agenda. Prices must continue to move in the same direction or the moving average will turn down and the trade ends. It performs poorly in sideways markets.

policy. Prices can drift up and down within a reasonably small range and the trend doesn't change.

Using a 40-day rolling breakout applied to XOM, we see nearly the same trades as when we used the moving average (see Figure 7.2), except that prices failed to make a new low in March, and the breakout trend held its long position.

The rolling breakout is not entirely immune from time change. The *rolling calculation period* moves forward in time. If prices become less volatile, then the highs and lows that trigger a new buy or sell signal will get closer together. Two methods that are completely independent of time are *swing charting* and *point-and-figure charting*, and the trading signals that they generate.

SWING CHARTING

Swing charting is based on identifying prices swings that are greater than a point value or a percentage. Anything larger than the swing size triggers a signal; anything smaller is ignored. In Figure 7.3 we've taken XOM again and

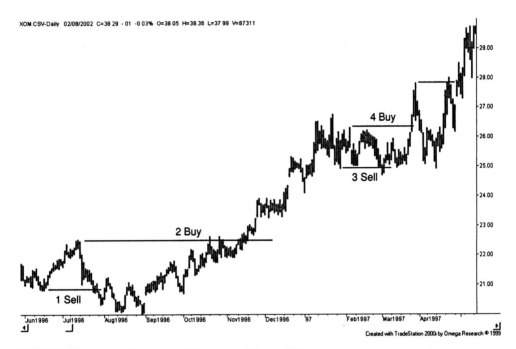

XOM.CSV-Daily 02/08/2002 C=38 29 - 01 -0 03% O=38 05 H=38.36 L=37 99 V=87311

Created with TradeStation 2000i by Omega Research © 1999

FIGURE 7.2 A breakout trend is event-driven. Using a breakout system, prices can move sideways as long as they do not make new highs or lows during the calculation (observation) period. It is intended to get a signal on a price event. Trading signals are shown in July and September but not during the sideways period from January to April 1997. These breakout rules use a 40-day calculation period.

shown the tops and bottoms of 5 percent swings using large dots, and 2.5 percent swings using small dots.

Calculating the Swing Changes

You should be able to take any chart and plot the swing highs and lows by following these rules:

1. Decide your minimum swing size. We'll use 5 percent to get the major swing points.

2. Start with any high or low price. Let's say prices are at a relative high of $23. We say that the *swing high* is $23 and the *swing direction* is *up*. This is just for the purpose of starting.

3. Prices drop to an intraday low of $22 (an *intraday low* is the low of the day, rather than the closing price). That is a drop of 4.3 percent; therefore, we do nothing. Prices must drop at least 5 percent before we take notice. The direction is still *up*.

4. Prices move higher, peaking at $25. We can ignore the previous drop because it did not fall 5 percent from the high of $23. We now have a new swing high of $25 and the direction is still *up*.

5. Prices now drop to $24, or 4 percent. We do nothing. The direction is still *up*. The swing high is still $25.

6. Prices drop again to $23 for a total of $2 off the high, or 8 percent. Because the swing exceeded our minimum swing size of 5 percent, the swing direction is now *down*. The previous swing high of $25 is now fixed. It cannot be changed.

7. Prices drop another 50¢. The direction is still *down* and the *swing low* is now $23.50.

8. As long as prices move lower, we simply record the low price as the *swing low*.

9. Prices now turn higher and close at $24, up 2.1 percent. There is no change in the direction or swing low.

10. If prices move to $24.68 (the low of $23.50 times 1.05), then the previous swing low is fixed at $23.50 and the swing direction changes to *up*.

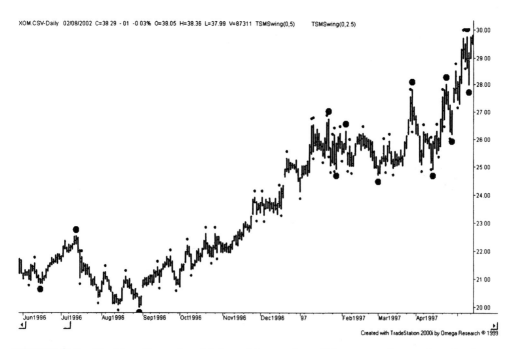

FIGURE 7.3   Marking the swing high and low points. Prices must change direction by 5 percent in order to create a new major swing high or low (the large dots). Changes of 2.5 percent can be considered minor swing points (the small dots).

In Figure 7.3 the swings points that are separated by 5 percent are shown with large dots. Reducing the size of the minimum swing from 5 percent to 2.5 percent sharply increases the number of swing points. You can choose your swing size to identify tops and bottoms that fit your style. Using 5 percent may be too large and 2.5 percent too small.

Swing Trading Rules

A swing system is not governed by a calculation period, only by a price event. It can be a simple picture where only the swing highs and lows are used (see Figure 7.4). The buy and sell signals are very similar to the breakout system:

Buy when the current upward price swing goes above the high of the previous upward swing.

Sell when the current downward price swing drops below the low of the previous downward swing.

A swing upward trend begins when prices make a new high, and a downtrend begins when they make a new low, the same as the buy and sell rules. The highs and lows of the swing are at least as far apart as the minimum swing

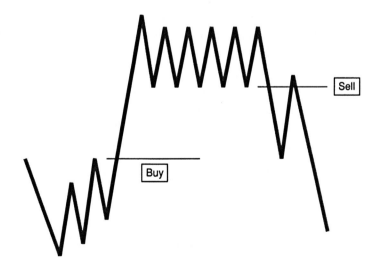

FIGURE 7.4 A swing chart. In a traditional swing chart only the swings are shown without any indication of how long it took to move from a swing high to a swing low. A buy signal occurs when the current swing high moves above the high of the previous swing. A sell is triggered when the current price moves below the low of the previous swing.

amount (2.5 percent or 5 percent in our example). As in the breakout system, if prices move back and forth, making moves less than the minimum swing level, then the current trend is unchanged and the price changes don't even appear on the chart.

POINT-AND-FIGURE CHARTING

Swing charting and point-and-figure charting may have been the first attempts at systematic trading. They both have very clear rules for entering and exiting and are known to have been used at the turn of the century (that is, the twentieth century). Breakout methods are still popular today, and they tend be more reliable indicators of price direction than moving averages.

Rules for Plotting Point-and-Figure Charts

Point-and-figure charts are plotted on graph paper. Each box is assigned a point size. If you assign a small number of points to a box, the resulting price patterns are more sensitive to change. This technique is still used by floor traders on the Chicago Board of Trade, where they plot the smallest possible price moves, trying to identify the trend before anyone else. A small box for IBM would be 10¢; a large box would be about $1. The initial chart for IBM is shown in Figure 7.5. To plot a point-and-figure chart, follow these rules:

1. Choose a box size. This should be no smaller than the minimum price move. You may begin by dividing the current daily price move (high to low) by 4 to get the box size. If the box size is, for example, 50¢, then fill

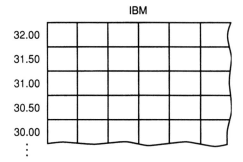

FIGURE 7.5 Setting up a point-and-figure chart for IBM. Start with an empty sheet of chart paper with square boxes. We use box sizes of 50¢ to get medium sensitivity.

```
39.50  X
39.00  X  O
38.50  X  O
38.00  X  O
37.50  X
```

FIGURE 7.6   Reversal from an uptrend. A reversal from up to down is plotted as a new column of O's beginning one column to the right and one box below the highest X. It must fill 3 boxes with O's to be a new downtrend.

in the left scale of the chart with values near the current price level in steps of 50¢. If you are plotting IBM and it is trading at $30, then start near the bottom of the paper at $15 or $20 and go up the chart by adding 50¢ at each box. The left scale should read $30, $30.50, $31, $31.50, and so on.

2. To begin, we see if today's price move was up or down. If *up*, put an "X" in each box where the traded price crossed the price marked on the box. If IBM traded from $38.25 to $39.55, then put an X in the box next to $38.50, $39.00, and $39.50. If today's move was down, then put an "O" in the boxes next to the price range.

3. If we began with a column of X's, we first see if the next trading day filled the next higher box or boxes. If yes, then we put an X in each of those boxes and ignore any downward move. Point-and-figure encourages "price persistence"; that is, it favors the continuation of the trend. If there is an uptrend (a column of X's), then you look first to see if a higher box was filled.

4. If we are in an uptrend (a column of X's) and prices do not fill another box higher, we then look for a trend reversal. To get a reversal, the low price of the day must be at least as low as the value three boxes below the highest X box. On our IBM chart, if the highest X box was $39.50, then a reversal doesn't occur unless prices print at $38.00. This is called a *three-box reversal* (although we are putting an O in the fourth box down from the highs). If a reversal occurred, we move one column to the right of the X's and begin a column of O's one box lower than the highest box with an X (see Figure 7.6).

5. We do just the opposite if prices are currently in a downtrend (a column of O's). We first look to see if the downtrend continues by filling a lower box. If not, we look to see if the high of the day would fill the fourth box up from the lowest box of O's. If there is a reversal, we move one column to the right, leave the lowest box empty, and fill at least the next three higher boxes with X's.

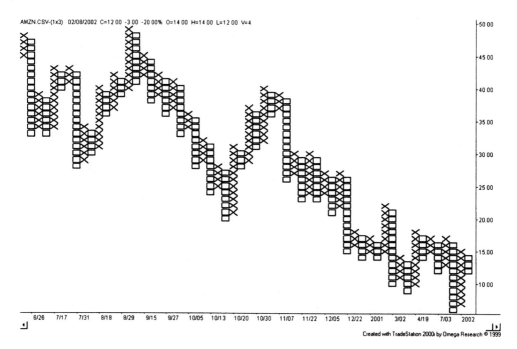

AMZN.CSV-(1x3) 02/08/2002 C=12 00 -3 00 -20 00% O=14 00 H=14 00 L=12 00 V=4

Created with TradeStation 2000i by Omega Research © 1999

FIGURE 7.7   Point-and-figure chart of Amazon. Upward trends are shown as columns of X's and downward trends as O's. This chart used a 25¢ box size. Note that each new column starts one box below or one box above the previous column and each has at least 3 boxes to begin a new direction.

A point-and-figure chart of Amazon.com, automatically produced by TradeStation, is shown in Figure 7.7. The O's are shown as rectangles.

Point-and-Figure Trading Signals

By now you can guess the rules for buying and selling with point-and-figure (all breakout methods are alike):

Buy when a column of X's *goes above* the high of the previous column of X's.

Sell when a column of O's *goes below* the previous column of O's.

By *goes above* we mean that the next higher box is filled, not just any price higher than the value of the previously filled box. *Goes below* means that the next lower box is filled. Trading signals can be seen in Figure 7.8. Once a *buy* signal occurs, you hold the long position until the next *sell*. You can't tell from the chart how long you should hold each trade. Time is not a factor in point-and-figure trading.

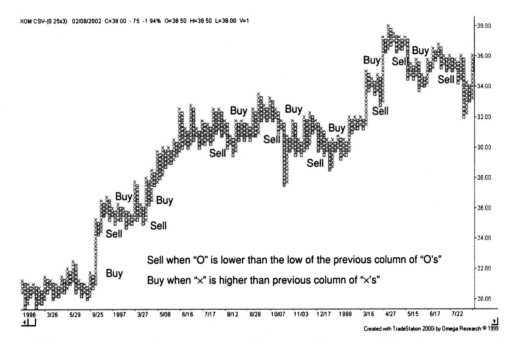

FIGURE 7.8 Point-and-figure buy and sell signals. This chart of XOM using a box size of 12.5¢ (⅛ minimum move) shows buy signals when the new column of Xs fills the box higher than the high of the previous column of X's. A sell signal is given when the new column of O's fills the box lower than the low of the previous column of O's.

SUMMARY OF EVENT-DRIVEN SYSTEMS

We will refer to event-driven systems and breakout systems together because they have the same major characteristics. They give buy or sell signals only when a new price high or low occurs. We make the assumption that price would only move to a new level if it was driven by an event. This may not always be true, but it is a successful working premise.

The trend is the single most important technical indicator, and breakout systems are the most successful trend-following methods. It is necessary to include one of them in your regular work.

Floor traders look at fast changes in price direction; therefore, they typically use a small point move as their box size. At one time most floor trades plotted point-and-figure charts on very large graph paper, taping the sheets together. Floor traders are only in for a few minutes or a few hours and they can get out quickly if the price changes direction.

The reliability of a breakout system, and all trend systems, increases as you look at longer time periods. Shorter periods can work, but market noise can fool you in more cases, and the dependability of the trend is far lower.

The principle of buying new highs and selling new lows remains sound, and most traders who use charts rely on a breakout, a swing chart, or a point-and-figure chart as part of their decision-making.

TRADING GAME TIPS

1. *It's good to have a bias.* You can have a fundamental opinion of where prices are heading and still be a technical trader. A bias can be very sensible. For example, when the Fed cut interest rates to under 2 percent, it removed a lot of profit potential from a long Treasury note trade. The potential profit fell to less than the likely risk of a trade. On the other hand, going short Treasury notes doesn't guarantee a profit because prices can drift sideways for a long time, but you'll want to trade only small positions long Treasury futures.

2. *Try to distinguish between a bias and wishful thinking.* The stock market is at very low levels, but a bias to the upside is wishful thinking. It may happen, but prices could still go lower. It's not the same as interest rates, where they are approaching a bottom of zero. Hopefully, the stock market will never get to the point where it is so low that it can't go lower.

3. *Are you still confused about the use of* limit *and* stop *when you're placing an order?*

   A *stop* order is used in the following situations:
   - When you are *long* and you are selling at a *lower* price (usually to exit the trade).
   - When you are *short* and you are buying at a *higher* price.

   You will want to buy at a higher price at the point where the trend turns up. Remember that a *stop* becomes a *market order* when the price is touched. You must use the word *stop* in your order.

   A *limit* order is used in the following situations:
   - When you are *long* and you are selling at a *higher* price (to take profits).
   - When you are *short* and you are buying at a *lower* price.
   - When you a trying to buy at a support level or sell at a resistance level.

4. *You can combine an MOC order with a price, but all conditions must be met to get an execution.*

- If you're long IBM at $52 and want to exit if prices close lower, but below a specific price, then you enter SELL IBM 48 STOP MOC. You will be executed at the closing price if it is anywhere below $48. It is unlikely you will get $48 as your price, but you won't be executed if prices dropped to $46 during the trading session, but closed at $49.
- If you have no position and you want to buy IBM on an upward break-out above $55 but only if it closes above $55, then if IBM is at 52, BUY IBM 55 STOP MOC.
- You wouldn't want to use this order to take profits on your IBM position because you would prefer to get a higher price anytime during the day. If you wait for the close, prices may have fallen back from their highs. If you are long IBM at $48, you would want to place the order SELL IBM 53. That gives you a $5 profit if IBM trades at $53 or higher during the day.

Questions

1. What is the key element that distinguishes a moving average trend from a swing trend?

2. If the swing direction is up, the high price is $50, and you are using a 3 percent swing value, at what price would the swing direction turn down?

3. If prices make a swing high of $30, a swing low of $25, and a swing high of $31, at what price would you get a swing sell signal?

4. Would you get more point-and-figure signals using a box size of $1 or 50¢?

5. If you had a point-and-figure box size of $1, and prices have just declined from $48.00 to $41.50, at what price would you begin a new column of X's.

6. Using a $1 box size, we plot a column of X's with the highest box filled at $28, followed by a new column of O's and then another column of X's. What is the lowest price that would give you a *buy* signal?

CHAPTER 8

Controlling the Risk of a Trade

You cannot trade successfully without controlling your losses. A *stop-loss* order is the most common technique for limiting your loss. You can never forget that there are no profits unless you can control your risk and your losses.

You will want to place a stop-loss order at a point where you believe that the trade has gone wrong. You do not place at stop-loss based on how much you can personally afford to risk on a trade. That's a different problem that will be covered later.

THE STOP-LOSS ORDER

The stop-loss order is a *sell* if you are long and a *buy* if you are short. It is placed *below* the current price level if you are long and *above* the current level if you are short. If prices go the wrong way, the stop-loss order will be executed and you should be out of your trade very close to that price.

If you are long 1,000 Amazon (AMZN) at $15 and there was support at $13, you would place the order:

SELL 1000 AMZN 13.00 STOP

If the price touches $13, your *stop order* becomes a *market order* and it is executed at the first available bid. You might choose to place your order at $12.95 to be sure prices move through support, or you could place your stop order at $13.10 to get out before prices dropped suddenly.

IMPORTANT CONSIDERATIONS ABOUT RISK

As a trend trader, using a moving average trendline, we don't always think of risk clearly. We know that slower trends allow larger price swings without changing the direction of the trend. Faster trends respond quickly to price changes. Those risks are implicit in the use of a trend method and can't be separated out.

One of the dilemmas of using a stop-loss to limit your risk to a "comfortable" amount can be shown best in an example. Suppose you've been following a trend system and you are long 1000 Amazon at $30 and now hold a $10 profit ($10,000 on your trade). You would like to protect those profits; therefore, you place a stop-loss at $28, risking only $2,000 of your gains. Sure enough, prices drop and you are stopped out. Prices continue down to $27.50, turn back up, and move above $40.00 to new highs. During the drop to $27.50 the moving average trendline never turned down. It would not have turned down until $22.00. You are now out of the trade but the trend is still up and prices are making new highs. What do you do? Do you jump back in and try to catch the rest of the upward move, or do you stand aside until there is a new trend signal?

None of these choices are good. If you going to trade the trend, then you must look at the risk in advance and decide how many shares you can buy and still hold the trade comfortably when prices move against you. *A stop-loss fights with the trend system.* The trend system wants to stay long and you want to get out. It just doesn't work.

You cannot trade more than you can afford to lose. Your position is too large if you are uncomfortable with the day-to-day risk.

LIMITING THE RISK OF A TRADE

A stop-loss works when you are using basic charting techniques to identify support and resistance lines. Stops can be used very effectively. There is an orderly process in deciding on how to apply a stop-loss, or whether to apply one for a specific trade.

Consider whether the *natural* buy and sell signals for your trading method provide adequate risk control. When the trade goes against your long position, does the system create a sell signal that gets you out with an acceptable loss? For example, you wanted to trade Amazon using a 200-day moving average, but when prices reached $90, the moving average was still lagging at

$40. It finally turned down when prices broke below $50, capturing only one-half of the profits. What could you have done?

1. Place a fixed dollar stop, the amount you can afford to lose.
2. Pick a support level on the chart that would signal a change of direction.
3. Draw your own trendline that would signal a change of direction.
4. Move the stop closer as profits accumulate in order to lose only a fixed amount of your peak profits.

All of these approaches have been used by traders, but not all of them are good solutions. The most important rules to remember are:

1. The best place to exit from a long position is the natural point where you would want to enter a short position.
2. The size of the stop-loss must be related to the speed of the trend. If you are trading a slow trend, then the stop must be farther away.
3. The stop should adjust to the volatility of the market. Your stop can be closer if the price changes are small or the market is quiet, and larger if prices are volatile.
4. A stop-loss must not be closer than 1½ times the current volatility (the high to low range). If you want it closer, you should simply close out the trade.
5. You must first decide how you would reenter the trade once you are out.

USING A STOP-LOSS WITH CHARTED TRENDLINES

The most successful stop-loss is a support or resistance line. The next best is a trendline. Figure 8.1 shows the evolution of a trade and the changing stop-loss levels.

Initial Placement of the Stop-Loss

Whether you enter a trend trade using a moving average trendline, a break-out, a swing method, or any other technique, the first stop should be below the most recent support level, and no closer than 1½ times the current price volatility. In Figure 8.1 the first buy signal is during the beginning of November at about $24. Recent lows in October give a clear support level just under $15. That's very far away, but a drop below $15 would clearly be a major

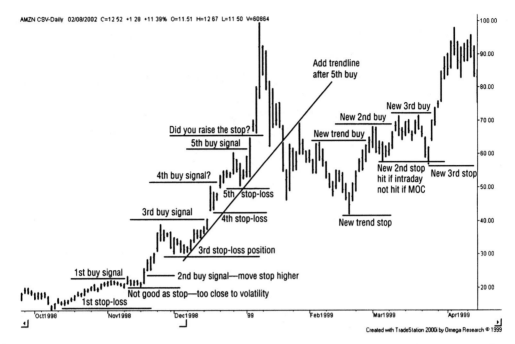

FIGURE 8.1 **Support levels used as a stop-loss.** As profits develop in a long position, the stop is raised as new support levels are established.

change of direction. You may place the stop as close as $2 below your entry price, given a daily volatility of $1.25; however, that would make your chances of getting stopped out very high, even though the trend may still be going up.

The market tells you what to do. If you don't like the trade because the natural stop is too far away, find another stock to trade; don't force the stop to be in a convenient place.

Raising the Stop-Loss to Protect Profits

Once the trade has been entered and the initial stop-loss placed, *you do not ever lower the stop-loss.* You can raise the stop level by following these rules:

1. If you are trading a breakout method and a secondary buy signal occurs (a breakout but not the first breakout to the upside), move the stop to the support level that would give a sell signal. In Figure 8.1 the second buy signal occurs soon after the first one, and the new support level is now very close. You would use that level because you're concerned about the risk. Experienced traders would not use that level because they see it as

too close. The trade looks good after the second breakout, and you want to give it a chance to develop without getting stopped out.

2. When a new support level is formed, you can raise the stop to that level. New support levels follow a price pullback. The third and fourth buy signals are good examples. Each occurs after the prices run up and then falls back part of the way. When prices move above the recent highs, we get another buy signal. The new support levels, which were the lows of the pullback, become the new stop-loss points.

3. Each time subsequent buy signals occur or new support levels are formed, the stop should be raised.

4. As the trade develops, you may be able to draw a significant trendline to add another view of where the stop should be placed. The stop-loss can be the higher of the nearest support level or the trendline. In Figure 8.1 a very nice trendline can be drawn after the fifth buy signal. Using the trendline, a stop-loss or sell signal would occur at $65, well above the last support level of $50. In this case the trendline is clear and a significant improvement over the support level.

Using the Closing Price for the Stop-Loss

Although your instincts may prefer exiting a trade at the moment it drops through your stop-loss, it is not the most profitable approach. Prices can be very volatile during the day. Much of this volatility is caused by moderate-size orders hitting the market during quiet periods. Yes, there are quiet periods. Most activity occurs at the open and falls off to a low at lunchtime. After lunch, volume increases until activity is again high in the last half-hour of trading. Volume during the day has a "U" pattern. Much smaller orders can move prices in the middle of the day.

To protect yourself against false breakouts, exit your trade only when the stop-loss level is broken as of the close of trading. If prices break below the stop during the trading session but close above your stop price, you don't get out. There is a special order for this type of trade, called a *stop close only*. If you want to move your Amazon stop up to $42 but only exit if prices close below $42, then your order is:

SELL 1000 AMZN 42.00 STOP CLOSE ONLY

Figure 8.1 shows an example in late March of an intraday penetration of the stop level but a higher close. Prices fell to $57 although the stop order was at $58. Prices closed higher than $58; therefore, the trade was not closed out. Because of the increased volatility, the stop was lowered to the low of the day, $57. This conflicts with an earlier rule, *don't ever lower the stop*, but there is always an exception.

If Volatility Increases

You want to keep your stop farther away if volatility is high and closer if volatility is low. When volatility increases, the stop should be farther from the current price, but *do not lower it*. Instead, *it should be raised at a slower rate* as new support levels are formed. That should be a natural process in charting. With higher volatility, prices make larger swings, and the support levels are farther away. This can also be seen in Figure 8.1 as prices decline from their highs. The price swings cause highs and lows to be farther apart than they were on the bull move.

  If you are concerned with the volatility of the market or concerned with how far away the stop is placed, you should exit the trade. Next time you should trade a smaller position or pick a stock with less volatility.

Fixed Dollar Stop-Loss and Changing Volatility

Look at using a fixed dollar stop-loss from another viewpoint. At the beginning of the Amazon chart a $2 stop-loss might have worked. Near the top of the chart, prices were moving $20 in a single day. If you keep using the same size stop-loss as volatility increases, you will get stopped out on the first price drop. You would net less than if you simply closed out your trade.

  Fixed stops are just as bad if volatility is declining. You start with a $30 stop-loss when the volatility is $20, and prices move lower. Volatility drops to $5 and your stop is still $30 away. Your risk is now greater than your profit potential.

USING A TWO MOVING AVERAGE SYSTEM TO REDUCE RISK

Another simple way to control the risk of a trend-following system is to use two trendlines instead of one. The rules for a two-trend system are:

1. Choose a long calculation period (between 50 and 200 days) and a short calculation period (between 5 and 30 days) for two moving averages.

2. *Buy* when both trendlines are up, and *sell* when one trendline turns down (the fast one will always turn down before the slow one).

The risk of this two-trend system is dependent on the speed of the fastest trend. The shorter the calculation period, the smaller the risk. Instead of one long trade that captures a big price move, this method will have a number of smaller trades. The total profits will usually be less that the single-trend approach, but so will the risk. The resulting reward-to-risk ratio may be much better with the two-trend approach—and you won't be giving back half of your profits at the end of a major price move.

An Amazon Example

Using Amazon from October 1998 through April 1999 (see Figure 8.2), we plot both an 80-day moving average (the straighter, smoother trendline) and a 10-day moving average. The trading rules are to buy when both trends are moving up and sell when the fast trend turns down.

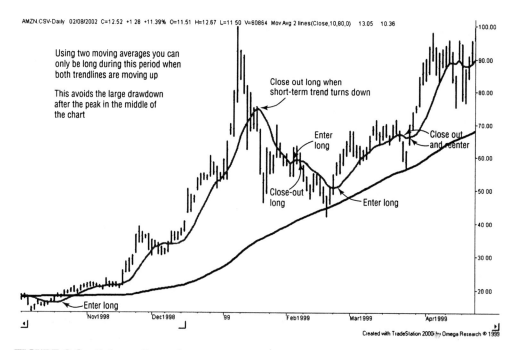

FIGURE 8.2   Using a 2-trend system to control risk. Instead of using a very slow trend and giving back a large part of the profits at the end of the trade, a 2-trend system generates many smaller trades, each with much lower risk.

The buy signal is taken at the end of October 1998 when the faster trendline crosses above the slower one. The entry price was $20. The faster trend doesn't turn down until mid-January, on the fifth day after prices penetrate the fast trendline moving lower. The exit price is about $70 while the slow trend is moving smoothly through the $35 level.

The fast trend briefly turns up again at the beginning of February and we enter a long and get out three days later when the trend turns down for a loss of about $3. In late February we get another chance to go long, this time holding the trade until late March for a profit of only $5 (we were executed far from the trendline on the days the trend turned up and down). The next buy signal lasts about one month and nets another $15. At the very end of the chart there are a few choppy price changes that should have cost about $5 in total.

These trades yielded a total profit of $62 per share. Meanwhile, the slower trend continued to move higher, and the current price is about $98, which gives a net open profit of $78. The word *open* needs to be emphasized. You have a larger profit in the slower trend, but you haven't yet closed out the trade. A lot can happen if you don't take your profits, yet a trend system won't let you out until the trend turns. If prices head down now, you will only capture about $70. You would have taken a greater risk than with the two-trend system and ended up with a smaller profit. *Long-term trends work, but two trends work better than one.*

THE REALITY OF TRADING

A stop-loss doesn't work when you're trying to protect yourself against disaster—when a price shock hits. When a truly unexpected, volatile event hits the market, prices jump. Very, very little trading occurs as the price drops far past your stop order. You don't get executed until prices stop dropping.

You ask, "Aren't I automatically filled when my stop is in the market?" No. As a seller, you're only filled when there is a buyer. When prices drop suddenly, such as on 9/11, there are only a few buyers and loads of sellers. You can only be sure you've been filled on a sell order if prices print higher. Then all the sell orders have been absorbed. In the case of a price shock, you can be sure of getting executed at the lowest price of the move.

So why use a stop order if it doesn't get filled? Sometimes the price pauses in a decline and lets you get out. That's better than not at all. If you use a stop-loss as part of your normal strategy and there are no price shocks, you should get filled near your price. Always set the stop-loss at the point where the reason for the current trade disappears.

A Few Good Reasons to Use a Stop-Loss

1. Using a stop-loss forces you to identify the risk of your trade. You must not enter a trade without knowing the risk.

2. A stop-loss works best when it is set at the point where the reason for the current trade disappears.

3. Used correctly, a stop-loss will reduce risk more than it will reduce profits. If you are stopped out, be sure you have a plan for reentering the next trade.

4. A stop-loss is not likely to save you in a price shock, but you might get lucky.

5. A stop-loss lets you sleep better.

6. Done correctly, a stop-loss is like the cost of insurance—you don't mind paying but don't want to collect.

THE TRADING TIPS

1. *Free exposure, a necessary ingredient for fast trading.* Fast trading requires concentration on entry timing. The first few minutes or hours are the difference between profits and losses. In order to create profits quickly, you need to look for opportunities where the market will give you *free exposure.* Free exposure is a burst of price movement. Without free exposure your losses may eventually outweigh your profits.

   Breakouts are the most common place to look for free exposure. When there is a clear trendline after a sustained downward move, or clear support and resistance marking a sideways period, you need to prepare for the breakout. For example, as prices get closer to the resistance level in a sideways move, you need to place your buy order below that level so that if prices rally to new highs, you are in the trade early and profit by being swept along with the movement. You may benefit from a gap if a lot of orders are clustered at the breakout point. You've gotten free exposure.

   What if prices don't break through resistance? If you are already in the trade and prices start turning down, then get out and take a small loss. When prices look as though they want to test the highs again, place your order ahead of others. It may take a few tries, but the end result is success.

2. *Don't day trade.* Day trading requires full immersion all day. You need to get the basics under control. Day trading speeds up the process so that mistakes occur much more often. It's best to evaluate the price patterns after the market closes and work out a plan. Place your orders before the open of the next day

3. *Be careful if your buy and sell orders can both be reached on a volatile day.* You'll need to look at an intraday chart at the end of the day to find out which order was executed first. It's important to be accurate.

4. *Include orders for both a profitable scenario and a losing one.* When you enter a trade, you must also know where you're going to exit. You don't always need to place your exit order on the same day you enter, but you must know where the trade goes wrong. On the day after you've entered your trade, start placing your stop-loss order to protect your risk. You can also place your profit-taking order if you have one.

5. *Don't be ambiguous.* "I think it's going to sell off" is not a reason for a trade. When you're logging your reasons on the trade blotter, keep it technical.

TRADING GAME #2

Now that you've had some practice trading, it's time to change the rules. We're going to reduce the number of stock and futures markets that you'll trade and increase the size of the positions. Risk now comes into play.

1. Forget all of the positions you are now trading.

2. You have $100,000.

3. You will trade only four stocks. Try to select them from different groups and make sure they are actively traded—for example, Amazon (AMZN), General Electric (GE), Microsoft (MSFT), and Exxon-Mobile (XOM).

4. Each stock trade will be 5,000 shares. No partial orders are allowed.

5. You may go short stocks (there is no uptick rule and no borrowing money; capital will count as though a short position was a long position).

6. You will trade two futures, the S&P 500 and Treasury notes. Pick the nearest contract to delivery. Delivery months are March (H), June (M), September (U), and December (Z).

7. You trade only 1 contract each of S&P and Treasury note futures. There will be no commissions.

8. You will start with no positions. Begin your accounting with no open trades and no history. Prepare the history as before.

9. Profits will count. In the first game it was important to try out the techniques. Now you need to pay attention to how near or far you place your stop-loss order. If you're placing your stops too close or too far away, the market will tell you that you're right or wrong.

10. No day trading, please.

11. Keep track of your capital in use. You could lose everything. Remember that 5,000 shares of a $50 stock is $250,000. It adds up. One contract of the S&P 500 may cost only $20,000 in margin to trade, but a 20-point move in one day is a profit or loss of $5,000, 5 percent of your capital. That adds up, too.

12. Continue writing a brief explanation with each order.

13. By now you should be able to keep the correct accounting of your positions. In real trading you must know your profits and losses every day before you enter the new orders.

14. Do not lose more than 20 percent of your capital on any one trade. A better risk is 10 percent. Large risk means that you're not diversifying, but trying to profit from one good trade. You should have a number of trades working at the same time. You should expect three of four trades to be profitable. If two of four are profitable you're still okay. If one of four is profitable, then you're not looking at each market as a unique opportunity. You need the diversification to control risk. Be sure your trades reflect the special patterns of each market.

15. Enter your orders clearly.

16. Don't forget: We are trading, not investing. Don't hold your trades long—two to five days is about right. Target a reasonable profit. Get out when it goes the wrong way.

Good luck!

Questions

1. The best place for a stop-loss is (*a*) as close as possible, (*b*) based on how much you can afford to lose, or (*c*) a support or resistance level.

2. What is the closest point at which you would place a stop-loss order? Why?

3. When you enter a new long position, where would you place your initial stop-loss?

4. If you have just entered a long position, when would you raise your stop-loss for the first time?

5. What is the advantage of using a stop close only order on your long position?

6. Why would you use a fast and a slow trend instead of just a slow trend?

7. If you've placed your stop-loss at $35 for your long position (entered at $40) and a price shock causes a sudden, large drop to $25, what are you likely to get as your exit price?

CHAPTER 9

One-Day Chart Patterns and Reversals

Watching a chart develop is fascinating. It is a study in human behavior. If that stock or futures market is traded in large volume, then it is a study in mass psychology. The classic examples of investor behavior have been reviewed many times, but none better than in Mackay's *Extraordinary Popular Delusions and the Madness of Crowds*, where he describes the history of the South Sea Bubble and Tulipmania. You may draw your own conclusions as to whether the Japanese Nikkei or the Nasdaq index were similar "bubbles."

Index markets have much greater liquidity than individual stocks. It was Charles Dow who decided to create an index to reduce the effects of manipulation in a single issue. His analysis was based on the reliability of index patterns. Although stocks are much more liquid than in Dow's time, the players are also far larger. Institutions with pension funds and large investment funds will overwhelm all other traders when they are entering or exiting one stock. They can create a pattern in one stock that reflects their own actions, yet that price movement can be absorbed into a larger index, such as the S&P 500, with little significance.

In this chapter we will look at one-day chart patterns, those reflected in a single bar showing the opening, high, low, and closing price of the day. Of course, that bar only makes sense when viewed relative to the previous bars. Some of these patterns only exist after the fact; that is, you can't tell they've occurred until you look back at the chart a few days later. These patterns have less value because they don't give immediate feedback, but they help to paint a larger picture. We'll see how anticipation of some of these patterns can give you free exposure, the ability to profit from the action of the masses.

GAPS

A *gap* is a day in which the low price is above the high of the previous day (upward gap) or the high is below the low of the previous day (downward gap). A gap is most often reaction to unexpected news. Gaps are more common in individual stocks than indices. Individual stocks likely will provide surprising news of quarterly dividends, guidance, new products, failure to get Federal approval for a new drug or acquisition, scandals, and countless other items.

A gap also can result from many buy orders clustered at the same place. This often happens when a stock has been trading in a clear sideways range. Traders will place buy orders at the point of a new high price, looking for a breakout to start a new upward trend. When prices touch that level, all of the orders are triggered, there are many more buyers than sellers, and the price jumps up.

Common Gap

Gaps occur often. They can be seen as a small white space on a chart. Most of them are not important. When you look back at a chart, many of these gaps occur within a trading range. They don't result in a new high or low price, and the patterns that follow don't begin a new trend or show any signs of being significant.

You can call a common gap simply a "gap" or a "plain old gap" or simply ignore it. A common gap is filled within a few days. That is, if prices jumped up, then they will drift lower with the next few sessions until the subsequent price lows overlap the gap. In the beginning of September 1999 (see Figure 9.1) Microsoft prices gapped higher by about 50¢ from their previous high of $92 (gap #3). In the next two days prices traded slightly higher and then *filled the gap* by trading below $92. Common gaps are always filled within a few days. You need to wait before you know that it was a common gap.

Breakaway Gap

The *breakaway gap* is the most useful of all gaps because it can be used at the moment it occurs. It is a price jump that breaks the previous chart pattern. In Figure 9.1 the breakaway gap (gap #2) in late August occurs after a $20 drop and a short sideways period. It is easy to recognize when it occurs, but not easy to trade profitably unless it occurs at the exact point of a resistance line.

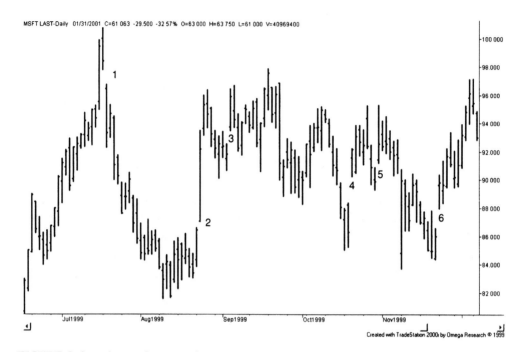

FIGURE 9.1   Microsoft gaps. There are six gaps during the period from July through November 1999. Three of the gaps, during September and October, would be considered common gaps. They did not result in new highs or lows, and the price movement that followed wasn't important.

A breakaway shows a change in investor attitude. Larger gaps occur when there is more participation and the breakout pattern is clear. When it is clear, traders bunch their orders together at the same obvious point. It is a strong, reliable trading signal.

Two Breakaway Gap Examples.   There are two obvious breakaway gaps in Figure 9.1, a sharp move up in late August (gap #2) and another smaller breakout in late November (gap #6). With gap #2, if you had waited for the end of the day to act, you would have been long just above $92, nearly $5 higher than the previous day. There would have been quite a few days in which prices traded higher and you could have made a small profit. Some traders would have been nervous when prices fell under $92 and taken a loss.

In the second case the breakaway gap was larger, but the day's trading range was smaller. You would be long on the close at $94. In this example each of the next 10 days would have been profitable although there were no new highs. To a short-term trader these look like breakaway gaps; for a longer-term view they might be common gaps. For the long-term trader a breakaway gap would occur on a jump above the highs at 98, or below the lows at 82.

Trading the Breakaway Gap. To take advantage of a breakaway gap, you need to be long before the upward breakout. Most profits are made by anticipating, not following. That's not an easy task. You need the profit from the jump and price flow if you are to get free exposure.

Anticipating the gap makes most sense when the trading pattern is clear, when there is a strong downtrend line that any fool can see, and when prices have been trading in an obvious sideways pattern. You can then place your buy order slightly below the point of breakout, inside the trading range. You might be wrong a few times and take a small loss, but the profit from the breakout should be enough to recover all the losses.

Figure 9.2 shows different types of gaps on an Amazon chart. The first breakaway gap in December 1998 occurs on a move through clear resistance just below $40. It is an opportunity for free exposure. The other breakaway gap in July 1999 is not as clear on the chart, but price might have fallen quickly through recent support right after the opening bell.

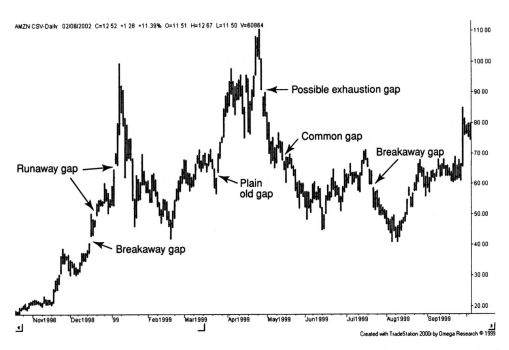

FIGURE 9.2 An assortment of Amazon gaps. This Amazon chart shows a good sample of different gaps. The breakaway gap occurs when prices move out of a previous sideways pattern, or change direction. A runaway gap occurs in the middle of a sustained trend.

Exhaustion Gap

A gap that occurs just after the peak of an extended, extreme run-up is an *exhaustion gap*. It is caused when traders realize that prices cannot to go straight up because the stock is already overpriced, and the buyers suddenly disappear. An exhaustion gap is usually followed by a substantial drop in prices, but that does not mean new highs won't occur after prices stabilize. It sets up an interesting trading pattern.

The price peak that precedes an exhaustion gap becomes a major clear resistance level. As prices move back toward that high, traders will be looking to sell at any opportunity. In Figure 9.2 we see an exhaustion gap two days after the high in April 1999. On the following day, prices trade up into the gap, closing slightly higher on the day, and afterward prices fall. There are two more exhaustion gaps in Figure 9.2, one following the peak in July 1999 and a small one in August 1999. Both of these secondary peaks show lower volatility and occur well below the highest price; therefore, we would treat them as a short-term indicator. When prices move above the high of the third peak, we quickly accept the fact that the recent top was not important.

A true exhaustion gap must be seen in context with other prices. It should follow inceasing volatility, preferably extremely high volatility. It should follow an unusually high price. Prices should continue to be volatile during the decline. The second and third exhaustion gaps in Figure 9.2 do not satisfy the high volatility and high price criteria needed.

Runaway Gaps

A *runaway gap* confirms a trend and indicates acceleration in the price move. It is a good confirmation of direction and, if you are long the Euro in December of 2000 (as in Figure 9.3), it quickly adds to your profits.

Runaway gaps are marked in Figures 9.2 and 9.3. They occur while prices are already in a trend. They may be caused by latecomers trying to jump on board a moving train. The sellers aren't interested because the trend is still moving up quickly; therefore, the buyers need to pay a higher price to join in. Being late to the party is never a good idea. In Figure 9.3, those who bought the Euro at .9250 would have been lucky to have captured any profit. It's more likely that a trader who was late getting in will be late getting out.

Spikes

A *spike high* is seen as a day in which the high is well above the high of the preceding and following days. It is at least a local top; it could be a major top.

FIGURE 9.3 Euro chart showing gaps and spikes. This Euro chart has a collection of gaps and spikes. Note that the first two spikes, in November 2000 (an upward spike) and April 2001 (a downward spike), were broken with breakaway gaps.

It usually can be seen the day after it occurs. In Figure 9.4, U.S. bonds show spikes in mid-June, mid-July, and mid-August. In each case it took more than a week before new highs exceeded the high of the spikes. Spike highs are most useful if the close of the day is near the lows. We then have some early warning that the spike high will be a top.

A Word of Caution about Spikes.   Spikes may seem infrequent and obvious because most potential spikes disappear into normal price patterns. That is, after an upward jump, prices continue higher or form a sideways pattern so that the potential spike becomes an invisible part of a larger price pattern. That makes a spike a less dependable pattern for trading.

In Figure 9.4 we can see that three days after each spike, the prices looked as if they might fall sharply. Instead, prices started back up, moving above the spike high before correcting and finally moving higher. Each of these cases proved a good short-term opportunity, but not the beginning of trend change.

On the far right of Figure 9.4 we see two volatile one-day price drops after the high. Had prices opened higher and remained higher after either day, we

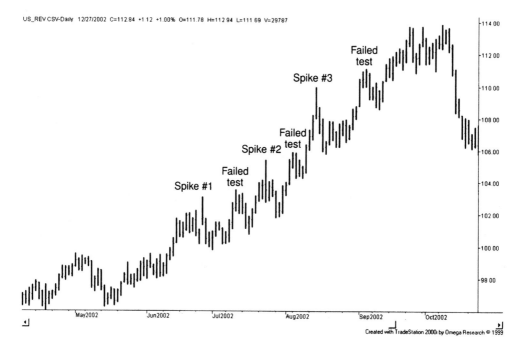

US_REV CSV-Daily 12/27/2002 C=112.84 +1.12 +1.00% O=111.78 H=112.94 L=111.69 V=29787

FIGURE 9.4   False tops in bonds. From June through October 2002, U.S. bonds show three spikes that form potential V tops after one to three days following the spike. Each spike was followed by an attempt to move higher, each time making new highs then falling back. Patterns look very different when you are trading than when you look at the chart in retrospect.

would see a downward spike. Don't act too quickly to accept a spike as a top or bottom. Even as a fast trader, buying on either day would have produced a large loss. You are safer if you treat them as if they will disappear, which happens much more often.

ISLAND REVERSAL

An *island reversal,* or an *island top,* is a single price bar, or group of bars, sitting at the top of a price move and isolated by a gap on both sides, before and after the island formation. Combined with high volatility, this formation has the reputation of being a major turning point. The gap on the right side of the island top can be considered an exhaustion gap.

You can find quite a few island tops in the Euro chart (see Figure 9.4), although most of them are at different stages during the strong trends. Island tops can disappear into the overall chart pattern along with other formations even though they are very good at defining a local top. Look at January 2001, just to the right of the highest point on the chart, and you can see an island

HO CF-Daily 01/02/2002 C=5786.00 +253.00 +4.57% O=5650.00 H=5800.00 L=5560.00 V=606

FIGURE 9.5 Heating oil shows an extreme island reversal. Although this pattern did not remain a top for long, it was an exciting moment in time.

top of two bars. In March 2001 there is another island top of eight bars formed as prices decline. There is an *island bottom* near the beginning of the chart, in October 2000, that is the low point of the chart.

Even the most extreme-looking island reversals may not remain the top for long. In August 1991 heating oil jumped 6¢ in one day (see Figure 9.5), stopped, and then reversed. It may look strange on the chart when we see it in context with later trading, but it was an exciting moment at the time.

REVERSAL DAY

A day in which there is a new high followed by a lower close is a *downward reversal day*. An *upward reversal day* is a new low followed by a higher close. Reversal days are a common part of technical conversation and appear to be an important sign of a change of direction. It is very likely that a reversal day will start a change of direction after a sustained trend up, or a move that peaks on high volatility.

The rapid drop of Tyco in January 2002 (see Figure 9.6) shows that a reversal day occurred at the top just before the final fall. During the decline

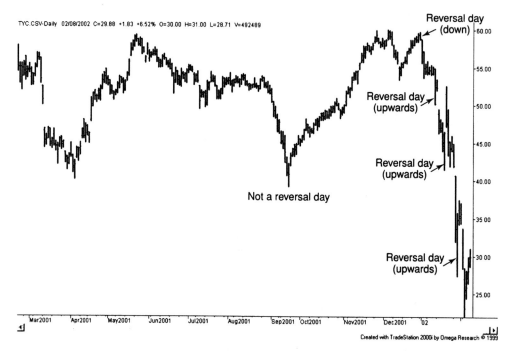

FIGURE 9.6   Reversal days. Upward and downward reversal days can be seen during the precipitous decline of Tyco. Reversal days are valuable when used selectively.

there were three upward reversal days, each followed by at least one higher day—no small accomplishment in a stock that is in a free fall. If a stock is trading on new lows for the current move and, then closes higher on the day, the selling pressure must be exhausted. We shouldn't be surprised to see the stock trade higher the next day. After all, prices don't go down or up every day without reprieve. There are always buyers and sellers.

Perception and Reality

The problem with a reversal day is that it is a very short term indicator. It does not tell you that the major trend has changed, only that the next day is likely to trade in the opposite direction.

Another important problem with reversal days is that we only look for them during special situations, particularly when prices are volatile or when we are near what we think is the top or bottom of a move. Reversal days happen often when we're not looking. If you study the reliability of reversal days, you would find that they have no special predictive qualities—no one has proved that they are profitable on balance. Yet, experienced traders know that they are important.

Limit your use of reversal days to special situations, those days when you are looking for prices to change direction. Then, only expect the next day to reverse. If prices fail to continue their new direction or show a tendency to reverse again, get out. A reversal day cannot win over the major trend; it can only signal a short pause.

THRUST DAYS AND RUN DAYS

An *upthrust* day is one in which the close is higher than the previous day's high. A *run day* is a more powerful version of a thrust day and it must have two qualities; (1) The high must be greater than the high of the *past N* days, and (2) the low must be lower than the low of the *subsequent N* days. Therefore, a run day is not known until N days after it has occurred. The importance of a run day depends upon N. The larger the value of N, the more important the run day.

Selecting the Important Thrust Days

A thrust day is a good concept for distinguishing a weak or strong move up (or down). Consider that the volume of trading varies across the day, and there can be very low volume through the middle of the trading day. A new high or low that occurs on a moderate-size order during a low-volume time could temporarily push prices to new highs or lows, breaking through a resistance or support level. If the price closes back inside the lines, perhaps even unchanged on the day, we would be suspicious that the breakout was false. If instead prices closed outside the previous range, above the resistance line, we would be confident that something new was happening. Therefore, a thrust day that also breaks a trendline or moves outside a range is important. It may be unimportant at other times.

Are Run Days Useful At All?

There are many chart patterns that confirm the trend. That is, they assure you the trend is still intact and you can hold your position. The jury is still out on run days. Although they are a well-recognized price pattern, they are not "timely"; that is, it is often too late by the time you can identify the pattern.

TYC.CSV-Daily 02/08/2002 C=29.88 +1.83 +6.52% O=30.00 H=31.00 L=28.71 V=492489

FIGURE 9.7 Run days. A 5-day run day is recognized when the high is greater than the high of the previous 5 days and the low is lower than the low of the following 5 days. Both thrust days and run days provide evidence of a trending market, although run days may not be timely.

In Figure 9.7 we see eight cases of a five-day run day. We use five-days to be more selective and to expect greater reliability. Don't forget that we can recognize this five-day run pattern only after it occurs. In the first case, the fifth day following the run day is a sharp move up, followed by a sharp reversal, and then a renewal of the upward trend. In each case shown, except for the last three, the fifth day following the run day seems to be a local high. After that, price dropped off for a few days before recovering and continuing the trend.

When to Use the Run Day Pattern

Run days suffer from the same problem as other chart patterns—they are less dependable when fewer days are used. In this case, when you use more days to recognize a run day, you may have waited too long for it to be a useful trading rule. A five-day run needs 10 days before it is identified. In the Tyco chart (Figure 9.7) the trend continued, if erratically, after the run days, but toward the end of the chart they correspond to where the trend was exhausted. A run day may be helpful for confirming a trend after the fact, but there are better patterns for trading.

WIDE-RANGING DAYS, OUTSIDE DAYS, AND INSIDE DAYS

Both wide-ranging days and outside days are typical of higher volatility. A *wide-ranging day* is a day of much higher volatility than recent days. An *outside day* must have both a higher high and lower low than the previous day. Examples of wide-ranging days and outside days can be seen in Figure 9.8.

Wide-Ranging Days

A wide-ranging day is likely to be the result of a price shock, some unexpected news, or a breakout in which many orders are piggybacked, causing a large increase in volatility. A wide-ranging day could turn out to be a spike or an island reversal. Because very high volatility can't be sustained, we can expect that a wide-ranging day will be followed by some type of reversal, even a one-day pause. When a wide-ranging day occurs, the direction of the

FIGURE 9.8 **Wide-ranging days, outside days, and inside days.** From October 1999 to June 2000, Tyco shows a variety of daily patterns.

close (if the close is near the high or low) is a strong indication of the continued direction.

Outside Days

An outside day often precedes a reversal. An outside day can also be a wide-ranging day if the volatility is high, but when volatility is low, it provides a weak signal. As with so many other chart patterns, if one day has a tiny trading range, followed by an outside day of normal volatility, there is very little information in the pattern. Selection is important.

Inside Days

An inside day is one where the high is lower than the previous high and the low is higher than the previous low. That is, an inside day is one where both the highs and lows are inside the previous day's trading range.

An inside day represents consolidation, or lower volatility. In turn, lower volatility is most often associated with the end of a price move. After a burst of activity and a surge of upward direction, prices have reached a point at which the buyers are already in and the price has moved too far to attract more buyers. Volume drops, volatility drops, and we see an inside day.

Very often, an inside day is followed by a change of direction, but that is not guaranteed. We only know that the event that drove prices up is now over. If more news surfaces to ignite prices, the next more could just as easily be up.

Figure 9.8 shows two inside days at the price peak on the top left of the chart. The first inside day is followed by a small move lower, then a small move higher, and then by another inside day. This last inside day precedes a major sell-off. On the right top of the chart there are two inside days immediately before another sharp drop. So far, this looks good.

Take a few minutes to look at the chart more carefully. There are at least 20 other inside days. Try to decide whether these other patterns are as reliable. We again face the issue of selection. Can we ignore certain inside days, yet quickly identify others so that we can trade? Is an inside day more reliable after a price move of 3 percent, or 5 percent?

A COMMON MESSAGE ABOUT ONE-DAY PATTERNS

Because these chart patterns are based on the events of a single day, they occur often. High frequency tends to make a pattern less reliable and less profitable. You cannot expect to profit from a one-day pattern unless you are selective about the situations that apply best.

During a quiet, sideways period of price activity, none of these patterns will be useful. When prices have moved quickly and volatility has increased, we look for a sign that the move is over. That allows us to take profits on the trade and, if you're an active trader, reverse your position. At those times, many of the one-day patterns, such as a key reversal or an inside day, will be highly reliable.

FEEDBACK PROCESS

Chart patterns confirm the trend, and yet the trend creates the chart patterns. It's a feedback process. Although many patterns are based on the way people trade, some patterns are the result of expectation. If you see a highly volatile up day, especially a reversal day where prices close lower, traders expect prices to change direction the next day. Therefore, they are encouraged to sell.

The recognition of patterns and the expectation of results make it difficult to decide whether all these patterns are true because of the way people trade, or because traders believe they are true. Does it matter?

TRADING GAME

Buy the rumor, sell the fact (anticipation vs. reality). XOM was trading higher than the market and then announced higher than expected profits from the merger of Exxon and Mobil (a year earlier). The market moves on anticipation. Once the news is out, everyone knows what should be done.

The reality of downgrading a stock. Any brokerage house, such as Goldman Sachs, announces a downgrade only after it has already liquidated the positions for its own clients. They would be foolish to tell everyone else first and then compete with them for a good price. That makes it a good opportunity to do the opposite—buy after others have sold. The advance liquidation plus those who get out because of the downgrade force the price down to unreasonably low levels (at least in the short term).

Money moves all markets the same way. During times when there is no special news about one of the stocks in the S&P, that stock price moves with the S&P. The use of futures and trusts (such as Spyders, SPY) allows traders to buy and sell the entire index of S&P stocks at one time. When that index goes out of line with the weighted average of the individual stocks comprising the S&P, *program traders* step in to correct that difference using *arbitrage*. This causes all stocks in the S&P to move together. Because of direct trading of the S&P Index as well a program trading, an individual stock may turn from up to down at the same resistance level seen on the S&P chart.

Questions

1. Define an upward gap.
2. When is a gap most likely to occur?
3. Name four gaps most often found on a chart. Briefly explain how to recognize each.
4. If today's price action is much more volatile than the previous month and the high is much higher than the high of the same period, would we call the pattern a *spike* or a *wide-ranging day*?
5. Define an *island reversal bottom*.
6. When are reversal patterns most reliable? (*a*) After a sustained move in one direction, or (*b*) after a highly volatile move?
7. Why would a *five-day run day* pattern be considered *not* timely for trading?
8. After a sustained upward price move, there are two inside days. What does this tell you?

CHAPTER 10

Continuation Patterns

Prices have trending periods that can be traded profitably. Each trend must have a beginning (where prices show a tendency to want to go higher or lower), a continuous sustained period during which we clearly see the direction, and finally an end. These phases reflect the confidence of the investors and their behavior. *Continuation patterns* are a set of formations that appear during these phases and both reflect and confirm the current stage of the trend. *A continuation pattern occurs within a long-term trend and is expected to be resolved by continuing in the direction the trend.*

SYMMETRIC TRIANGLES

Triangles are large formations that occur throughout a trend. At the beginning of a trend there is greater uncertainty and a *symmetric triangle* is most likely to appear. A symmetric triangle (see Figure 10.1) is formed by a price consolidation, that uncertainty results in decreasing volatility in a such way that prices narrow to the center of the previous trading range. The breakout from a symmetric triangle often marks the beginning of a longer-term trend.

DESCENDING AND ASCENDING TRIANGLES

Even during a clear downward trend, prices will rally. Because the trend is clear, sellers are anxious to step in and sell these upward moves, looking for

FIGURE 10.1 Symmetric and descending triangles. These patterns, shown on a back-adjusted price chart of gold futures, are formed as confidence in the trend direction increases. The symmetric triangle comes near the beginning of a trend, followed by more than one descending triangle. These patterns are resolved in the trend direction.

the trend to continue. The top of the rally is likely to be the last support point at which prices broke out of a previous pattern. The recent lows of the new trend form a temporary support level, and prices may bounce off that level while short-term traders play for small profits. This action forms a descending triangle. As more traders are convinced that prices are still heading lower, the rallies off support are sold sooner, causing a narrower pattern, until prices finally break below support. The *descending triangle* is complete. In an upward trend an *ascending triangle* would be formed.

Size of the Triangles

A triangle should take no less than two weeks to form; however, they can span a much longer period. In the gold chart (see Figure 10.2) there are triangles of mostly two to three weeks, but the descending triangle in the middle lasts three months. The descending triangle evolved as traders decided that gold was still in a downtrend.

GC_REV.CSV-Daily 02/20/2002 C=292 60 -1 00 -0 34% O=294 00 H=294.30 L=291.10 V=32744

FIGURE 10.2 More triangles in a falling gold market. There are more triangles hidden in the gold chart that is shown. These triangles can vary in size, some encompassing others. Because they reflect trader confidence and behavior, you must expect some inconsistencies.

After the large descending triangle was resolved, a symmetric triangle appears. Traders are again uncertain of the direction. Once resolved, prices begin a steep descent. We may have chosen to redraw the small descending triangle as a larger one to include the previous symmetric triangle. We also might find another descending triangle just before the last major drop in mid-February.

Triangles can be very consistent indicators of investor confidence. Because they reflect human behavior, they are not always perfect in appearance and not always perfect in pattern.

FLAGS

A *flag* is a smaller pattern than a triangle and is formed by a correction in a bull market or a rally in a bear market. Flags are congestion areas that lean away from the direction of the trend. At the beginning of a trend the flags and pennants may not lean away from the direction of the new trend formed by

FIGURE 10.3 Upward flags in a downtrend. Flags are smaller formations than triangles and are formed opposite to the trend direction. They can be as small as one week or as long as two months.

two parallel lines, similar to a channel. If the first flag after an upward break-out leans down, it confirms the new upward trend.

Figure 10.3 shows a series of three ascending flags, each larger than the previous one, in a downward trend. In a downtrend, the most important part of the flag is the bottom line, or support line, because it must be watched for a break and a renewal of the downtrend. The top line that forms the flag can be drawn parallel to the bottom line or across the peaks, if there is more than one peak.

PENNANTS AND WEDGES

Pennants are irregular triangles normally leaning toward the trend, similar to a descending triangle in a downtrend. During a sustained trend, triangles are large, clear formations, and flags are frequent, smaller changes of direction with parallel sides. Pennants are catch-alls. They are formations that occur during the trend, but the lines converge rather than form parallel sides. They usually lean toward the trend, but that's not a requirement. If it looks like a formation but you can't quite identify it, call it a pennant.

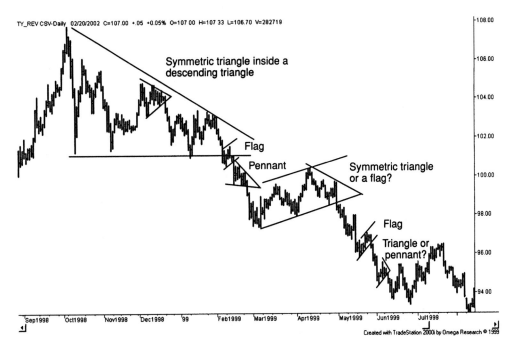

FIGURE 10.4   An assortment of continuation patterns. All of these patterns are resolved by prices moving lower. A pennant can be found in the middle of the chart.

In Figure 10.4 there is an assortment of continuation patterns applied to Treasury note futures, all resolved by a break down of prices. A small, classic pennant can be found in the center of the chart, pointing down. Following the pennant is a move up that could be interpreted as a large flag or a symmetric triangle. If you don't think that the triangle is exactly symmetric, you can call it a pennant.

In the General Electric (GE) chart, Figure 10.5, there is a large pennant in the middle. Pennants, just as other continuation patterns, represent a pause in a trend, followed by a consolidation. The way in which investors enter the market, whether carefully or anxiously, ultimately will determine which continuation pattern is formed.

WEDGES

If the pattern looks as if it's a large pennant but does not come to a point, then we can call it a *wedge*. In an upward trending market the wedge should be rising. A strong upward wedge will have both lower and upper lines rising, as

GE LAST-Daily 01/31/2001 C=45.980 -72.583 -61.22% O=46.750 H=46.950 L=45.560 V=21346100

Rising wedge

Rising wedge

Pennant

Created with TradeStation 2000i by Omega Research © 1999

FIGURE 10.5   A strong rising wedge. The strong wedge formation has both the lower and upper lines rising, as seen in this chart of General Electric near the end of 1999.

shown in the center of the GE chart, Figure 10.5, near the end of 1999. The earlier wedge has a horizontal upper line, bridging the pattern between a wedge and a rising triangle. In either case, investors are testing resistance and buying sooner as prices drop. The result is a continuation of the upward trend.

A typical rising wedge would have a lower line that is at a steeper angle than the upper line, as seen in the GE chart, Figure 10.6. The earlier wedge formation shown is nearly symmetric. If we study the bigger picture, we can see that the uncertainty at the beginning of the trend is reflected in the symmetric formation. The rising wedge occurs after the trend is well established and investors can anticipate a continuation. The third, smaller pattern in Figure 10.6 may be treated as a wedge or a pennant.

CONTINUATION PATTERNS ARE NOT A SCIENCE

It is not important to be able to classify the pattern exactly, because not all patterns are clear. It is very important to understand that a trend will create large patterns that lean in the direction of the trend and small correction

GE LAST-Daily 01/31/2001 C=45.980 -72.583 -61.22% O=46.750 H=46.950 L=45.560 V=21346100

Created with TradeStation 2000i by Omega Research © 1999

FIGURE 10.6 Typical rising wedge. More often, a rising wedge shows a steeply rising lower line and a moderately declining upper line. You might also see this as a large pennant. The early wedge is more symmetric, indicating that the direction of price is not yet clear.

patterns that lean away from the trend. If the patterns take on a symmetric form or begin to lean in the wrong direction, the market is telling you that the trend is weakening, or it is over.

TRADING TIPS

Don't avoid selling short. There is a lot of money to be made quickly as prices decline. Prices tend to drop faster than they rise. Being short GE and long XOM could give you valuable diversification and greatly reduce your risk. Because they are part of the S&P index they may move together most of the time, but you can profit from the *spread*, where GE is *relatively weaker* than XOM.

*Be careful about using a single-spike low for your support leve*l. A spike represents an extreme. A downside spike exists because a lot of traders came in and sold on the price drop. However, it's a wide-ranging, extreme day, and the bottom of that spike is an unreliable number. You might do best to ignore the spike for the purposes of support and resistance levels. There may be hesitation as prices test the lows of the spike, but it's not likely to stop the decline.

Questions

1. How does a continuation pattern help you trade?
2. At what points in a trend is a symmetric triangle most likely to occur?
3. Which triangle is most likely to occur in the middle of an upward trend, a symmetric, ascending, or descending triangle?
4. Describe a flag in an uptrend.
5. What is the difference between a pennant and a triangle?
6. During a downtrend, which way does a wedge point?
7. What should you do if a descending triangle is formed during an uptrend?

CHAPTER 11

Top and Bottom Formations

T he most elusive and unrealistic goal of trading is to buy at the bottom or sell at the top. Prices rarely stop where you expect. The only way to see a top or bottom is after they occur. In this chapter we will look at the most popular top and bottom formations and see which ones are the best candidates for trading, and when they can be used.

We have already seen some of the top and bottom patterns, although they may have occurred at different places in the price move. Spikes and reversal days, island reversals, and "V" tops and bottoms are simple formations. Rounded tops and bottoms and head-and-shoulders formations take longer to develop but are very reliable.

"V" TOPS

The classic top is an inverted "V" although it is called a *"V" top*. It is a sharp run up with a single day marking the high, and then an equally fast price drop. It is always accompanied by high volatility and usually high volume. The final peak may also be an upward spike. There is a classic "V" top in Amazon during January 1999, shown in Figure 11.1, and another potential, smaller formation in April that looked as though it was a "V" top two days after, which quickly disappeared into a broader formation of no particular pattern. You can't tell a "V" top, after one day down. The final peak in late April 1999 is broader than a classic "V" top but may still go under the same name.

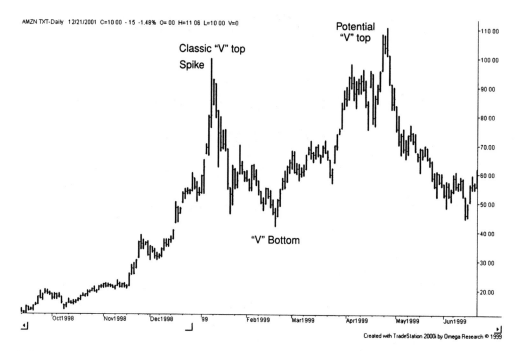

AMZN TXT-Daily 12/21/2001 C=10 00 - 15 -1.48% O= 00 H=11 06 L=10 00 V=0

FIGURE 11.1   Classic "V" top in Amazon. The top in January 1999 is a classic "V" top; the highest top in late April is slightly broader, the result of a three-day price pattern. Just before the last top, in early April, was a potential "V" top that disappeared after three days.

The Blow-Off

A "V" top with an extended spike at the top is thought of as a *blow-off*. High volatility, high volume, and a pattern of accelerating upward prices must reach a point where the momentum can't be sustained. The range on the last day is wider than previous days, and the following day opens much lower and remains lower. The market thinks about whether it can muster enough energy to continue the run-up, decides that it cannot, and collapses. Everyone changes their opinion from bull to bear on the same day, and each wants out before the others. Prices drop faster than they rose during the last part of the bull market.

"V" BOTTOMS

"V" bottoms are much less common that their upside counterparts. They occur more often in futures, where supply and demand can change dramat-

CL_REV CSV-Daily 02/20/2002 C=20.43 - 69 -3.27% O=20.86 H=20.90 L=20.35 V=151308

FIGURE 11.2 **"V" bottoms in crude oil.** Just as with "V" tops, a "V" bottom is the a clear statement that prices have gone too far, too fast.

ically and leverage causes surges of buying and selling. Both "V" tops and bottoms should be read as a sign that prices have gone too far, too fast. Both buyers and sellers need time to reevaluate the fundamentals to decide where prices should be. "V" bottoms are followed by a rebound and then a period of sideways movement. Two good examples can be found in the crude oil chart (Figure 11.2).

DOUBLE TOPS AND BOTTOMS

A *double top* is just what you would expect, one price peak followed a few days or weeks by another peak, stopping very close to the same level. A *double bottom*, more common than a double top, is the occurrence of two price valleys with the lowest prices at nearly the same level. Because prices are more likely to settle for a while at a lower price than a high one, prices often test a previous support level, causing a double bottom.

Double Tops

Tops and bottoms occur at the same level because traders believe that the same reason prices failed to go higher the first time will be the reason they fail the second time. At extreme tops and bottoms this is true. The very high or low prices are not supported by the fundamentals of the business or by the supply and demand numbers. They are pushed to extremes by crowd psychology without regard to reason. Traders, looking for a place to sell at an unreasonably high price, target the previous point where prices failed. As prices move higher to test that level, increased speculative selling causes the buyers to realize that something is wrong, and they back away from the market, causing prices to drop and forming a double top.

Although a classic double top is thought to peak at exactly the same price, selling in anticipation of that test of the top may cause the second peak to be lower than the first. Figure 11.3 shows one type of double top in crude oil. Although some double tops are two sharp peaks, this one looks as though it was gathering energy yet still failed to make new highs.

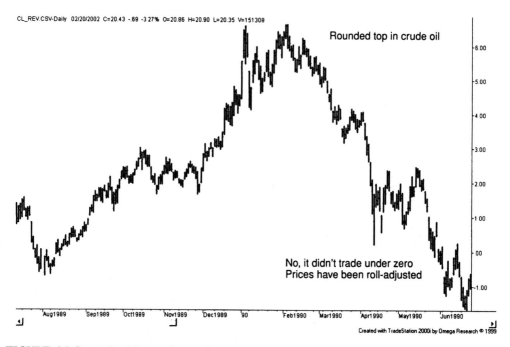

FIGURE 11.3   A double top in crude oil. The double top, formed at the beginning of 1990, turned into a rounded top. Prices have been created by *back-adjusting* individual futures contracts; therefore, the scale on the right doesn't show the actual prices in 1990. The pattern, however, is identical.

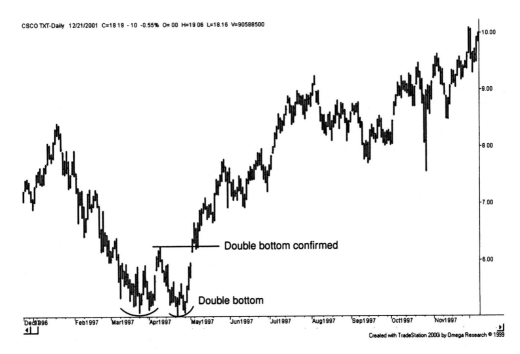

CSCO TXT-Daily 12/21/2001 C=18 19 -10 -0.55% O= 00 H=19 06 L=18.16 V=90588500

Double bottom confirmed

Double bottom

Created with TradeStation 2000i by Omega Research © 1999

FIGURE 11.4   A double bottom in Cisco. In this double bottom pattern there are four failed attempts to move lower, followed by a faster break upward. When prices penetrate the highs between the two bottom patterns, we have a confirmation of the bottom. Our first profit target would be an equal distance above the confirmation, at about $7.50.

Double Bottoms

Bottoms are more orderly than tops. They should be quiet rather than volatile. They are caused by prices reaching a level that is low enough for the normal investor to recognize that there is little additional downside potential. Economists might call this the *point of equilibrium*. Neither buyers nor sellers are convinced that prices will continue to move. They wait for further news.

Double bottoms will often test the same price level because large position traders accumulate more stock, or increase their futures position, each time the price falls to their target level. Once prices are low, there is less chance of absolute loss. Selling a double top can be very risky. The greatest risk when buying a double bottom is that your timing is wrong. If prices don't rally soon, you've used your capital poorly.

Cisco shows a double bottom in Figure 11.4, although it lacks the clear decline in volatility that we would like to see. The small spikes down show four attempts to go lower, followed by a faster move up. When prices cross above the highs formed between the two bottom patterns, we have a completion, or *confirmation*, of the double bottom.

TRIPLE TOPS AND BOTTOMS

Triple tops and bottoms are considerably less common than double tops and bottoms, and much less likely to turn at exactly the same price. Figure 11.5 shows a classic triple top in natural gas. There are many other patterns that comprise this top, including an island reversal as the first peak, a spike as the second, and finally a lower, wider peak that ends the move.

If you look at the days following the first two peaks, each looked as though it marked the top. After the first island reversal, prices dropped $2; after the second peak there was another large gap down and a one-day loss of more than $1. We can say only that investors were very nervous at $10.

A triple bottom that can be traded is most likely to occur at low prices and low volatility, much the same as a double bottom. Prices show an inability to go lower because investors are willing to accumulate a position at a good value.

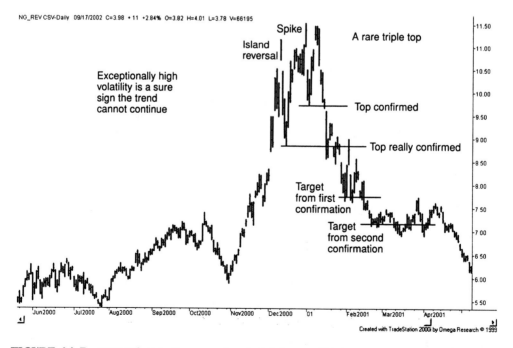

FIGURE 11.5 Natural gas shows a classic triple top. Triple tops can contain other patterns. In this chart, the first peak is an island reversal and the second is a spike. The third peak fails to reach the highest price, making it easier for traders to sell.

THE DANGER OF TRADING DOUBLE AND TRIPLE TOPS

We can find many examples of double tops and a fair number of triple tops. There is a lot of money to be made by selling these tops at the right place. Before you start planning your next coup, think about why a triple top is so rare. It's because prices continue higher and the potential triple top disappears into a strong bull market pattern. You need to be very selective about trading tops. Few of them actually become tops when you look back at the chart.

TARGETING PROFITS AFTER TOPS AND BOTTOMS

We're going to use volatility to decide when to take profits. Volatility is considered reasonably stable by traders because it seems to increase slowly and decrease slowly. It can remain at the same level for extended periods. When prices are running up sharply, we expect volatility to continue to increase until the top is formed. That gives us a tool to target a retracement price and, in turn, tells us when to take profits and exit the trade.

Figure 11.5, natural gas, is a perfect example of a volatile top formation that offers a trading opportunity. The first pullpack after the island reversal brought prices to $8.20, followed by the a test of the top that formed the second peak. If we had tried to sell the test of the first peak, we would have seen prices go slightly higher and most likely we would have stopped out the trade.

The second retracement was only to $9.00, followed by another run up. We won't try to sell the highs because the risk is too great and the last time we would have been forced out. Instead, we sell when the high fails and the price moves below the first retracement low of $8.20. The break of $8.20 is called *confirming the top*. It creates a final triple top formation. We could have picked the price of $9.00 as a selling point if you are an aggressive trader, but prices could still be jumping around. When it drops from $9.00 to $8.00, you can be sure that prices aren't going to make another test of the highs.

Calculating the Profit Target

We find the profit target by measuring the height of the top formation and projecting it downward from the point marking the end of that pattern, the levels where the *top is confirmed*. In Figure 11.5 there are two confirmations, the first at $9.00 and the second at $8.20. If we mark the top at $10.75, we have two volatility values, $1.75 and $2.65, the differences between the top and the confirmation levels.

We can now find the profit targets by subtracting the volatility from the confirmation levels. For the first trade we get $9.00 − $1.75 = $7.25, and for the second $8.20 − $2.65 = $5.55.

The first target is realistic. Prices are very volatile and a drop of $1.75 could occur very quickly. The second target is less realistic, although prices get to that level after stalling at about $6.50. When targeting a much larger decline, and beginning at a much lower point, it is unrealistic to expect volatility to continue at the same high level. In the decline of natural gas from January through March, we can see that volatility also drops.

When targeting a price that is half the starting point (from $10.75 to $5.55), you must expect volatility to decline. A good estimate is to expect volatility to halve because our second target would be a decline to half the top price, we need to reduce our target by 25 percent (the average decline over the period). That gives us a conservative goal of $6.85, which falls right in the middle of the sideways range that begins in mid-February.

Adjusting for volatility is simply an attempt to be realistic. It's best to be right more often and not try to squeeze every penny out of a trade.

Profit Targets after a Bottom Formation

We apply the same principle to calculate the profit target for bottom formations. We measure the distance from the bottom to the confirmation point and then project that value upward from the confirmation price. If we go back to Figure 11.4, the double bottom in Cisco spanned the price range from about $5.00 to $6.25. We project the volatility of $1.25 up from the breakout at $6.25 to get the target of $7.50. Because volatility should expand as prices rise, we can use the exact volatility calculation as a conservative measure.

ROUNDED TOPS AND BOTTOMS

When prices change direction over a longer time period, they can create a rounded top or bottom pattern. A *rounded top* reflects a gradual change in market forces from buyers to sellers. It is a very clear sign that any attempt to move prices higher has been abandoned. Rounded tops often lead to faster and faster price drops as more investors liquidate or initiate shorts.

In Figure 11.6 we see two classic rounded tops in the German DAX stock index. The first is an example of gathering downside momentum as more investors become aware of the decline. Prices drop faster after a break of the double bottom.

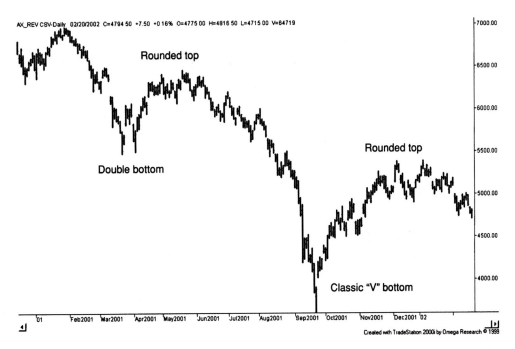

AX_REV CSV-Daily 02/20/2002 C=4794.50 +7.50 +0.16% O=4775.00 H=4816.50 L=4715.00 V=64719

FIGURE 11.6 Two rounded tops. It is unusual to see two rounded tops, one following the other, but this chart of the German DAX shows prices gradually turning from up to down, then accelerating to the downside. A rounded top is a strong sign of a weak market.

ROUNDED BOTTOMS

A *rounded bottom*, similar to a rounded top, is an extended formation where prices gradually turn from down to up. In Figure 11.7 we see a rounded bottom in the Japanese yen followed by a breakaway gap. Because rounded bottoms are a long formation, traders look for a breakout to signal a change in the supply and demand balance. A breakout, whether in stocks or futures, indicates that something new has entered the picture.

Irregular Rounded Bottom

Not all rounded bottoms are perfect. Sometimes you need to look past a few odd spikes or gaps to see the bigger picture. In Figure 11.8 we can identify an irregular rounded bottom. The key to this formation is the way it emerges from the pattern beginning in mid-February 1992 until it accelerates at the beginning of April 1993. The extended bottom formation in crude oil, and the gradual change of direction, marks a shift in investor attitude. Once an upward breakout occurs, we do not expect to see these lows again for some time.

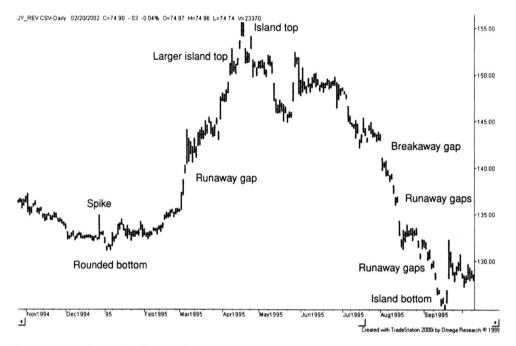

FIGURE 11.7 A classic rounded bottom in the Japanese yen. This extended rounded bottom from late 1994 through early 1995 was followed by a breakaway gap, indicating a change in supply and demand. Some other classic chart patterns are marked.

FIGURE 11.8 A somewhat irregular rounded bottom. Crude oil shows an irregular but rounded bottom. The key element is the gradual rise in prices at the end of the formation. Once prices break out of this extended bottom, we don't expect to see another test of the lows for some time.

WEDGE TOP AND BOTTOM PATTERNS

We have seen a wedge formation as a continuation pattern, but a large ascending wedge can mark the top of a move and a large descending wedge the bottom. The dominant characteristic of the wedge is that volatility is declining toward the end. If we look ahead to Figure 11.10 we see a declining wedge in the Japanese yen. Volatility compresses until a breakout is inevitable. There are no profit targets associated with the breakout of a wedge, but when it appears, it's a good chance that a breakout is about to occur.

THE HEAD-AND-SHOULDERS FORMATION

The most desirable and predictable of all top and bottom formations is the *head-and-shoulders*. A head-and-shoulders top has three peaks, the left shoulder, head, and right shoulder, where the head is higher than the shoulders (see Figure 11.9). The low points between the left shoulder and the head, and the head and right shoulder, form the *neckline*. The neckline is the sup-

FIGURE 11.9   Head-and-shoulders top pattern. A classic head-and-shoulders top is seen in the Japanese Nikkei. The height of the top is projected from the breakout of the neckline to get the profit objective. Another bottom formation, although not a head-and-shoulders, is treated in the same way, projecting a target from the confirmation point of the bottom pattern using volatility.

port line for the head-and-shoulders top. When prices break the neckline we expect a continued drop.

Head-and-Shoulders Profit Target

In exactly the same way that we have calculated profit targets for other top and bottom patterns, we find the target for head-and-shoulders top by measuring the volatility of the pattern and reflecting it down from the break of the neckline. In Figure 11.9, the peak of the Japanese Nikkei index was at about 22,750, above the neckline by 2,750 points. If we project the same 2,750 below the neckline at the point of the breakout (20,250), we get a price objective of 17,500, right at the lows of the first decline. We could have reduced our target because we expected volatility to decline as prices dropped, assuring us that prices would reach our target.

Head-and-Shoulders Bottom

A head-and-shoulders bottom is an upside down version of the top. It is not as common and not as exciting to trade as the top formation, although it also is dependable. Profit targets are calculated in the same way, measuring the distance from the bottom of the head to the neckline, and then projecting that distance above the neckline from the point of the breakout.

Skewed Head-and-Shoulders Top

As we've come to realize, chart patterns are not always as clear as the classic versions, and it is necessary to recognize some of the variations in order to increase your trading opportunities. In Figure 11.10 we have a *skewed head-and-shoulders top*. The left shoulder and head begin in the classic way, but the right shoulder is wider than we would expect. The entire pattern is slanted up far more than the previous example, as you can see when the neckline is drawn. It is not until after the third attempt at highs on the right shoulder that prices break through the neckline. After that, prices behave well, moving quickly to the price objective.

A Clear Bottom, but Not an Identifiable Pattern

Rather than keep a checklist or a template of patterns to match against each chart, you must learn to see a bottom or top formation in many different shapes. Figure 11.9 has a clear bottom at the end of 1998. Prices make a low

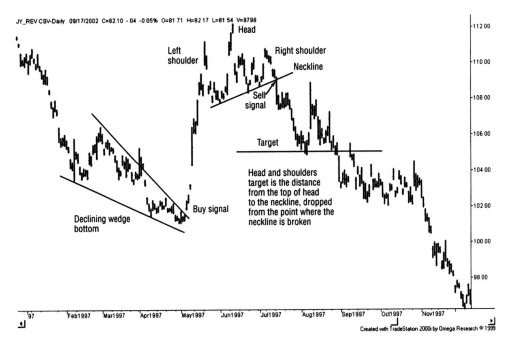

JY_REV CSV-Daily 09/17/2002 C=82.10 - 04 -0 05% O=81 71 H=82 17 L=81 54 V=8798

FIGURE 11.10 **A skewed head-and-shoulders top and a declining wedge bottom.**
Not all head-and-shoulders patterns develop in the same way. This one has an extended right
shoulder and a steep upward neckline. Once the breakout of the neckline occurs, prices act in
the normal way, reaching the price objective quickly. The declining wedge formation is also a
reliable pattern for expecting a change of direction.

at the beginning of October, rally, and then test the lows in January. The bottom is confirmed when prices cross above the high formed between the two lows, and then move up to a price objective measured from the volatility of the confirmed bottom pattern.

We apply the same principles for all top and bottom formations. We wait until there is a breakout of the formation, and then we expect prices to move at least a distance equal to the volatility of the top or bottom pattern. For a head-and-shoulders formation, a double bottom, a rounded bottom, or any combination, the principle is the same.

TRADING GAME TIPS

Risk versus reward. By now you should have a worksheet with quite a few trades. Look at the average profit and the average loss. There should be one of two patterns:

1. You have more losses than profits, but your profits are bigger than your losses.

2. You have more profits than losses, and your losses are bigger than your profits.

Either pattern is good if you come out with a net profit. If you're a trend follower, you'll have more small losses. A good ratio of the size of profits to the size of losses is 2.5. If you're an active trader, or scalper, then you'll take profits often but allow more risk. That ratio could be .75. If you have this pattern but are not profitable, your ratio isn't right. Your profits need to be a little bigger, or your losses a little smaller. If you target profits that are too close, then the commissions eat into your profits and you end up behind.

If you don't have either pattern, take another look at your trading style. Don't shift between taking profits quickly and then holding for the big trend move. Stay with one style.

Don't use a limit order to protect risk. A limit order is used to get a good price by buying on a decline. If you want to get out because prices are going the wrong way, close out the trade right away. Don't fool with the order. The first one out is the best.

Don't put your stop too close. If your stock trades in a $3 range each day, put your stop a minimum of $4.5 to $6 away from the market. You don't want to get stopped out the same day just because of market noise.

Questions

1. True or false? It is best to sell a "V" top on the day it makes its spike at the top of the move.

2. Define an island top.

3. Which is riskier to trade, (*a*) selling a double top or (*b*) buying a double bottom?

4. The price of a stock falls through support at $30, and then forms a double bottom with a low of $21. After better economic news, prices rally and break through resistance at $30. You buy. What is your price objective?

5. If the volatility of a double top was $10 and prices moved through support at $40, the point where the double top was confirmed, what would be your maximum profit target? What would be a more realistic target and why?

6. Describe the classic calculation for a head-and-shoulders top profit target.

CHAPTER 12

Retracements, Reversals, Fibonacci Numbers, and Gann

P rice movement is a combination of two steps forward and one backward. The more serious students of price patterns say that it moves two steps forward and 1.618 steps backward. Whoever is right, prices rarely move in one direction without reversing.

Anticipating the size of a retracement is an attempt to capitalize on the mass behavior of the investors. The continuous flows of funds in and out of the markets are not at random points, but reflect the risk tolerance of each participant. When seen as the action of a large group, the places where prices stop and reverse, in both their forward movement and backward steps, seem to cluster at specific levels.

We will look at the most popular ways to measure the ebb and flow of prices beginning with the simplest and moving to the esoteric. The method you choose to use can be at either end of the list, or anywhere in between. Accept and use only what you think is reasonable.

Retracements are most important after a sustained price move or during a clear trend. It is necessary to gain the support of the investing masses in order to expect consistent patterns.

PERCENTAGE RETRACEMENTS

The most important reversal that follows a sustained trend is a retracement of 100 percent—prices give back all of their gains. A 100 percent pullback means that the reason for the previous trend has disappeared. This is most common for shorter moves, where prices are driven by a single news event that turns out to be false. It happens often and can produce a large price swing, but lasts only a few days.

False news can be quite common. The government revises its previous GDP numbers each time it releases new ones. Each year the media report a major problem with crops, the result of too little rain or too much rain. In the end technology wins, and there is a record harvest. There are constant rumors of large companies being the target of a Securities and Exchange Commission (SEC) probe, or they are about to announce the correction of an accounting irregularity. When the news turns out to be false, the market simply returns to the price level before the news.

For seasonal commodities, such as crops, there are longer patterns of rising and falling prices. In 1988, a shortfall in the soybean crop with dwindling warehoused stocks caused prices to double (see Figure 12.1). After two years of good harvests, inventories were restored and prices returned to original levels, a 100 percent retracement.

In 2001, a typical seasonal pattern in soybeans (see Figure 12.2) shows a rally during the growing months, June through August, based on lack of rain. By the end of August prices stopped going up when traders realized that the

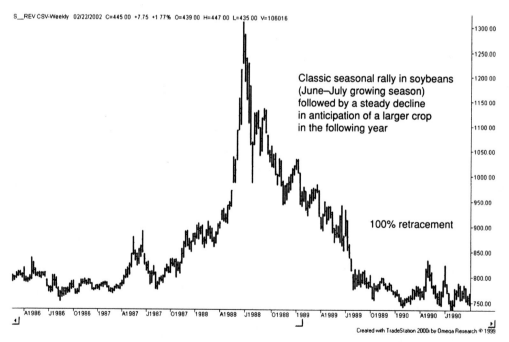

FIGURE 12.1   Classic soybean supply problem. A poor crop in 1988 limits supply and drives prices higher. It took two years of good harvests to restore the inventory of soybeans and return prices to previous levels.

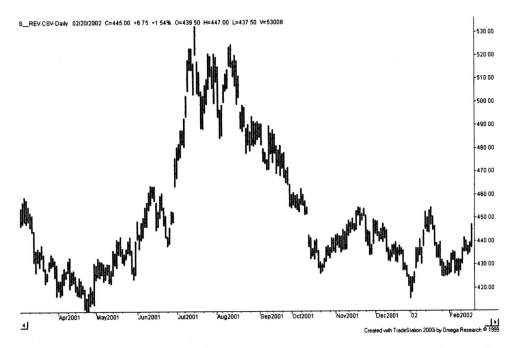

S__REV.CSV-Daily 02/20/2002 C=445.00 +6.75 +1.54% O=439.50 H=447.00 L=437.50 V=53008

FIGURE 12.2   A 100 percent retracement in soybeans during 2001. Typical seasonality turns concerns about the weather into price uncertainty. Soybean prices rally during the growing season, from June through August, when the outcome of the crop is still unknown. By the end of August there is a good estimate on the final size of the crop, and prices drop back to normal levels. This 100 percemt retracement shows there was no problem in the end.

weather problems affected only a small part of the crop, but a large amount of news coverage on CNN and CNBC. As harvest begins, and the crop size looks normal, prices fall back to the same level as in the spring, another 100 percent retracement.

We will look at other examples of soybean prices because for many years they were the most actively traded market. Farmers, grain elevators, and speculators have been doing the same thing since the mid-1800s and there are many examples in soybean patterns. Many patterns used to analyze stock and index prices come from agricultural futures markets. Traders adopt any technique that works. The much greater liquidity of soybean futures compared to individual stocks during the middle of the 1900s makes the futures patterns clearer.

Other Percentage Retracements

There is a significant difference between a 100 percent retracement and a *partial retracement*. A full retracement says that the previous rally was based on bad information. But what does a 50 percent retracement say? That the information was *half* right?

Retracements are a common occurrence in a trend. They have been compared to the ebb and flow of a tide. Investors buy until they have bought too much, and then the sellers come in to correct the overbought situation until the price is back to a level that attracts more investors. The history of technical analysis is full of well-known traders who have concluded that there is a profitable pattern in the retracements. Among these, Schabacker favored a one-half or one-third pullbacks; anything larger was considered a trend reversal. Gann, whom we discuss later, chose inverse powers of 2, giving ½, ¼, ⅛, and so on as his key levels. Angus considered ¼ as the most important. Dunnigan and Tubbs liked ⅓, ⅔, and ¾. Elliott advocated the Fibonacci ratios of .618 and .382.

The obvious problem is that if we use all of these retracement levels, the price is bound to stop at one of them. How can you trade that? If you stay with the principle that the most basic retracements are the most likely to be important, then you'll always be safe. Then 100 percent is the most important, and 50 percent is the next in line. After that we have ⅓ and ¼, each of less importance. Certainly ⅛ is too small to consider. The exceptions are the

FIGURE 12.3 Retracements for soybeans. A weekly chart shows the bigger picture of retracements for soybeans. Most of the popular retracement percentages can be found easily.

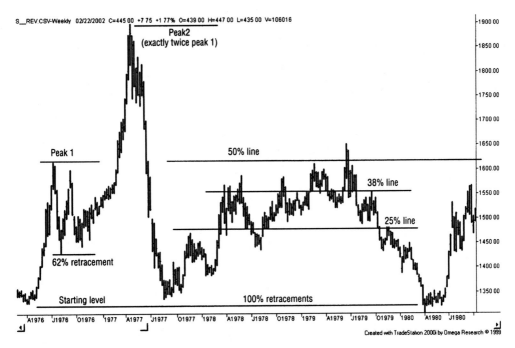

FIGURE 12.4   Soybean retracements in the late 1970s. Are the lines significant, or are there so many that one is likely to be at the place where prices stop and reverse?

Fibonacci ratios, which we discuss separately in this chapter. There seems to be good support for expecting mass behavior to be reflected in the Fibonacci ratios.

Including Fibonacci, the most important retracements are 100 percent, 50 percent, and 61.8 percent. Figures 12.3 and 12.4 show various retracements measured on two periods of soybeans. Markets that have high volume are most likely to conform to standard retracements. That means index markets, such as the S&P 500, would also show 50 percent and 61.8 percent pullbacks, but individual stocks may not. Mass behavior is a function of broader participation and a big picture of economic price movement.

S&P Retracement Levels

The S&P has very high trading volume; therefore, we would expect retracement levels to conform to the rule of large numbers. In Figure 12.5, the swing highs and lows are marked with letters beginning with *A* and *C* at the top, with *B* the low between them. From there we see that a drop to *D* is a decline of 100 percent of the range from *A* to *B*, followed by a retracement of 50 percent back to *E* (support becomes resistance). Throughout the decline we can find

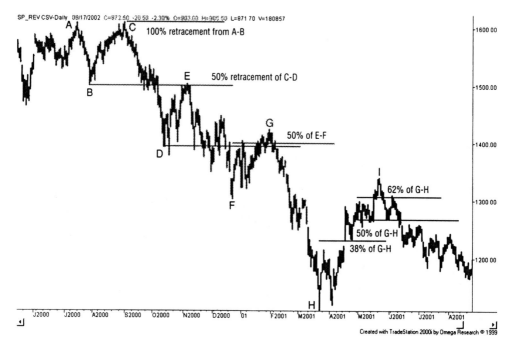

FIGURE 12.5   S&P retracement levels. Highs and lows are shown with letters, and the obvious retracements are measured from combinations of highs and lows. The S&P shows a reasonable number of 50 percent retracements.

numerous examples of retracement that conform to our expectations of 100 percent, 50 percent, and less importantly, 62 percent.

Each time we look for retracements, we need to ask ourselves, "How can we trade it?" If we expect a rally to stop at a 50 percent retracement, we automatically sell at that price. However, what if prices continue to rally? Anticipating where a retracement will stop isn't a good policy. If the price advance slows down, volatility drops, and volume falls, all at a point very close to your expected retracement level, then you can sell. If a new high follows on an increase in volume, then you get out and try again later. Common sense is needed, in addition to a retracement target.

TRADING AT EVEN NUMBERS

It is said that prices advance and decline to even numbers. A stock is more likely to stall at $10 than at $9.25; the price of gold resists moving below $300, but once it has traded lower, it struggles to go back above $300, and then slows at $310 and $320. A study by the New York Federal Reserve confirms the increase in trader activity around even numbers.

It makes sense that investors are more likely to place orders at an even numbers. We simply don't tell a broker to buy at $12.375 but would more likely buy at $12.25 or $12.50. Even more investors would choose $12.00 or $13.00. When Martha Stewart placed her well-known order to sell Imclone stock, it was at $60, not at some odd value.

A good trader can take advantage of this obvious bias for placing orders by avoiding even numbers and looking for free exposure when prices move through those levels. Think of them as mini-breakouts. If you want to sell a breakout of Imclone at $60, place your sell order at $60.25 and be ahead of the crowd.

FIBONACCI AND HUMAN BEHAVIOR

Fibonacci (Leonardo Pisano) observed nature and reproduction to create his famous *Fibonacci summation series*. We will discuss the basis for this series and some of its features in order to give you a better understanding of why it has been broadly accepted

The process is said to begin with two rabbits (1,1) who then reproduce (added together) to get 2, giving the starting series of 1, 1, 2. The last two numbers are added to get 3, then 5, and so on, until the final series is: 1, 1, 2, 3, 5, 8, 13, 21, 34, 55, 89, 144, ...

There are two remarkable aspects of this series:

1. These numbers occur with surprising frequency in nature.

2. The ratios of the adjacent numbers in the series are unique.

You will find Fibonacci ratios used throughout technical analysis, and you will find them throughout nature and art.

Fibonacci Ratios

The most important facts to remember about Fibonacci ratios are:

- The ratio of one number in the series to the following number, $N/(N+1)$, approaches .618.
- The ratio of one number to the previous number, $(N+1)/N$, approaches 1.618.
- Multiplying the first two ratios together gives the value 1.0.
- Pythagoras, the famous mathematician, left behind a triangle with Fibonacci proportions and the words "The Secret of the Universe."

Fibonacci in Nature

There are countless occurrences of the numbers 3, 5, 8, 13, and 21, as well as combinations of those numbers occurring in our life. A few common ones are:

- The human body has 5 major projections, both arms and legs have 3 sections, there are 5 fingers and toes, each (mostly) with 3 sections, and there are 5 senses.
- In music, an octave means eight, with 8 white keys and 5 black, totaling 13.
- There are 3 primary colors.
- The United States has 13 original states, and 13 is an unlucky number.
- The legal age is 21, and the highest salute in the army is 21 guns.
- According to the Kondratieff wave, the business cycle is 55 years.
- The normal sunflower has 89 curves, 55 in one direction and 34 in another.
- The genealogical pattern of the beehive and the leaf pattern of the sneezewort are perfect representations of Fibonacci numbers.
- The chambered nautilus is a perfect Fibonacci golden spiral (all measures are Fibonacci ratios).

Fibonacci in Art

Occurrences of Fibonacci ratios in art may be more important than those in nature because they reflect human behavior and perception. It is said that Fibonacci may have created his series after observing ancient structures.

- The Great Pyramid of Giza has 5 surfaces, 8 edges, for a total of 13. There are 3 edges visible from any side. It is 5,813 inches tall (5-8-13), and the inch is the standard Egyptian unit of measure; the ratio of the elevation to the base is .618.
- The Parthenon, sculpture of Phydias, and classic Greek vases are all made to Fibonacci ratios. Leonardo da Vinci used them extensively.

Fibonacci in Behavior

In documented tests, when asked to pick a number between 0 and 100, the results of a large sample number clustered around 0, 38, 50, 62, and 100. This appears to be a natural response.

Fibonacci and Price Retracements

Why all this bother about Fibonacci numbers? It is because, when we look back at the retracements in Figures 12.3, 12.4, and 12.5, we can see numerous examples of 62 percent and 38 percent retracements. You can find more if you study the charts carefully. Most importantly, traders watch for those numbers. Perhaps it's self-fulfilling, but we care only that retracements stop at 62 percent more often than you would expect. R.N. Elliott, creator of the Elliott Wave Theory, relied heavily on Fibonacci ratios.

FIBONACCI TIME TARGETS

While we're discussing Fibonacci ratios, there is another way to use these values to target price movement. Instead of projecting a *price target*, we can project the *time* when the target will occur, that is, the date when prices will turn from an uptrend to a downtrend.

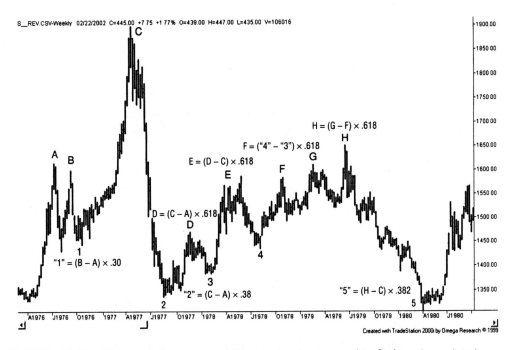

FIGURE 12.6 Fibonacci time targets. Fibonacci ratios are used to find turning points in the trend by projecting the distance between two clear price peaks forward 1.618 percent of the distance between the two previous peaks.

As an example, suppose that the "Q's" (the Nasdaq QQQ) peaked at 1250 on March 30, declined and then peaked again at 1240 on June 30, 91 days later. The most likely time for another peak or valley (we can't tell you which will occur, only that it will be a turning point) will be 147 days after the last peak ($91 \times 1.618 = 147$), on or about October 26. If prices have been in an uptrend prior to October 26, we can expect that date to be a top; if it is in a downtrend, we can expect a bottom. If prices were drifting sideways ahead of October 26, then nothing is expected.

Figure 12.6 shows a number of different time targets calculated from highs (marked with letters) and lows (marked with numbers). The ratios .382 and .618 are used, although .618 is most popular.

To get our *time targets*, we normally measure the distance between the highs and multiply by .382, .618, or 1.618 to get the projection for the next high or low. We can do the same using the lows, but the highs are considered more important. The location of the low may not be as clear.

If you are thinking about trying all of the major ratios, 100, 61.8, 50, and 38.2, you will get a lot of targets. Prices are likely to turn within a day or two of one of them, simply because there are so many. To prove a theory, use only the most important scenarios.

W.D. GANN—TIME AND SPACE

Both W.D. Gann and R.N. Elliott are extremely popular with technical analysts. Both formed their trading approaches by the mid-1930s. Gann published individual, small studies of market movement; Elliott's book *The Wave Principle* was published in 1938.

Gann has contributed a variety of retracement theories and price targets to the literature. His philosophy was "Conserve your capital and wait for the right time." It is important to remember that Gann believed in seasonality, and all his work applies to commodities markets. However, there are interesting universal concepts:

1. Traders like whole numbers. There are more orders clustered at 5 and 10¢ points than at values in between. There are more orders at $.50 and $1.00 than at 5 and 10¢.

2. Natural price divisions for support and resistance are most often 0 percent and 100 percent. After that, 50 percent, 25 percent, and 12.5 percent are most important, in that order.

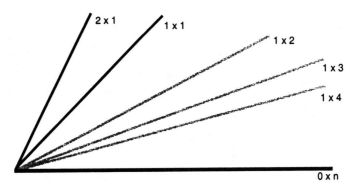

FIGURE 12.7 Gann's geometric angles. Using graph paper, Gann decided that the most important support levels were those formed by drawing lines through the corners of the boxes. These are also called *fan lines*.

3. Geometric angles form support levels. Using square graph paper for your chart, lines are drawn upward to the right through the corners $(1 \times 1$ angle) to create 45° support lines. Steeper angles are drawn through the corners of multiple boxes $1 \times 2, 1 \times 3, \ldots$, and lower angles are 2×1, $3 \times 1, \ldots$, and 1×0. When shown together, these support lines are called *fan lines* (see Figure 12.7).

Gann Squares and Hexagons

Gann had an interesting way of finding price targets that included an implied volatility calculation. Using soybeans, he began with the lowest recorded cash price of 44¢ per bushel and placed that in the center of the square. He then added 1¢, moving first to the right, then up and counterclockwise until he included all prices at which soybeans have traded. This method, called the *squaring of price and time*, is based on the *cardinal square*. It can be seen in Figure 12.8.

The two diagonal lines passing through the center of the chart, as well as the vertical and horizontal lines through the center, are the prices that Gann used to forecast major support and resistance levels. You should note that, as the square gets larger, the prices along the diagonal, horizontal, and vertical lines get farther apart. For example, along the vertical beginning at the center, we read 4, 47, 58, 77, 104, 139, 182, 233, 292, 359, and 434, representing percentage increases of 6.8, 23.4, 32.7, 35.0, 33.6, 30.9, 28.0, 25.3, 22.9, and 20.9. Based on what we know now, we would expect the volatility

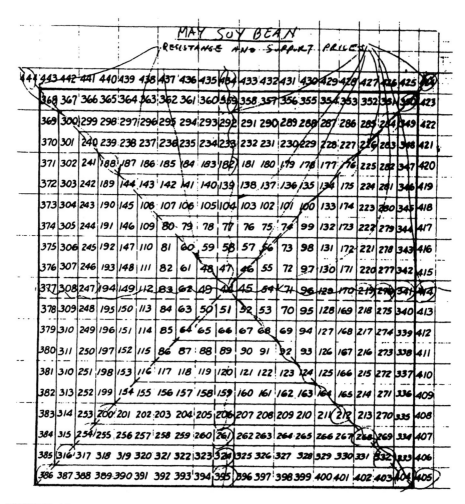

FIGURE 12.8 Gann's square. Starting from the lowest traded price, Gann moved right and then up in a counterclockwise direction, creating a price square. Key levels of support and resistance are expected to fall on the horizontal, vertical, and diagonal lines. The price change between the levels in the square shows the increase in volatility relative to price. (With permission from Figure 14.19, p. 369. P.J. Kaufman, *Trading Systems and Methods*, 3rd edition. New York, John Wiley, 1998.)

of prices to keep at an equal percentage, or increase slightly. Considering this was done in the 1940s, it's pretty good.

We could speculate that that Gann created the square by first writing down the key resistance levels, and then working out the geometric pattern that would cause these levels to fall on a diagonal, vertical, or horizontal. Gann also used the hexagon for other markets, which might give us a few moments of doubt.

AFTERTHOUGHT

Many traders perform best when they have a system to watch, even when they don't follow it rigidly. A system provides a valuable structure for traders. It can serve as a guide to avoiding stupid decisions, such as holding a trade too long that fights with the trend. For example, you may be watching a breakout system and get a buy signal as prices jump through a key resistance level. Rather than buy immediately and guarantee a horrible fill, you wait for the fast move to end and prices to pull back before buying. You're not trading against the trend, just using common sense to improve your entry.

Many traders perform well by knowing the trend and knowing where the system entered the trade. They have a knack for doing better. In the long run, this type of trading will not do as well as the system when prices are running. That is, in a very trending market, getting into a trade quickly gives the higher profits. When the trends aren't as clear, during a noisier market, waiting for a better price will be a more profitable strategy.

In the final analysis, trading around a trend system does worse during a trending market and better in a sideways market. It smoothes out performance and ends up being very close to the same net profit.

Questions

1. What are the three most likely percentage retracement levels?
2. What significance would you put on a 100 percent retracement?
3. Write the first 6 numbers of the Fibonacci summation series.
4. In the Fibonacci summation series, for large numbers in the series, what is the ratio of the Nth value to the previous value?
5. If prices moved from a low of $35 to a high of $55, then retraced to $45, and started to move higher, a Fibonacci ratio of .618 would tell you to expect prices to reach what level?
6. If a high occurred on December 4, a low 20 days later, and another high 15 days after the low, in how many days would you expect a new high or low according to the Fibonacci ratio .618?
7. In a Gann square, the key support and resistance levels are supposed to fall where?
8. As you move outward in Gann's square or hexagon, the various support and resistance levels represent (a) an increase in (b) unchanged, or (c) a decrease in volatility?

CHAPTER 13

Volume, Breadth, and Open Interest

Price change is the most important indication of what is happening to a stock, index, or commodity. When price goes up, there is more demand or less supply. We spend a lot of time looking at a price pattern, drawing or calculating trendlines, and turning the chart upside down to see if we've exhausted every combination.

Adding volume to the picture introduces an entirely new dimension. Volume has nothing to do with price. It tells you about the extent of participation in the day's price change. If we think about it in extremes, we would have less confidence in a move up if only one person was buying than if 1 million investors were buying. By adding volume to our trading decision, we can add important reliability.

Chart patterns are more dependable when price movement is the result of broad participation. We will extend this same principle to market breadth and to futures market open interest.

THE BASIC PRINCIPLES OF VOLUME

The standard interpretation of volume has been part of the trading culture from its beginning. Volume is always considered in combination with price movement:

Volume	Price	Interpretation
Rising	Rising	Volume confirms price rise
Rising	Falling	Volume confirms price drop
Falling	Rising	Volume indicates weak rally
Falling	Falling	Volume indicates weak pullback

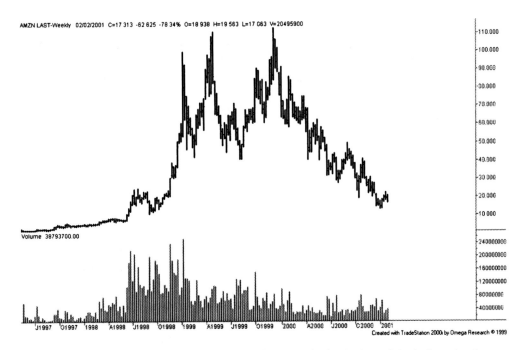

AMZN LAST-Weekly 02/02/2001 C=17 313 -62 625 -78 34% O=18 938 H=19 563 L=17 063 V=20495900

FIGURE 13.1 Amazon price and volume chart. At the beginning of the bull market in Amazon, volume sharply increased along with prices. After the first peak, volume clearly dropped and continued to drop on the second peak. It wasn't until June 2000 that volume started to rise again, confirming a downtrend although with less participation.

Therefore, *volume confirms direction*. When volume declines, it indicates that a change of direction should follow.

Amazon.com gives a good example of the bigger picture of volume. In Figure 13.1 we can see the sharp increase in volume in May 1998 just ahead of the major upward move in Amazon prices. At the beginning of 1999 prices make their first peak on high volume, but then volume starts to fall sharply. When prices make their second peak in April 1999, volume is much lower. Higher prices and falling volume are considered signs of a *weak* rally, and prices again drop sharply. When the third peak occurs in December 1999, volume is even lower. A major decline follows. Fewer and fewer investors and traders were willing to participate in the second and third attempts to push Amazon prices higher. It's important information that can be applied to faster trading as well.

The Problem with Volume

Before we get too far into the merits of using volume, let's address its problems so that we can watch for pitfalls along the way.

What do you do if there is a very small increase or decrease in volume? You treat it as any other increase or decrease in volume. The amount doesn't seem to matter.

What if the price is unchanged? You continue using your analysis from the previous day.

What if price moves up by just 1 point? It still seems best to apply the basic rules. Any higher close is important. Ignoring the day doesn't work as well.

What if volume is erratic from day to day? Volume can vary a lot from day to day. You can choose to use it just the way it is, or you can smooth the volume with a three-day moving average just to be sure that you're not fooled by one low volume day between two strong days. With certain analysis you can also limit your use of volume to extreme changes, very high volume days, or large drops in volume. We'll discuss this more later.

With all of these problems, volume is still important. You need to find the best way to use it rather than find an excuse for not using it.

Volume Is a Predictor of Volatility

Most often high volume and high volatility occur at the same time. It's easy to see that one confirms the other. Sometimes volume can be high, and the price can end nearly unchanged for the day. We need to look at that day as a sign of potential volatility—a lot of traders with opposing opinions just happen to offset each other. Tomorrow, if there is an imbalance in the buys and sells, prices could explode in either direction. Therefore, *high volume means high risk.*

More Examples of Volume Interpretation

Microsoft.   Using volume becomes clear when you look at more examples. In Figure 13.2 there are periods in Microsoft where the price made significant moves and where volume spiked or dropped sharply. The first example is in December 1999, where we get a sharp rally from about $90 to $120. Volume triples just ahead of the rally and then starts to drop as the price rise continues. As prices round out at the top, we can see volume drop sharply into the holiday season. Volume then starts to increase as prices decline. Happy New Year! It will be a long time before Microsoft sees that price again.

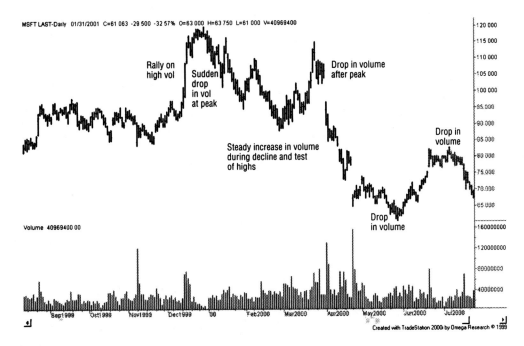

FIGURE 13.2 Examples of price and volume for Microsoft. The first pattern of rising price and volume followed by a sharp drop in volume is a classic case, as are the two drops in volume at the far right. The middle pattern is not as clear. You shouldn't force an interpretation.

There are two other clear examples at the right of the chart, where volume dropped at the end of a downtrend and during the following uptrend. The case in the middle is not as clear, but can be interpreted after the fact. Volume increases toward the end of the downtrend, but seems to continue to increase through the next rally. Some of you may find this pattern consistent with the rules and others may not. Volume doesn't solve all problems.

AOL.   The AOL chart in Figure 13.3 is typical of the erratic pattern of volume that is difficult to interpret. Although there is an underlying decline in volume from late April through September of 1999, there are continual volume spikes that identify local tops and bottoms (mostly bottoms). When prices finally start back up in October of 1999, volume still seems to decline steadily. We know now that AOL was destined to see much lower prices, but volume would tell you that the move from $40 to $95 was a weak rally and should be avoided. You might find that being right in the long run but missing a big move is an unsatisfying experience. Fortunately, there are a lot of other stocks from which to choose so that your capital doesn't sit idle.

AOL CSV-Daily 02/08/2002 C=27.36 +1.91 +7.50% O=25.45 H=27.70 L=25.40 V=298429

FIGURE 13.3 AOL price and volume example. Although erratic, volume delines steadily after the first price peak. Unfortunately, volume also declines on the second rally from $40 to $95, suggesting a weak rally. In the long run that was true, but making the decision to stand aside might not be easy.

VOLUME SPIKES

Madness is the exception in individuals but the rule in groups
—Nietzsche*

A volume spike is just what you would expect, a single day on which the volume was much higher than the previous day—at least twice as high, perhaps 3 or 4 times as high.

A volume spike means that everyone has jumped into the boat at the same time. Experienced traders will tell you that *when the public jumps in, it's time to get out.*

You can see volume spikes on the three charts that we've already studied. Let's look again at the last one, AOL. We see the highest volume days in April, August, and September 1999, and in January 2000. What is common about

---

*Quoted by Donald Cassidy, *Trading on Volume*, New York, (McGraw-Hill, 2001).

these spikes? They occur at the bottom of a price move. After a spike, prices reverse. In Figure 13.2 spikes occur at both tops and bottoms.

A spike doesn't tell you how long or how severe the following reversal will be. It just tells you that the current move is exhausted. It may turn out to be a major top or bottom, or simply a local turning point.

Volume spikes are a good example of extremes. It is easier to identify and trade an extreme. If you start to spend a lot of time trying to decide if volume is confirming or rejecting a price move, then it's not clear enough to trade. Put it aside and try to find another stock or another way to make the trade.

The theory of a spike is that when everyone has entered the market, there is no one left to buy (or sell) and prices must reverse. The crowd is always wrong—at least their timing is always wrong.

VOLUME INDICATORS

There have been many attempts to clear up the erratic behavior of volume and create a clinical "signal" of when volume is confirming or rejecting the price move. Most of this involves some smoothing of the numbers and seems sensible. A few of these methods have been very popular.

Volume Oscillator

Visualizing the pattern of volume can be very helpful, and the simplest way to do this is with a *volume oscillator*. A volume oscillator is a two-step process:

1. Calculate the 14-day moving average and the 34-day moving average of volume.
2. Plot the difference between the 14-day and 34-day averages.

Looking at the Microsoft chart in Figure 13.4 from mid-January 2000 through the end of March 2000, we see an increase in volume as prices drop, and then a clear drop in volume when prices begin to rally in mid-March. As prices reached their peak at the end of March, the volume oscillator had fallen to near zero.

On-Balance Volume

By far, the most well-known of all volume indicators is *On-Balance Volume* (OBV), made famous by Granville. It is simply the accumulated volume, where volume is added when prices rise and subtracted when prices fall:

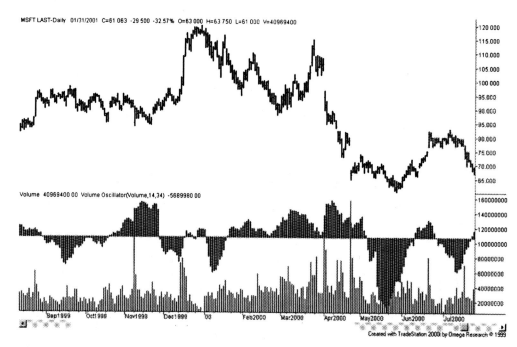

FIGURE 13.4 A volume oscillator. Using the difference between a 14- and 34-day average of volume, the volume oscillator is a good visual representation of the increases and decreases in volume. From February through May 2000 volume favored the downside. A sharp decrease in volume at the end of May signaled the end of the downtrend.

If today's price change > 0, then OBV = OBV + today's volume

If today's price change < 0, then OBV = OBV − today's volume

Once we have created the OBV line, we interpret the OBV to make trading decisions instead of using the price. In Figure 13.5 the OBV is plotted along with the volume at the bottom of the chart. You'll notice that it looks very much like the price chart rather than the volume chart, even though it is created from volume. The obvious difference between the price chart and the OBV line is that the peak is shifted from the end of 1999 to the end of March 2000. On the OBV line, the low in November is more significant than it appears in the prices, and it shows a breakout of the lows at an early point.

Volume Accumulator

The Volume Accumulator (VA), created by Mark Chaiken, uses buying or selling strength as a way to assign volume to the buyers or sellers. If the

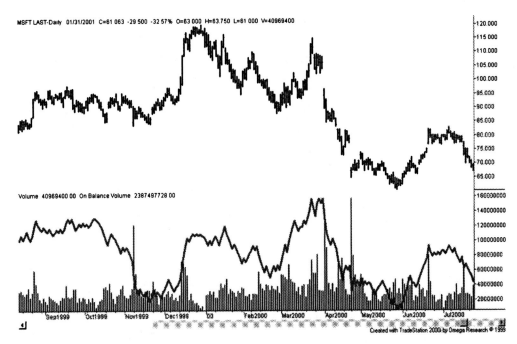

FIGURE 13.5 On-Balance Volume. On-Balance Volume (OBV) is created by adding the volume when prices rise and subtracting the volume when prices fall. You then use the OBV line to make trading decisions, rather than price.

close is above the middle of the trading range, then the percentage above the middle determines how much volume goes to the buyers; if it is below the middle of the range, then that percentage of volume goes to the sellers:

$$VA = ((close - low) / (high - low) - .50) \times 2 \times volume$$

If close = high, then all volume goes to the buyers.
If close = low, then all volume goes to the sellers.
If close = middle of the range, then no volume is added.

If you want to check your arithmetic, when prices close three-fourths of the way up in today's range (for example, a high, low, and close of 44, 40, and 43), then 50 percent of the volume is added to the indicator VA.

An Unexpected Comparison between On-Balance Volume and the Volume Accumulator

We should expect the OBV and VA lines to be very different because the calculations of the VA are so much more complex. In Figure 13.6 it seems

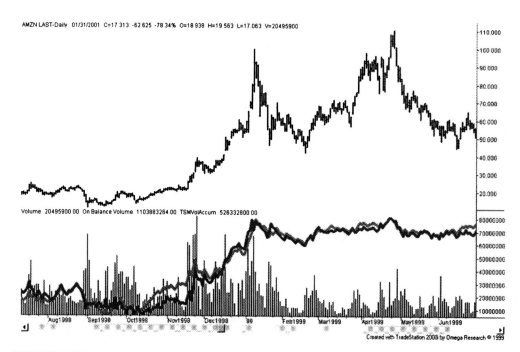

FIGURE 13.6   Comparison of the On-Balance Volume and Volume Accumulator.
On-Balance Volume (gray line) and the Volume Accumulator (dark line) are remarkably the same, even though the calculations seem different. Both are intended to be used for trading instead of price.

remarkable that there should be so little difference between the two indicators. Sometimes we can be fooled into thinking that two apparently different methods yield different results. Our first hint of this was when we looked at the difference in performance of four trending methods. The conclusion was that, if the market trended, any of the methods would work. We'll see many more examples where we can simplify our trading by using only one method.

Further Comparisons.   It's not always the case that the Volume Accumulator is the same as On-Balance Volume. In Figure 13.7, On-Balance Volume starts higher, drops lower, and then stays lower than the Volume Accumulator. Across the entire chart, the Volume Accumulator shows an upward trend, while On-Balance Volume shows a break in June 1994. Look at the chart carefully and try to decide how you would use either of these indicators to your advantage.

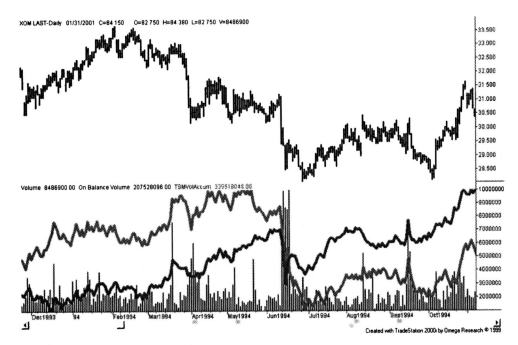

FIGURE 13.7 **Recent-Exxon Mobil volume patterns.** In this example, the OBV and VA show very different patterns. OBV shows a sell in January 1994, while VA holds an uptrend throughout the entire interval. Neither is better than a simple price trend for this one-year interval.

September 11

It is always interesting to see how indicators performed on September 11, 2001. In the charts of XOM (Figure 13.8) and the S&P (Figure 13.9) we see slightly different pictures.

On September 10 XOM was trading at $41.42 on volume of about 10 million shares. Markets were closed September 11 and reopened on September 17 to a rapid sell-off. The bottom came on September 21 when XOM traded at a low of $35.01 with volume of 21 million shares. The spike in Figure 13.8 shows the day. By October 11, prices were back at $41.77, up 19 percent, erasing the entire decline that began September 11. Other spikes in Figure 13.8 mark local turning points, except in mid-December.

The S&P 500 show a slightly different picture of building volume from the reopening of the New York Stock Exchange until the bottom on September 21. Volume in Figure 13.9 comes from the total futures contracts traded. The S&P index doesn't trade; therefore, there is no volume.

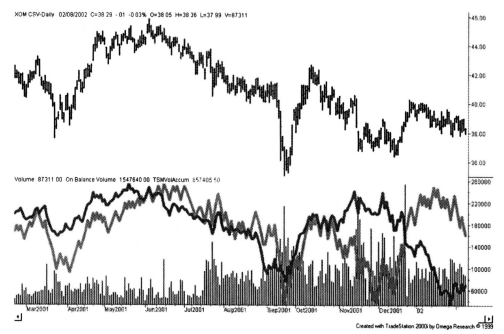

FIGURE 13.8 XOM on September 11, 2001. Prices fell sharply when the NYSE reopened on September 17, hitting a low on September 21 with a volume spike. By October 11, prices had fully recovered the 19 percent drop that occurred from September 11 to September 21.

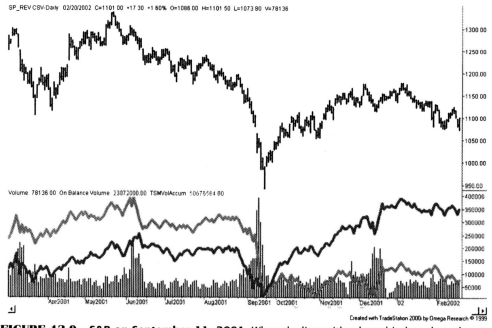

FIGURE 13.9 S&P on September 11, 2001. When dealing with a broad index, the volume spike following the September 11 attack is clearly the major event on the chart and signals a reversal. Although the volume spike was an accurate signal, you would need nerves of steel and deep pockets to buy on September 21.

Because the S&P represents a much broader market than XOM, volume after September 11 is clearly much higher than any other time. The entire market was swept away by selling over five days, only to bounce back to a price higher than before the attack on the World Trade Center.

Volume Indicators on September 11.   How did the OBV and VA indicators perform during the crisis? On the XOM chart they both rally when the market reopens after September 11, but the VA continues higher and then falls while OBV drops and rebounds. The OBV actually has the same pattern as the prices. The indicators move in opposite directions, proving that they are not the same indicator in disguise as it appeared at first. On the S&P chart, the OBV drops after September 11 and doesn't recover. The VA follows the price pattern.

Prudence.   Volume spikes tend to be an accurate indicator of price reversals and September 11 was no exception. Afterward, it looks as if it was a lost opportunity; the chart clearly shows a buy signal. Don't fool yourself. You could only buy between September 17 and September 21 if you had nerves of steel and deep pockets. There was enormous risk. Try to remember that when you're looking back at this chart in five years.

The Crash of 1987

As you gain experience, you'll suffer through other extreme events. The crash of October 1987 seems to have been pushed aside by the more recent bull market of the 1990s, but it was devastating at the time. In Figure 13.10 we see a volume spike on the day of the crash, but it doesn't rise above the other volume bars as far as we would expect. Would you have taken it as a buy signal?

On-Balance Volume gained credibility during the 1987 crash by turning down ahead of prices. The Volume Accumulator didn't react soon enough and hardly reacted during the crash. We would prefer an indicator that worked in extreme price moves.

Automatically Identifying a Volume Outlier

A *volume outlier* is the statistician's name for a *spike*. If you are trying to automate your trading rules in order to test them, it's easy to recognize an outlier:

1. Calculate the average volume over 20 days (call that N days), beginning five days ago. You will not be using the last five days to avoid volume that is creeping higher.

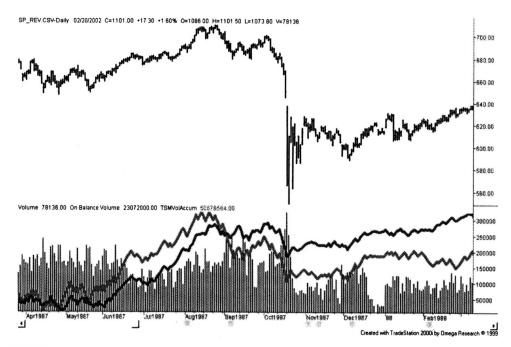

FIGURE 13.10   The crash of 1987. The volume spike is on the right day, but may not be as clear as we need to buy. The OBV indicator (gray) gains credibility by turning down ahead of the crash. The VA doesn't seem to respond.

2. Compare today's volume with your average volume from 6 to 25 days ago.
3. If today's volume is 2 to 3 times higher than the average for a stock, or 1½ to 2 times higher for an index, you have a volume spike.

Notice that individual stocks will show spikes that are far above the average, but a broadly traded index market has consistently high volume; therefore, spikes are not as extreme.

MARKET BREADTH INDICATORS

Market breadth measures the imbalance between the number of advancing and declining stocks on a given day. In general, more advancing issues should add confidence to an upward price move. A net increase in the S&P 500 while more issues are declining should generate concern that the upward move is poorly supported.

The information for advances and declines is published along with stock prices each day. You also may want the volume of advancing issues and the volume of declining issues. Both of these values can be found in the *Wall Street Journal* under "Trading Activity."

Market breadth indicators are best used as a confirmation of price direction. The table below shows that the interpretation of market breadth is the same as the relationship between volume and price.

Market Breadth	Price	Interpretation
Rising	Rising	Breadth confirms price rise
Falling	Falling	Breadth confirms price drop
Falling	Rising	Breadth does not confirm price rise
Rising	Falling	Breadth does not confirm price drop

Advance-Decline Index

The most well-known and simplest of the market breadth indicators is the advance-decline (AD) index. It is a running count of the number of advancing issues minus the number of declining issues at the end of each day:

$$AD(today) = AD(previous\ day) + advances(today) - declines(today)$$

Sibbett's Demand Index

The volume of stocks advancing compared to the volume of stocks declining may be considered more a "robust" measurement than simply the number of issues advancing and declining. Throughout technical analysis we'll see indicators that are equally weighted and their counterparts that use relative value.

Sibbett's Demand Index, (DI), uses the sum of the past 10 days' upside and downside volume because these volume numbers, just as with total market volume, can jump around quite a bit. A 10-day sum is really the same as a 10-day average, only the numbers are 10 times as large:

$$DI = \frac{sum(upside\ volume,\ 10\ days)}{sum(downside\ volume,\ 10\ days)}$$

where upside volume and downside volume are found in the *Wall Street Journal* under "Trading Activity."

Arm's Index—TRIN

The *Arm's Index*, called *TRIN*, combines the number of advancing and declining issues with the volume of the advances and declines. Its value is often quoted on television and has gained popularity among technicians:

$$\text{TRIN} = \frac{(\text{number of advancing issues} / \text{number of declining issues})}{(\text{volume of advancing issues} / \text{volume of decline issues})}$$

Bolton-Tremblay Index

The *Bolton-Tremblay Index* (BT) recognizes that there are also unchanged issues each day. Without including the unchanged issues, we have an incomplete picture. This index also takes the square root of the change value, a familiar technique that reduces the importance of a few extremely large changes:

$$\text{BT} = \frac{(\text{advancing issues} - \text{declining issues})}{\text{unchanged issues}}$$

where

$$\text{if BT} > 0, \text{ then BT} = \text{BT} + \sqrt{\text{BT}}$$
$$\text{if BT} < 0, \text{ then BT} = \text{BT} - \sqrt{\text{BT}}$$

Schultz A/T Index

Schultz takes the same advancing, declining, and unchanged data and represents it as a "bullish index." By putting the advancing issues in the numerator, the *Schultz A/T Index* (SAT) would be 100 if all issues advanced:

$$\text{SAT} = \frac{\text{advancing issues}}{(\text{advancing issues} + \text{declining issues} + \text{unchanged issues})}$$

Is One Breadth Index Better Than Another?

These five breadth indicators show some of the ways data can be massaged into an index. There are dozens of others that have not been mentioned.

There is no doubt that we should be more confident of a price rally when a large number of issues are advancing, or the total number of shares traded is much greater for the advancing issues. We should be concerned when market breadth drops, as we would when volume drops, during any price move up or down.

Does it make a difference whether we include the unchanged issues in the index? Is the total volume traded on advancing issues a better picture than simply the number of advancing issues? Does the square root used in the BT Index make the result more accurate? To find the answer, we should remember the charts that compared the On-Balance Volume with the Volume Accumulator. Sometimes one looks better than the other, and sometimes they look the same. Neither seemed to be perfect.

Breadth is an interesting measurement, but don't expect it to solve too many problems. Most often, it will simply confirm the current price move. When it does stand out by conflicting with rising prices, volume and other indicators also should show weakness.

OPEN INTEREST IN FUTURES

The stock market has a fixed number of shares that can be traded, the amount issued by each company. In futures markets the concept is different. When a new buyer trades with a new seller, they create a contract between themselves. That contract is one unit of *open interest*.

Each buy or sell in futures may create or liquidate a unit of open interest. If a new buyer finds a new seller, then a new contract is added to the total open interest. If a new buyer finds an old seller, then his unit of open interest (his outstanding obligation) is transferred to the new buyer and there is no change in open interest. When those contracts are liquidated, they are removed from the open interest.

The larger the open interest, the more outstanding contracts exist and the larger the participation in the market. A day trader who buys and sells but holds no positions overnight does not affect the open interest, which is calculated at the end of the day. The table summarizes these relationships.

Buyer	Seller	Change in Open Interest
New	New	Increase in open interest
New	Old	No change in open interest
Old	New	No change in open interest
Old	Old	Decrease in open interest

A new buyer (seller) is a trader with no market posiition seeking to be long (short); an old buyer (seller) is a trader who had previously entered a short (long) position and seeks to exit.

Futures contracts, as with stock options, are traded for a specific delivery month, such as March, June, September, and December. When we use futures volume and open interest data, *we must always use the total of all contracts for that market,* not the volume or open interest for the nearest or most active contract. *Total volume* and *total open interest* are interpreted as follows:

Volume	Open Interest	Interpretation
Rising	Rising	Confirmation of trend
Rising	Falling	Position liquidation (the end of a trend)
Falling	Rising	Slow accumulation of a position
Falling	Falling	Congestion phase, denies a trend

An increase in open interest means greater participation in a move. It is possible to have high volume during the day because of day trading activity, but more open interest means that traders are going home with their position. High open interest during a trend means that the market is in strong hands and the trend is likely to persist. When it is in weak hands, it is likely to fail.

ARE THERE TOO MANY INDICATORS?

There is an underlying theme in the interpretation of volume, breadth, and open interest. Increasing values confirm price direction, and decreasing values deny that direction. That is a valuable concept.

However, which of these indicators should we use? Does a volume indicator tell you more than a simple volume spike or a sharp drop in volume at the top of a move? If we look back at the OBV and VA in Figure 13.7, the final results don't seem to be as good as simply using a moving average price trend. The VA implies that you should be holding the long position throughout, while the OBV is late exiting a long and entering a short.

In the final analysis, when volume spikes or drops sharply lower during a rising market, we get a reliable indicator of a change of direction. None of the indicators seem to improve on this simple interpretation.

Become Familiar with One Indicator

The most important part of any indicator is the way you use it. When we looked at different moving average techniques, we concluded that they all worked when prices trended. All of these indicators will show the same result in slightly different ways. Pick one that seems most sensible to you, watch it, and become familiar with it. Most often, it will simply confirm price movement, but once in a while it will show you that the direction of prices is not supported by much activity. If it helps only a few times, it's valuable.

ADVANCED TOPICS

How Do You Recognize an Extreme Volume Day Using Excel?

An extreme volume day is one that has a much wider range, from high to low, than previous days. You can recognize an extreme day if

$$\text{Today's volume} > \text{factor} \times \text{average(volume from } t - 6 \text{ to } t - N)$$

where *factor* should be at least 2.0 and N should be at least 20. Therefore, today's volume is extreme if it is 3 times greater than the average volume of the 15 days from 6 days ago to 20 days ago.

This satisfies the idea that today's volume is much higher than normal. It also avoids using the most recent five days in the average. Sometimes the volume increases gradually until it reaches an extreme. If you measure each day against the previous day, you might not recognize an extreme, so we don't look at the most recent few days.

Low-Volume Periods

Low volume is important because it is associated with lack of direction for prices. To recognize a low-volume period we need to have the average volume over the past few days below a threshold value. That threshold varies with the individual stock. Therefore, a low-volume day occurs when

$$\text{Average volume over the past } N \text{ days} < \text{threshold}$$

where the average might be 250,000 shares and N should be at least 5.

Questions

1. What interpretation do you place on falling prices and falling volume?
2. Would you say that volume trends are (*a*) clear and easy to interpret or (*b*) require smoothing to avoid erratic values?

3. If volume was high and prices closed unchanged, would you consider the risk of trading (*a*) low, (*b*) normal, or (*c*) high?

4. A volume spike usually corresponds with what price pattern?

5. How do you calculate On-Balance Volume?

6. Of all the volume patterns and indicators, which appears to be the most definitive?

7. If prices are falling, what would the market breadth need to do in order to confirm the decline?

8. In futures trading, if a new buyer meets an old seller, what happens to the open interest?

CHAPTER 14

Momentum and MACD

I n this chapter we'll focus on *momentum*, the *speed* of the price. Changes in the speed can be seen in different momentum indicators. Momentum indicators make up a very valuable set of tools. The most well-known variation of a momentum indicator is the *moving average convergence-divergence* (MACD), which gives extremely reliable forecasts of price changes.

MOMENTUM

Momentum is *speed*. Then the momentum value M is the change of price over a specific time period, such as a week:

$$M = \text{price(today)} - \text{price}(N \text{ days ago})$$

If N is 5, then we have the weekly momentum, the price change over a one-week period. An important feature of momentum is that its value can be as large the biggest price move over the N days used in the calculation.

A momentum indicator plotted below the prices in Figure 14.1 shows that momentum is smoother than price. The more days used in the momentum calculation, the smoother the line. A 5-day or 20-day momentum has the same effect as looking at weekly or monthly prices instead of daily prices. The weekly prices appear smoother than the daily and the monthly smoother than the weekly.

FIGURE 14.1   Momentum. In this chart of AOL the prices are on the top and the 20- and 40-day momentum lines on the bottom. The 40-day momentum is smoother and has peaks and valleys at about the same place as the price series. The 20-day momentum (gray) reaches its peak sooner than prices because the price swings last more than 20 days.

Interpreting Momentum

The momentum line doesn't lag as we saw with a moving average. A 10-day momentum simply answers the question, "How high or low is today's price compared to 10 days ago?" In Figure 14.1 the scale to the right of the momentum lines shows that the momentum was as high as 20 and slightly below –10. For both the 20 and 40-day momentum lines that means prices over any 20- or 40-day interval never gained more than $20 or fell more than $15.

The thinner gray line is a 20-day momentum. It peaks at the place where the largest move occurs over a 20-day period. The heavier line, a 40-day momentum, peaks at the largest move of a 40-day period. The scale on the right measures the net price change over 20 or 40 days.

Steadily Increasing Prices.   One special feature of momentum that must be understood is that *if prices continue higher at the same rate after 40 days, the 40-day momentum indicator will go sideways.* Therefore, prices could be increasing, but the momentum line is not increasing.

For example, the price of International Widgets starts at $10 and increases by $1 every day. After 40 days it is $50 and the 40-day momentum is 40 (50 − 10 = 40). On the next day it again increases by $1. The price is $51 and the 40-day momentum is 40 (51 − 11 = 40). As long as the price increases by the same amount, the momentum remains the same. It's the same as driving a car. As long as you hold the accelerator at the same pressure, the car moves forward at the same speed. *If the speed is unchanged, the momentum value is unchanged.*

Acceleration. If the speed is the same when the momentum line is moving sideways, then prices must be accelerating (increasing in speed) when the momentum line is rising. It will also be accelerating to the downside when momentum is falling below zero. We will refer to speed and acceleration throughout our study of momentum.

Momentum as a Trend Indicator

Momentum can be used as a trend indicator. We showed in Figure 14.1 that the longer the momentum calculation, the smoother the momentum line. It's not as smooth as a moving average, but it is smoother than the actual prices. *When the momentum moves above zero, the trend is up. When it moves below zero, the trend is down.* If a 20-day momentum line moves above zero, then the price today is higher than the price 20 days ago, a legitimate reason for saying that prices are rising.

You may notice that the momentum lines show a lot of small, erratic moves. When using momentum to decide the trend, you may want to use a small buffer zone, a filter, around zero so that a little erratic movement does not cause you to change position unnecessarily. For example, you can go long AOL when the momentum goes above 2 and short when it goes below −2. That will prevent jumping in and out if the value gets stuck around zero, as it might if prices are going sideways.

Comparing Momentum to a Moving Average

To be sure that momentum really acts as a trend, we should compare it with a moving average. In Figure 14.2 20-day and 40-day moving averages are plotted along with prices on the top of the chart, and the previous 20-day and 40-day momentum indicators are shown at the bottom.

To compare the slower moving average with the slower momentum (the thicker lines), we look at where the moving average changes direction and

FIGURE 14.2 Comparing momentum with moving averages. To compare the trends of momentum with a moving average, we match the point where the moving average changes direction with the point where the momentum crosses the zero line.

where the momentum crosses zero. In April 2001 the moving average turns up at about $42; the momentum crosses the zero line moving higher at just about the same day. When the moving average turns down in July, the momentum falls below zero at about the same time. You'll find that the same is true of the faster 20-day trends.

We concluded at the end of Chapter 4, Calculating the Trend, that if the market is trending, any of the trend calculations would be profitable. We can now add the momentum trend to that list.

Detrending a Price Series Using Momentum

Momentum can be used to remove the trend from a price series. A *detrended* series allows us to see the cyclic or oscillating patterns clearly. It is a method used by economists.

If we create a one-day momentum, we are looking at the one-day price changes by subtracting today's price from the previous price. In mathematics this is called the *first difference* in price. The first difference also gives you the speed. In Figure 14.3 the first differences of AOL are shown in the center panel. It is easy to see the daily volatility of price changes, but the overall

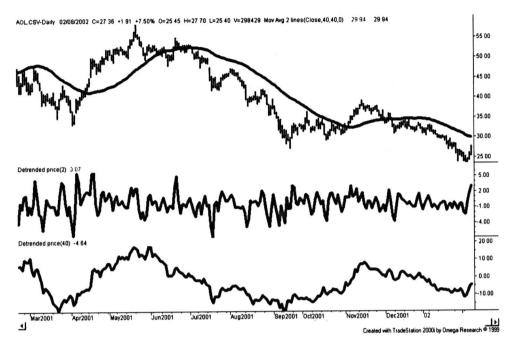

FIGURE 14.3   The detrended AOL price series. Classic detrending is simply the one-day price changes (center panel), but you can also detrend AOL by subtracting the 40-day momentum from the current price (the bottom panel). Both methods remove the downtrend. The bottom panel using momentum shows the cyclic pattern clearly, while the one-day changes show volatility.

trending pattern is sideways. The trend has been removed. We can also detrend the AOL series by subtracting a longer momentum value. In Figure 14.3 the bottom panel shows the new series when a 40-day momentum is subtracted from the original price series. By using a longer momentum calculation, we also remove the trend bias but keep the cyclic pattern.

By subtracting a momentum line of a different speed, we can choose to see specific patterns in AOL that were not as obvious in the original series. We will use this technique to create the well-known indicator, *MACD*.

MOVING AVERAGE CONVERGENCE-DIVERGENCE

The *moving average convergence-divergence* (MACD) indicator is a smoothed difference between two smoothed trendlines. It is formed by creating a faster and slower smoothed trendline from the original price series, subtracting the slower one from the faster one, and finally applying another smoothing to the new series. If we choose the slow calculation period as 40 days, the fast period as 20 days, and the final smoothing as the 9-day equivalent, the MACD is calculated as follows:

Step 1. Choose the two calculation periods, for example, slow = 40 and fast = 20. Calculate the percentage smoothing values using $2/(N+1)$, where N is 40 or 20.

Step 2. Calculate the slow trendline using the smoothing value .0243.

Step 3. Calculate the fast trendline using the smoothing value .0476.

Step 4. The *MACD line*, the slower oscillating line in the bottom panel of Figure 14.4, is calculated as the fast trendline minus the slow trendline. When the market is moving up quickly, the fast smoothing will always be above the slow and the difference will be positive. This is done so that the MACD line goes up when prices go up.

Step 5. The *signal line* is the 9-day smoothing (using a percentage of .10) of the MACD line. The signal line is slower than the MACD; therefore, it can be seen in the bottom panel of Figure 14.4 as the lower line when prices are moving higher.

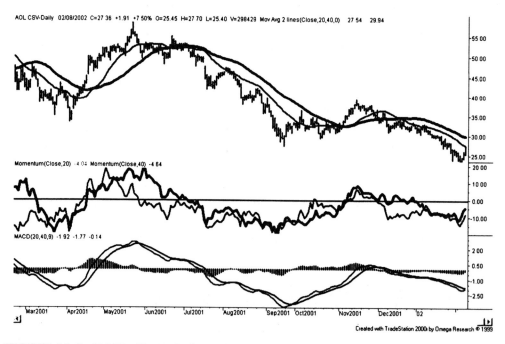

FIGURE 14.4   MACD. *The MACD line* is the faster of the two trendlines (gray) in the bottom panel; the *signal line* is the slower (dark). The histogram is created by subtracting the slower signal line from the MACD line. This histogram shows the relative strength or weakness of the MACD compared to the signal line.

Reading the MACD Indicator

We normally see the MACD as it appears in the bottom panel of Figure 14.4. The MACD line is higher in an uptrend and lower in a downtrend. The histogram is created by subtracting the slower signal line from the MACD line. When the histogram is above zero, it confirms the uptrend.

The 40/20 MACD line is similar to the 40-day momentum line. We can compare the MACD in the lower panel with the 20- and 40-day momentum in the center panel and see that the peaks and valleys are in about the same place, but the MACD line is much smoother. The MACD is a variation of momentum because it is the difference between two trendlines.

Trading the MACD

The most common use of the MACD is as a trend indicator. For that purpose, we use only the MACD and signal lines in the following way:

> *Buy when the MACD line (faster) crosses above the signal line (slower).*
>
> *Sell when the MACD line crosses below the signal line.*

We can look at the bottom panel of Figure 14.4 to see that the buy signals that occur right after a bottom, in April and October 2001, generated large gains. Unfortunately, there were a lot of other crossings that generated losses. It is clear that we need to be more selective about these signals.

One easy way to pick the good trades is to say that we only take the sell signals that occur after the MACD goes above 2.00, and only the buy signals after the MACD has fallen below –2.00. That gives us a very nice *buy* signal in April, a *sell* in May, and a *buy* in October. However, if someone were looking over our shoulder, we would be accused of "fitting" the data. We looked to see what worked for this chart and made up a rule to profit from it. Using +2.00 and –2.00 works for this chart, but some other charts will have peaks that may be as high as +10. What looks as if it's a top on this chart will turn out to be the middle of another chart.

If you have some other way of deciding that prices are near a top, then you can select the signal crossover as your point to sell. One likely method is to look for a strong resistance level on your price chart. If prices slow as they rise into resistance, then you have a good chance that the MACD sell signal will work. Using a much longer time period for your chart will also give you a better view of the possible range of MACD values.

DIVERGENCE

Divergence is one of the great concepts in technical analysis. *Divergence shows when prices are about to change direction.*

It is easier to show divergence in an illustration than in words. In Figure 14.5 there is a *bearish divergence* in Amazon formed in October through December 2000. It is *bearish* because it anticipates a drop in prices. To see this divergence on the Amazon.com chart, follow the rules:

1. Find the swing highs on the chart. This can be done simply by looking at the highest peaks. In Figure 14.5 there are five significant peaks, the largest in April and December 1999, medium peaks in October 1999 and February 2000, and a small peak in July 1999.

2. Find two consecutive peaks that are rising. They are July, October, and December.

3. Draw a line connecting the October and December peaks.

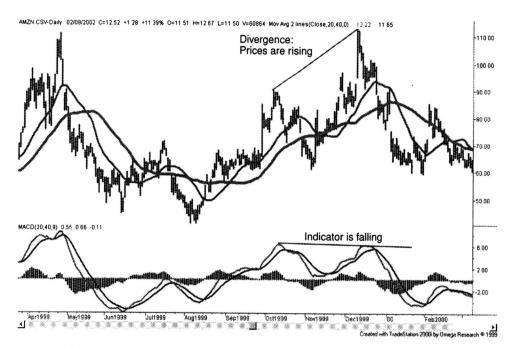

FIGURE 14.5   MACD divergence. In this divergence, prices are rising sharply while the MACD is falling. Sell the next crossover of the MACD line and signal line.

4. Look at the MACD line directly below the October–December line that you drew in the upper part of the chart. There always will be a peak in the MACD corresponding to a peak in prices. Connect the two peaks in the MACD line.

5. The line drawn across the price highs is rising sharply. The line across the MACD peaks is falling slightly. Whenever these lines are angling in opposite directions, you have *divergence*.

Bearish divergence occurs when the price moves higher and the indicator moves lower. This divergence is important because the MACD is not confirming the upward move, but indicating that prices want to go down. Prices drop from $110 to $60 in a few weeks.

Bullish divergence is the opposite formation. Prices are dropping, but the MACD is rising. Prices want to change direction. Figure 14.5 has an equally successful bullish divergence. Can you find it? The bullish divergence has lower price lows in June and August with clearly rising lows in the MACD at the same time. The August price low marks the bottom of the move, and a substantial rally follows.

Divergence is one of the most successful of all indicators. When you study it closely, you find that the divergence is formed when the new high price peaks get farther and farther apart. Although not as apparent, a bearish divergence also is recognizing an irregular but rounded top formation.

Divergence is most profitable when it is very clear, as it is in the bullish divergence example. If the price peaks are nearly at the same height, the peaks are not very big, or the MACD line is nearly horizontal, then the success of the divergence is doubtful. Unfortunately, the clear divergence signals never occur as often as we would like them, but they have a high degree of success. Watch for them.

Another Amazon Example of Divergence

Earlier in 1999 Amazon shows another clear bearish divergence (see Figure 14.6). Prices show peaks in January and April 1999. At the same time the MACD peaks are clearly declining. Note that Amazon had a test of the January highs three weeks before the major peak. At the time the second MACD peak was much lower and a divergence seemed likely, but prices didn't quite move above the first peak. As it turned out, this was not the

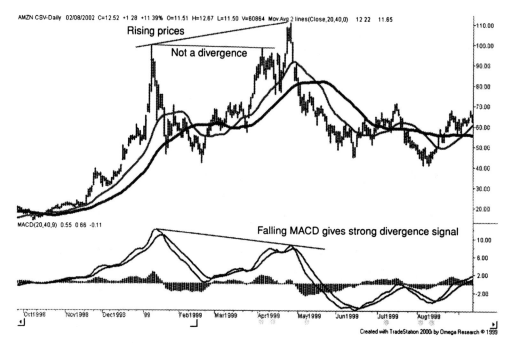

FIGURE 14.6   Another example of divergence in Amazon. In this bearish divergence, the MACD is much weaker on the second peak, indicating a strong divergence signal. Before the actual divergence, there is another peak that may be taken as a divergence; however, prices did not make a new high.

top of the market, and the divergence signal would have been premature. Once the second price peak has been made in the bearish divergence, we look for the MACD line crossing the signal line heading down. We can now *sell*.

Anticipating the Divergence

As you become more comfortable with recognizing a divergence, you'll want to trade it as early as possible. So far, we enter a bearish divergence after we see the second MACD peak form and recognize that it is lower than the previous MACD peak. We can do better than that.

When a current price rally moves above the high of the previous rally (which happened about December 1 in Figure 14.5), we look at the MACD. The MACD value is less than 4.0 when prices break out to the upside. The previous MACD high was above 6.0. If prices were to turn now, we would have a strong divergence (the new MACD peak being much lower than the previous peak). We should start selling now.

Don't sell everything at one time. Divide your capital into three parts:

1. *Sell the first third when prices make a new high and the MACD is much lower.*
2. *Sell the second part when the MACD line gets to within 15 to 20 percent of the previous MACD high.*
3. *Sell the third part when the MACD line crosses the signal line heading down.*

If you only have one choice, you are better taking the second signal. If you have two choices, take the first and second. If you look at the price when the MACD crossed the signal line, the third sell signal, you'll see that your fill would have been disappointing. Prices already had dropped significantly.

Exiting a Divergence Trade

A bearish divergence is a special case of prices being overbought. Prices have reached new highs but have slowed down and give every sign of wanting to reverse direction. As with other overbought situations, once prices have returned to a neutral position, the trade is over. For divergence, that happens when the value of the MACD reaches zero. It is a mistake to think that prices will go from overbought to oversold.

The Divergence Disappears. Not all trades are profitable. Although a divergence signal is reliable, it is not perfect. If you've sold a bearish divergence and prices start back up and the MACD value goes above the previous MACD peak, then the divergence formation has disappeared. The MACD peaks are now rising, and you must exit your trade. Take your loss and look for the next divergence trade.

Combining Divergence with a Trend. One very effective strategy is to combine divergence with a trend. If you use a trend for you basic positions, watch for the formation of both bullish and bearish divergence patterns. If you are long, then sell if a bearish divergence forms and watch the trend to see if it also reverses. The best case is that when the MACD reaches zero, the trend has turned down and you can hold your short position and continue to follow the trend.

HIGH-MOMENTUM TRADING— A GAME PLAYED BY PROFESSIONALS

We started this chapter looking at momentum. Momentum is the change in price over some time interval, a number of days or hours. Momentum is strongest as prices gain speed in a clear uptrend, or as they gain speed during a dramatic drop.

We saw that momentum has peaks based on the span of the momentum calculation. If we use a 10-day momentum, the peaks show the largest 10-day net moves; if we use a 20-day momentum, the peaks will be higher than the 10-day peaks and will show the largest 20-day moves.

One quirk about using a short momentum period, for example, 10 days, is that the momentum line will remain high if prices continue rising for more than 10 days. If there is a 20-day rally, then the last 10 days will all post high momentum values.

In Figure 14.7, a chart of AOL, the 10-day momentum is shown along the bottom, and two horizontal lines have been drawn at +15 and −15 to show the extremely high and low momentum values. It would be possible, although

FIGURE 14.7   Trading high-momentum periods. Professional traders will buy when prices are moving fast and hold the trade for a short time. High-momentum periods, when the momentum value is above the horizontal line, show where prices are rising quickly and accelerating.

risky, to sell when momentum crosses the upper band and buy when it crosses the lower band. We saw in previous charts that momentum usually doesn't remain at a high level for long.

Trading above the Threshold

Some professional traders have made a business of trading in the direction of the trend only when momentum exceeds a *high threshold level* (for example, +15) rather than looking for a change of direction. There is a lot of money to be made because prices are moving fast. There is also a great deal of risk. High-momentum trades are held for only a short time—a few minutes or a few hours for day traders, two or three days for longer-term traders.

Price patterns have changed over the past five years. There are many more day traders. When one stock breaks out above a previous high, everyone sees it as an opportunity for profit. Buy orders start to flow and volume increases. Stocks that are normally ignored can attract large volume when prices make a new high. Traders ride the rising price for as long as possible, watching to see when volume begins to drop, and then they exit. They may just target a modest profit and get out.

It's a fast game that requires tools that allow you to scan a wide range of stocks looking for one that has made a new high after a long, quiet period. You need to stay glued to your screen, enter fast, and exit fast. It's a business for the professional trader, and it's not easy.

TRADING GAME TIPS

Gold shares and gold prices. Is there a relationship between gold shares and gold prices? Yes, if the company is not so diversified that the mining operation is only a small part of its revenue. You can then watch the cash price of gold and look for support and resistance levels that occur at the same place for both the share price and the physical gold price (see Figure 14.8).

General Electric and electricity prices. Don't think for a moment that the price of GE has anything to do with the price of electricity. GE is a massive financial company. Light bulbs and electricity round off the end of its balance sheet.

Questions

1. If the last five prices of IBM were $40.25, $40.75, $41.25, $40.75, and $41.50, what is the value of the five-day momentum?

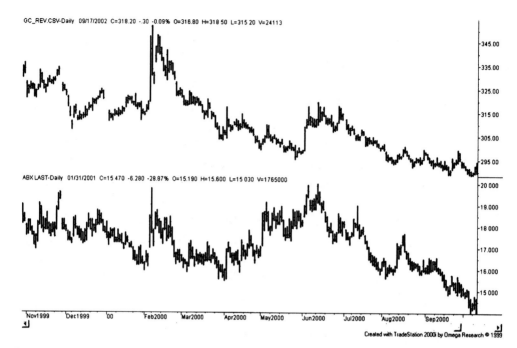

GC_REV.CSV-Daily 09/17/2002 C=318.20 -.30 -0.09% O=316.80 H=318.50 L=315.20 V=24113

ABX LAST-Daily 01/31/2001 C=15.470 -6.280 -28.87% O=15.190 H=15.600 L=15.030 V=1765000

Created with TradeStation 2000i by Omega Research © 1999

FIGURE 14.8   Barrick Gold (ABX) compared to physical gold prices. You can gain extra insight, as well as confirmation of technical signals, by comparing gold stocks with the price of physical gold.

2. Which one of the 20-day or 40-day momentum lines can potentially have the highest value?

3. When two consecutive momentum values are 1.50 and 1.50, are prices (*a*) increasing, (*b*) unchanged, or (*c*) decreasing?

4. When two consecutive momentum values are 2.50 and 1.50, are prices (*a*) increasing, (*b*) unchanged, or (*c*) decreasing?

5. If you are using momentum as a trend indicator, at what point does the trend turn up?

6. If you are using the MACD as a trending indicator, when do you get a *sell* signal?

7. How would you improve the reliability of a standard MACD trending sell signal?

8. Describe an MACD bearish divergence.

9. What would make you consider one bullish divergence as *stronger* than another?

10. If you were anticipating a *bearish divergence* and planned to make two sales, when would you sell?

CHAPTER 15

Overbought/Oversold Indicators and Double Smoothing

When we watch the way a stock price moves, we form expectations. When the price breaks out above a previous high, we expect continued higher movement because something new has happened. When prices move up exceptionally fast, we expect them to stop and reverse. Prices can't accelerate upward forever. We call a market that has gone up unusually far or unusually fast *overbought*. A stock that has dropped in the same way is called *oversold*.

We can decide that a stock or index is overbought or oversold in two ways. The "quants" will statistically measure the fluctuations in price movement over the past, create a profile, and then say that the current move is extreme. Before mathematical analysis was so easily done on a computer, overbought and oversold conditions were decided by *market sentiment*. Market sentiment is still popular and just as valid today.

MARKET SENTIMENT—OPINION AND CONTRARY OPINION

Market sentiment is the driving force of the market. Prices don't go up unless investors believe they will go up and are willing to back up their opinion with money. Although there is a constant flow of funds into pension plans, which works its way into the market, investors will draw money out if they see a gloomy forecast for the next six months. We might conclude at first that if consumer confidence is rising, then we should buy and if it is falling, we should sell.

Is the public always right? We expect prices to rise if the general public is comfortable putting their pension money into the market in large numbers, allocating a larger percentage to stocks and putting less into fixed income, such as bonds.

What happens when prices have been rising steadily, as in the mid-1990s, and the public becomes enamored by the returns of the stock market, when they expect to get more than 20 percent each year? Isn't that an *overbought* situation?

Contrary Opinion

Contrary opinion is a theory that when the public is overly confident in its belief that the market will continue higher, it is time to sell or, at least, time to get out of your long stock holdings and look for a place to sell. Extreme cases justify this approach. The most famous of all events in which the public was wrong are documented in Charles Mackay's *Extraordinary Popular Delusions and the Madness of Crowds* (originally published in 1932 but available in a Noonday Press paperback). It's a bit scary to think that the rise and fall of the Internet stocks, still an incomplete story, may qualify as another great financial bubble.

The *contrarian* is the investor who believes in doing the opposite of the majority of investors. Some of the qualities of contrarian investors are:

- They are value investors.
- They look for undervalued stocks or opportunities where prices are away from value.
- They are attracted to prices after a sustained run up or down.
- Once they identify an opportunity, they use other technical tools for timing; being undervalued does not mean the stock price will rise any time soon.
- After they buy, they wait patiently for prices to turn from down to up.

To be successful, contrarians must not act in the same way as everyone else.

Bullish Consensus

One of the tools for measuring public opinion is the *Bullish Consensus* by Earl Hadady. The Bullish Consensus assesses the impact of the opinions of professional market analysts and brokerage houses by ranking the bullishness of their analyses and weighting the results by the circulation of each one's market letter:

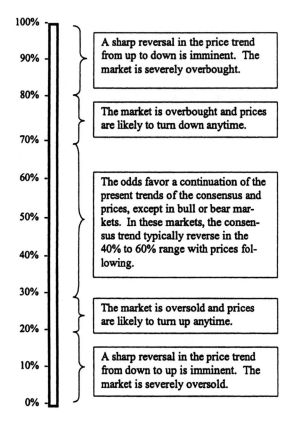

FIGURE 15.1   Interpretation of the Bullish Consensus. (With permission from Figure 6.1, p. 69, R. Earl Hadady, *Contrary Opinion*, New York, John Wiley, 2000).

$$\text{Bullish Consensus} = \frac{\text{sum of (each source} \times \text{relative weight} \times \text{bullish opinion)}}{\text{sum of (each source} \times \text{relative weight} \times 100)}$$

Bullish Consensus values range from 0 to 100 percent. It is considered neutral at 55 percent because of the bullish bias in the stock market that has resulted in a 5 percent rise over the long term. In Figure 15.1, an imminent downtrend is expected when the Bullish Consensus is greater than 90 percent, and an imminent uptrend when it is below 10 percent. Positions are never entered without confirmation.

The obvious problem with the Bullish Consensus is timeliness. First, the analysts must evaluate the individual stocks and write their reports; the reports are then published and distributed. They are usually sent by mail. The elapsed time must be no less than two weeks. Then the reports must be ranked for bullish content.

OSCILLATORS: OVERBOUGHT/OVERSOLD INDICATORS

Oscillators are the best tools for identifying contrary options without reading through all the available market letters—and a much more definitive and timely solution. Some oscillators measure the current price relative to previous highs and lows, while others try to extract a more complex "quality" of the price. We'll look carefully at the two most important of these indicators, the *stochastic* and the *Relative Strength Index*.

The Stochastic

Not to be confused with the stochastic random process, this stochastic was created by George Lane and is a widely used technical indicator for determining overbought and oversold conditions.

The basic calculation, called the *raw stochastic* (also called %*K*), gives the relative position of the closing price within the range of the previous *N* days.

$$\text{Raw stochastic} = \%K(\text{today}) = 100 \times \frac{\text{close}(\text{today}) - \text{lowest low of past } N \text{ days}}{(\text{high} - \text{low}) \text{ range of past } N \text{ days}}$$

where range is the highest high of the past *N* days (not including today) minus the lowest low of the past *N* days (not including today). Dividing by the range creates a value from 0 to 100. For example, if we are using the past 10 days (called a *10-day stochastic*), the raw stochastic has the value:

- 100 if today's close is higher than the high of the past 10 days.
- 0 if today's close is lower than the low of the past 10 days.
- $0 < \%K < 100$ if today's close is between the high and low of the past 10 days.

Calculating the 10-Day Stochastic for Nokia. Using an Excel spreadsheet, we can calculate a smoothed version of the raw stochastic called %*K-slow* (or %*D*), and an even smoother version called %*D-slow*. In Figure 15.2, the historic prices for Nokia are imported into columns *A* to *D*. We are then ready for the calculation of the raw stochastic:

A	B	C	D	E 10-day	F 10-day	G 10-day	H 10-day	I	J
Date	High	Low	Close	High	Low	Range	Stochastic %K	%K-slow	%D-slow
1/2/1996	2.50	2.45	2.50						
1/3/1996	2.55	2.41	2.44						
1/4/1996	2.39	2.29	2.34						
1/5/1996	2.30	2.19	2.21						
1/8/1996	2.23	2.19	2.19						
1/9/1996	2.20	2.14	2.19						
1/10/1996	2.20	2.07	2.16						
1/11/1996	2.27	2.15	2.27						
1/12/1996	2.26	2.18	2.19						
1/15/1996	2.21	2.10	2.12	2.55	2.07	0.48	10.4		
1/16/1996	2.25	2.12	2.25	2.55	2.07	0.48	37.5		
1/17/1996	2.30	2.18	2.20	2.39	2.07	0.32	40.6	29.5	
1/18/1996	2.30	2.23	2.29	2.30	2.07	0.23	95.7	57.9	
1/19/1996	2.33	2.25	2.30	2.33	2.07	0.26	88.5	74.9	54.1
1/22/1996	2.37	2.27	2.37	2.37	2.07	0.30	100.0	94.7	75.8
1/23/1996	2.37	2.31	2.34	2.37	2.07	0.30	90.0	92.8	87.5
1/24/1996	2.37	2.34	2.37	2.37	2.10	0.27	100.0	96.7	94.7
1/25/1996	2.40	2.30	2.30	2.40	2.10	0.30	66.7	85.6	91.7
1/26/1996	2.35	2.26	2.35	2.40	2.10	0.30	83.3	83.3	88.5
1/29/1996	2.36	2.30	2.35	2.40	2.12	0.28	82.1	77.4	82.1
1/30/1996	2.41	2.37	2.37	2.41	2.18	0.23	82.6	82.7	81.1
1/31/1996	2.38	2.30	2.34	2.41	2.23	0.18	61.1	75.3	78.5
2/1/1996	2.45	2.35	2.43	2.45	2.25	0.20	90.0	77.9	78.6
2/2/1996	2.45	2.38	2.41	2.45	2.26	0.19	78.9	76.7	76.6
2/5/1996	2.45	2.39	2.45	2.45	2.26	0.19	100.0	89.6	81.4
2/6/1996	2.48	2.45	2.45	2.48	2.26	0.22	86.4	88.4	84.9
2/7/1996	2.44	2.31	2.36	2.48	2.26	0.22	45.5	77.3	85.1
2/8/1996	2.39	2.31	2.34	2.48	2.26	0.22	36.4	56.1	73.9

FIGURE 15.2   Excel example of 10-day stochastic. The stochastic has three variations, the raw calculation, *%K*, a three-day smoothing of *%K*, called *%K-slow* or *%D*, and a three-day smoothing of that called *%D-slow*. The raw values, *%K*, fluctuate faster between 0 and 100 percent, while the slowest, *%D-slow*, fluctuate the least.

1. In column E find the 10-day high, not including today, using the function *@Max*.

2. In column F find the 10-day low, not including today, using the function *@Min*.

3. Calculate the high-low range by subtracting column F from column E and putting it in column G in the same row.

4. The raw stochastic *%K*, in column H, is = (close − 10-day low) × 100 / range.

5. In column I, the *%K-slow* is the three-day average of *K*.

6. In column J, *%D-slow* is the three-day average of column I.

If we look at the raw stochastic in column H of the spreadsheet, we see that values reach 100 percent three times. This means that prices are at the highest level, or higher than prices during the past 10 days. For the first occurrence of 100 percent on January 22, 1996 the closing price of $2.37 was the high of that day and higher than the highs of the past 10 days. On January 24, 1996 the same high of 2.37 was equal to the high of the past 10 days. When calculating the stochastic, today's close is compared to the range of the previous 10 days; the range does not include today's values.

The smoother values in columns I and J will reach 0 or 100 percent less often but will also lag because of the smoothing.

Charting the Stochastic.   The stochastic is an interpretation of the price chart that removes the trend and scales the prices between 0 and 100. In Figure 15.3, the price of AOL appears on the top and the raw and smoothed stochastic values appear on the bottom. You should first notice that the stochastic peaks and valleys fall at about the same place as prices, but the stochastic values run sideways while AOL prices first go up and then down.

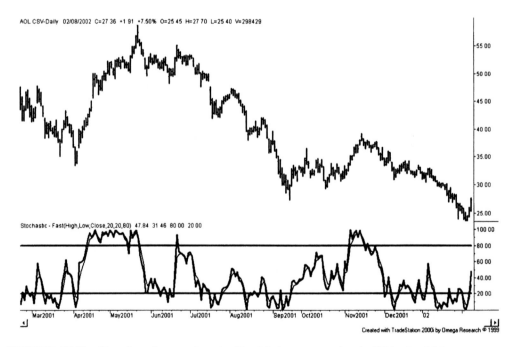

FIGURE 15.3   Charting the stochastic. The 20-day raw stochastic %*K* is the thicker gray line along the bottom. The 3-day average %*K*-slow is the thinner dark line that appears smoother.

Two horizontal lines have been drawn at 20 percent and 80 percent to indicate an *oversold* and *overbought* levels. Whenever prices approach the lows of the past 20 days, the stochastic falls below the 20 percent line. When it nears the highs, it moves above the 80 percent line. Most analysts use the two slower stochastic values and avoid the raw stochastic because the raw value tends to jump around. On the other hand, because it is not smoothed, you can react quickly to current market action, rather than waiting a day or two for a lagged confirmation.

Trading the Stochastic.   The smoothed stochastic trading signal is similar to the signal line used with the MACD. If you look back to Chapter 14, you will see that the MACD smoothed signal line was created in order to get a buy or sell signal. As with the MACD, the best signals follow after the stochastic reaches an extreme:

1. After the smoothed stochastic *%K-slow* has moved above the 80 percent line, sell when the *%K-slow* line crosses the *%D-slow* line moving down.
2. After the smoothed stochastic *%K-slow* has moved below the 20 percent line, buy when the *%K-slow* line crosses the *%D-slow* line moving up.

In Figure 15.4 we see an example of the slow (*%D*, the heavier line) and slower (*%D-slow*, the thinner line) stochastics applied to the S&P from the beginning of 2002. At the beginning of 2002 the S&P was mostly sideways, and the stochastic shows swings from below 20 to over 80. During this period the peaks are easier to trade than the valleys because the stochastic moves above the 80% line and turns down quickly. Stochastic peaks correspond to price peaks.

The oversold points are a problem. As prices decline, the stochastic tends to stay below 20 percent, occasionally moving higher but rarely reaching 50 percent. This is the typical pattern of the stochastic during a downtrend. As prices make new lows, the stochastic value must near zero. Because these two stochastic lines are smoothed, they don't touch zero as often as the raw stochastic.

Clearing Up the Confusing Signals.   The stochastic works best in a sideways market, where prices are not reaching new highs or new lows. During a upward-trending market the stochastic will usually remain above 50 and during a downtrend below 50. Traders will use the stochastic with a trendline (a moving average or breakout) to decide which stochastic signals are good.

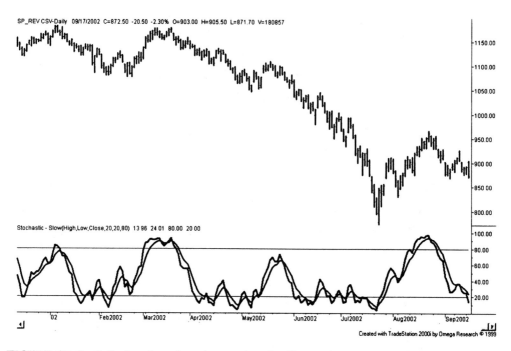

FIGURE 15.4 Sell signals using the stochastic. The stochastic generates good signals during a sideways market, but will stay at low values during a downtrend and high values during an uptrend. To trade the stochastic successfully, you'll need to use a trend to find the direction of prices and then use the stochastic to time your entry.

If the price is trending down, as the S&P in Figure 15.4, you want to sell when the stochastic moves below 80 after being higher, or when the faster stochastic line crosses the slower line heading lower the first time after the faster line has been above 80.

During March 2002 the S&P stochastic reached about 90 and both stochastic lines crossed twice above 80. The proactive trader will take the first crossing as a sell signal. The more conservative trader will wait until the faster or slower stochastic crosses below 80. If you take the first signal, then you have the advantage of selling while prices are rising—you get a good price—but with greater risk. If you wait for a confirmation, you are safer but prices are already heading down and your entry could be much lower. You'll need to try both ways and decide for yourself.

Comparing the 20-Day Stochastic with a 20-Day Momentum. When you plot the faster stochastics (%*K* and %*D*) along with momentum, the peaks and valleys occur at the same points (see Figure 15.5). Neither the stochastic nor the momentum indicators have a lag; that is, neither is the result of smoothing or averaging. They tend to peak where prices peak and are therefore more responsive to price change than averages.

The main difference between the stochastic and momentum is that the stochastic is be scaled between 0 and 100. Even though the AOL rally in November 2001 was much smaller than the previous one in May, the stochastic values reached the same levels near 100 percent. This makes it easier to say the prices are overbought.

When you look at the way momentum shows the same two rallies, the one in November peaks at about 7 percent and the May rally touches above 15 percent. Because momentum is more variable, it is not a good candidate for an overbought/oversold indicator.

A Brief Review of the Stochastic.   The stochastic will be an important tool for timing, but it has three different calculations and some confusing names, used differently throughout the industry:

1. The raw stochastic is the fastest. It is called *%K*, *%FastK*, and *%K-fast*. It is the only stochastic called *fast*.

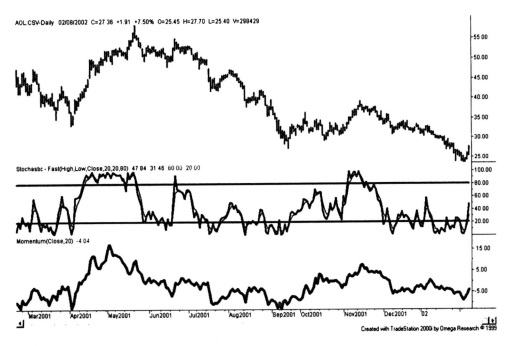

FIGURE 15.5 Comparing the 20-day stochastic with a 20-day momentum. The peaks and valleys of both indicators fall at about the same point, but the stochastic is scaled between 0 and 100; therefore, it has the ability to show when it is overbought and oversold using simple 80–20 lines.

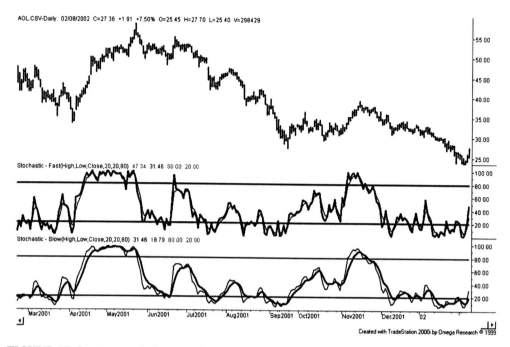

FIGURE 15.6   Fast and slow stochastics. The center panel shows the raw (%*K*) and slow stochastic (%*D*). The bottom panel shows the slow (%*D*) and slowest (%*D*-slow) stochastics.

2. The next slower stochastic is %*SlowK*, which is simply a three-day average of %*K*. It is also called %*D* and %*K-slow*.

3. The slowest stochastic is called %*SlowD* or %*D-slow*. It is a three-day average of %*D* and it is used as the *signal line*.

Figure 15.6 shows the faster stochastics in the middle panel and the slower ones along the bottom.

When trading, use the stochastics as follows:

1. *Sell in a downtrend* when the stochastic crosses the signal line above 80 percent, or when the stochastic moves back below 80 after being higher.

2. *Buy in an uptrend* when the stochastic crosses the signal line below 20 percent, or when the stochastic moves back above 20 percent after being lower.

3. In a *sideways market* use both *buy* and *sell* signals.

An Example of Stochastic Timing.   Although the AOL charts showed periods where the stochastic indicator was confusing, the stochastic has gained popularity because it also can have extended periods where the signals are very clear. These tend to be sideways patterns, and prices often go sideways.

In Figure 15.7 we see AOL in the last part of 2000, where prices had only a slight downward bias. We trade by combining the trendline and the fastest stochastic line (the thinner of the two). During the sideways period from June into October we sell when the stochastic falls below 80 after being higher and buy when it moves above 20 after being lower. When the downtrend becomes clear in mid-October, the stochastic is used only to enter shorts. When the stochastic falls below 20, the trade is closed out.

Stochastic Divergence. We used divergence with the MACD when we found that there were too many signals and they were not always reliable. *Divergence* selects those patterns that are likely to forecast a turn in prices. Divergence is associated with a broadening pattern, or a rounded top or bottom. It shows when prices are rising but at a slower rate.

Divergence works well with the stochastic. The fastest stochastic line is best because it has less lag. The raw stochastic line (the thinner one at the

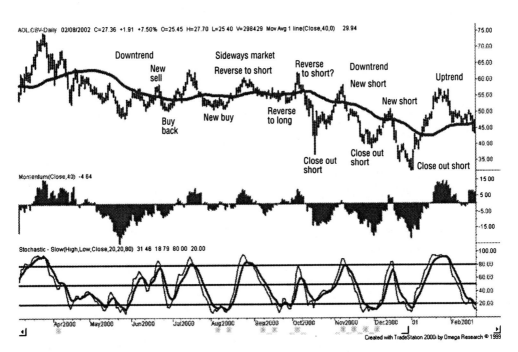

FIGURE 15.7 Combining the stochastic and a trendline. The stochastic is a very good indicator for timing but needs a trendline to select which signals are best. During the sideways period both buys and sells are used. When the downtrend becomes clear in mid-October, only the sell signals are taken.

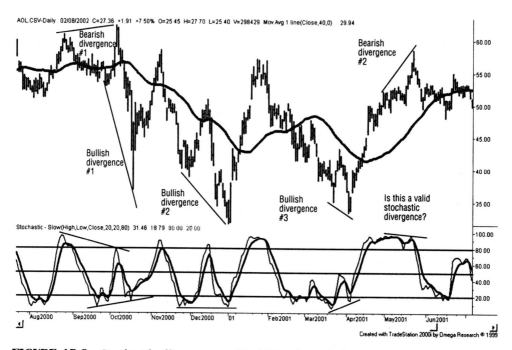

FIGURE 15.8   Stochastic divergence with AOL. A bearish divergence occurs when prices are rising and the stochastic is falling. In this chart there are two bearish and three bullish divergences, all profitable trading signals.

bottom of Figure 15.8) must always be in the extreme zone before there can be a divergence.

A sell signal (a *bearish divergence*) occurs when there are two declining stochastic peaks at the same time that prices are rising. In August and October 2000, the raw stochastic indicator first peaked near 100 and then peaked again at about 80. When you connect the two peaks with a straight line, the line clearly angles down.

If you look above the two stochastic peaks, you see prices rising. Prices peak at about the same place as the stochastic peaks (because the raw stochastic doesn't lag) and if you connect those peaks, you see that prices are rising. The combination of rising prices and a falling stochastic creates a divergence. The sell signal occurs when the raw stochastic line crosses the slower stochastic line after the second peak. In this example prices are falling quickly at the same time as the sell signal, but there is still room for profit. In Figure 15.8 there are two bearish divergences (sell) signals and three bullish divergence (buy) signals. All of them are profitable.

Stronger and Weaker Divergence Signals.   A bearish divergence is stronger when the angle between the rising prices and the falling stochastic is greater, that is, when prices are rising faster and/or the stochastic is falling faster.

Divergence only works when the prices and the stochastic are moving in opposite directions. It is not enough to have a strong relative difference, where prices are declining slightly and the stochastic is declining sharply. One must be going up and the other down.

Bearish Divergence Rules.   There are specific rules for recognizing a divergence signal (this describes a bearish signal, but the bullish signal is just the reverse):

1. The first stochastic peak must be greater than 80.
2. The second stochastic peak should be at least a 15 percent lower (but no less than 5 percent lower). For example, if the first peak is at 90, the second should be at 70 or 75.
3. The price peaks that occur at the same time as the stochastic peaks must be clearly rising.

Using Faster and Slower Stochastics for Divergence.   Do we get better divergence signals when we use a faster or slower calculation period for the stochastic? In Figure 15.9 a 10-day and a 20-day fast stochastic are shown along the bottom, the 10-day above the 20-day. Because the 10-day calculation causes the stochastic to change faster, it creates clear and frequent peaks and valleys on the chart. The angles are clearer. In May 2001, the 20-day stochastic has a rounded formation with a very small dip in value, while the 10-day stochastic shows a drop to 60 in between two peaks of 90. In this case the faster stochastic works better and is likely to give us more trading opportunities.

Relative Strength Index

Created by Wells Wilder in 1978, the *Relative Strength Indicator* (RSI) is used more often than the stochastic. It is most often used the same way as the stochastic, but has some extra features. The RSI is a ratio of the upward price movements to the total price movement over 14 days. It has a slight smoothing feature, and is a little more difficult to calculate. The way to calculate the RSI is:

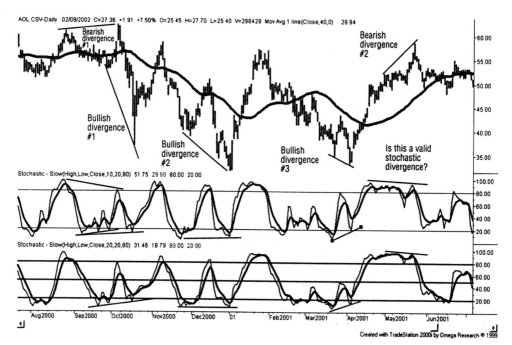

FIGURE 15.9   Comparing the divergence signals for a 10-day and a 20-day stochastic.
A faster 10-day stochastic is more sensitive and gives a clearer picture. The bullish divergence in
December 2000 can be seen and the one in May 2001 is now clear.

$SumU$ = sum of price changes for all those days closing higher (positive numbers)

$SumD$ = sum of price changes for all those days closing lower (positive numbers)

Then

$$RS = \frac{SumU}{SumD} \text{ (the ratio of up changes to down changes)}$$

and

$$RSI \text{ (first calculation)} = 100 - \frac{100}{1 + RS} \times 100 \times \frac{RS}{1 + RS}$$

Once the first calculation has been made, the following values of $SumU$
and $SumD$ use the *average off* method, requiring only the previous values of
$SumU$ and $SumD$, and the current price change:

$$SumU(\text{today}) = SumU(\text{previous}) - \frac{SumU(\text{previous})}{14} + \text{today's upward change}$$

$$SumD(\text{today}) = SumD(\text{previous}) - \frac{SumD(\text{previous})}{14} + \text{today's downward change}$$

Date	Close	Changes	10-day *SumU*	10-day *SumD*	RS	RSI	
1/2/1996	2.50		0.000	0.000			
1/3/1996	2.44	−0.06	0.000	0.060			
1/4/1996	2.34	−0.10	0.000	0.160			
1/5/1996	2.21	−0.13	0.000	0.290			
1/8/1996	2.19	−0.02	0.000	0.310			
1/9/1996	2.19	0.00	0.000	0.310			
1/10/1996	2.16	−0.03	0.000	0.340			
1/11/1996	2.27	0.11	0.110	0.340			
1/12/1996	2.19	−0.08	0.110	0.420			
1/15/1996	2.12	−0.07	0.110	0.490			
1/16/1996	2.25	0.13	0.240	0.490	0.49	32.9	Initial
1/17/1996	2.20	−0.05	0.216	0.491	0.44	30.6	Iterative
1/18/1996	2.29	0.09	0.284	0.442	0.64	39.2	Iterative
1/19/1996	2.30	0.01	0.266	0.398	0.67	40.1	Iterative
1/22/1996	2.37	0.07	0.309	0.358	0.86	46.4	Iterative
1/23/1996	2.34	−0.03	0.278	0.352	0.79	44.2	Iterative
1/24/1996	2.37	0.03	0.281	0.317	0.89	47.0	Iterative
1/25/1996	2.30	−0.07	0.253	0.355	0.71	41.6	Iterative

FIGURE 15.10   RSI spreadsheet example.

If the current change is up then SumD is reduced by $\frac{1}{14}$. If the current change is down then *SumU* is reduced by $\frac{1}{14}$.

The RSI calculation seems like a lot of numbers, but it is easily done on a spreadsheet. Figure 15.10 gives an example that you can test yourself. The formulas that go into the key cells are (for 10-day calculation period):

Iterative SumU = IF($C14>0,D13 − (D13/10) + $C14, D13 − D13/10)

Iterative SumD = IF($C14<0,E13 − (E13/10) − $C14, E13 − E13/10)

Any number of days can be used instead of 14, but 14 is standard.

Comparing the RSI with the Stochastic.   Which is better, the RSI or the stochastic? We can find the answer by comparing some charts showing both the RSI and the stochastic one above the other. In Figure 15.11, a 20-day RSI can be seen in the center panel and a 14-day stochastic in the bottom panel. You will find that while the patterns of the two indicators often match, the calculation periods will be different.

In Figure 15.11 many of the peaks and valleys for the 20-day RSI and 20-day stochastic are similar. The stochastic moves more freely between 0 and 100; however, the most important extremes are in the same place.

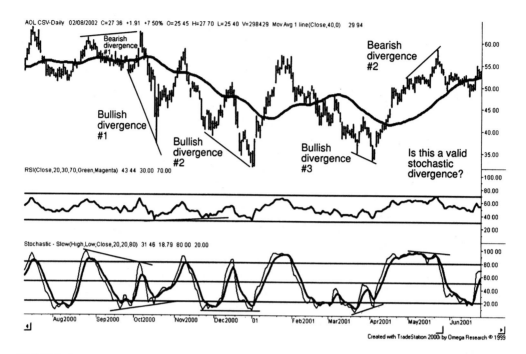

FIGURE 15.11 **Divergence signals for the 20-day RSI and the 20-day stochastic.** The RSI has only one bullish divergence signal and no bearish signals, while the stochastic has three bullish signals and two bearish signals.

As a trader, you'll see that the stochastic produced five divergence signals, while the RSI only had one. That's an important difference if you're trying to make money.

Speeding Up the RSI Calculation. We said earlier that we could make the two indicators similar by changing the speeds. In Figure 15.12 the RSI calculation period is reduced from 20 days to 10 days, while the stochastic is left at 20 days. The patterns are much closer in appearance.

Do these new RSI peaks and valleys produce more divergence signals? Look for yourself. It doesn't seem to help. The stochastic seems to be the better indicator for finding divergence signals.

Anticipating Divergence: a Reminder

Divergence signals are usually entered when, for example, the faster stochastic %*K-slow* crosses the slower %*D-slow*; however, they can be anticipated for greater profit with an occasional, relatively small loss:

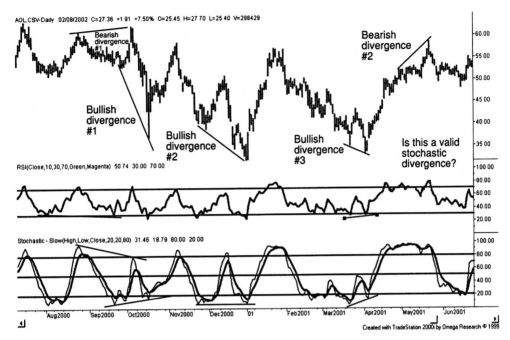

FIGURE 15.12 Comparing a 10-day RSI with a 20-day stochastic. The peaks and valleys of the RSI are now very similar to the stochastic but the stochastic is still better at showing divergence signals.

1. When prices make a new swing high (a high greater than the previous high peak), look at the position of the faster stochastic.

2. If the faster stochastic is well below the level of its value at the time of the previous price peak, then there is a potential divergence.

3. Sell while the stochastic is still rising.

4. Close out the trade with a loss if the current stochastic value becomes greater or equal to its value at the previous price peak. This will happen if prices start to move higher at a faster rate.

DOUBLE-SMOOTHED MOMENTUM

Originally, we saw that momentum was unbounded and erratic. It is similar to most other trends but not quite as smooth. There is a technique called *double smoothing* that will turn a questionable indicator into a very valuable one.

The success of double smoothing is that it creates a trendline that has less lag than a moving average. Less lag means that you can react faster to changes in the direction of prices. Double smoothing does this by averaging the momentum rather than the prices.

Momentum is speed. It shows faster movement and more sensitivity than prices. If you take the first difference in prices (a one-day momentum), then you speed up price movement. If you then average the momentum, you smooth out the prices and slow down the speed. First speeding them up and then slowing them down results in no lag.

However, a momentum indicator that is smoothed once is still not quite enough. If we now average the new result, we are averaging something that has already been averaged. We have smoothed it twice. For convenience we use percentage smoothing rather than a moving average. Figure 15.13 shows Microsoft with 20-day and 40-day momentum indicators in the center panel, and a double smoothing of the 20-day indicator in the bottom panel. The

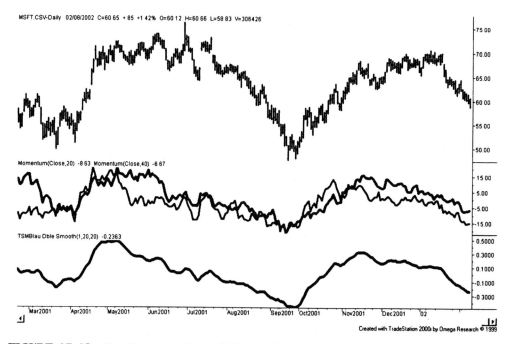

FIGURE 15.13 Double smoothing of Microsoft. The 1-day differences in Microsoft prices are smoothed once using a 20-day period and the result is smoothed again using a 20-day period. The resulting trendline does not have the lag of a moving average. In this case, the double-smoothed line is not yet as smooth as we would like it to be.

double-smoothed indicator begins with the one-day price differences and smoothes them with a 20-day period (smoothing value of .0476). It then smoothes the new values by .0476 again.

This first example of double smoothing does not produce a trendline that is as smooth as a moving average. It also has different value than the original prices; therefore, it can't be plotted along with prices in the upper panel. That's not a big problem because we only need to see the direction of the trendline to decide whether prices are going up or down. Most important, the new double-smoothed line does not have a lag. The highest point and lowest point of the trendline in the bottom panel correspond to the highs and lows of the price chart.

Smoothing the Final Smoothed Indicator

By starting with the 10-day momentum rather than the 1-day momentum (the first differences), we can smooth the indicator even further without adding any noticeable lag. We follow these steps:

1. Calculate the values of the 10-day momentum.
2. Smooth the momentum values using a 20-day percentage smoothing.
3. Smooth the values in step 2 using a 20-day percentage smoothing.

The result appears in Figure 15.14. The double-smoothed trendline in the bottom panel is much smoother using the 10-day momentum rather than the 1-day momentum. It is now possible to use the simple turns in the trendline for buy and sell signals. At the same time, only a very small lag is introduced. This method was developed by Bill Blau and deserves your attention.

TRADING GAME TIPS

The most reliable MACD signals are divergences. They don't occur often enough, but they are worth waiting for. After that, look for the normal sell signal (the MACD line crossing the signal line) when it occurs at a high value or after a noticeable price run.

Use more than one technique. You're still learning what methods are best. Try using both a moving average and support-resistance. Keep track of the MACD, looking for divergence. Look for a volume spike. You need to watch everything before you settle on a few choice methods.

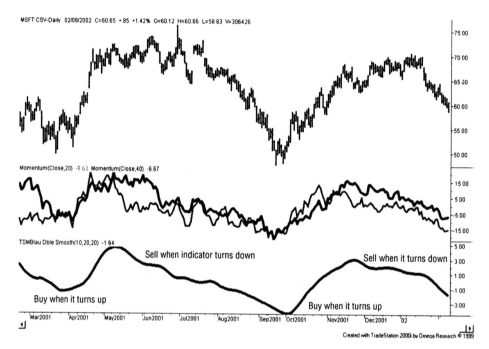

FIGURE 15.14 Double-smoothed 10-day momentum. Using a 10-day momentum instead of 1-day creates a much smoother trendline (bottom panel) without the lag normally associated with moving averages.

TRADING GAME #3

We're now going to trade the way it's really done. You'll be able to go long or short, add to your positions, and take off part of your size. Trade as much as you want to, but be sure to watch your risk. Be careful of the futures positions; losses in the S&P can add up fast. You'll learn to manage your position size and your risk.

You'll want to keep watching a few active stocks, but also ones that give diversification. Try a pharmaceutical, a defense stock, Wal-Mart, and an energy company. Continue to trade the S&P futures, but now add crude oil (CL) traded on the New York Mercantile Exchange. Crude oil futures give you a macro picture of price direction and a little excitement when the Mideast pot is stirred.

The new rules are:

1. Begin with no positions. Begin a new spreadsheet for your accounting.
2. You now have $1,000,000.

3. You will trade four stocks (your choice) and two futures, SP and CL.

4. You may trade any size on any trade. You may add or remove partial positions.

5. You must state your current position before each new order (e.g., NP, L 5000, S 1000).

6. Each new order or partial position must be entered on your accounting as a new trade (e.g., buy 5000 RTN, and then buy 2500 RTN are two separate lines).

7. You may go short stocks (there is no uptick rule and no borrowing money; use of capital will count as though a short position was a long position).

8. You must keep an accounting of your capital used for trading and your free capital.

9. Try to evaluate the return-to-risk ratio for performance as the game proceeds.

10. Profits and losses will be important feedback in deciding if you are trading correctly.

11. Don't risk more than 5 percent of your investment on a single trade. That's bad management.

12. Be thoughtful about your position size. You could lose everything.

13. There will be no commissions.

14. No day trading!

15. Your accounting should now be perfect. Know your positions and know your current account balance, including open profits and losses. That's called *marked-to-market* daily.

16. Enter your orders clearly. If an order is not what you intended but is a valid order, it will be executed! Be careful.

17. Don't forget: We are trading, not investing.

Questions

1. When contrary opinion indicates that the market is oversold, do you (*a*) buy immediately, (*b*) sell immediately, (*c*) use a timing indicator to give you a specific buy signal, or (*d*) use a timing indicator to give you a specific sell signal?

2. What is the greatest disadvantage of the Bullish Consensus indicator?

3. Explain the raw stochastic in words.

4. Name the three stochastic calculations from fastest to slowest.

5. What is the primary difference between the stochastic calculation and momentum values?

6. Explain the chart pattern that gives you a bullish stochastic divergence signal.

7. In a stochastic bearish divergence, the second stochastic peak should be lower than the first by at least what value?

8. The Relative Strength Index is a ratio of what two values?

9. Explain the steps need to create a double-smoothed trendline using a 10-day momentum.

10. What is the advantage of double smoothing?

CHAPTER 16

Managing Your Entry and Exit

It is not only important that we know when to enter and exit a trade; we also must know how much to trade, and whether to enter the entire position at one time or feed that order into the marketplace.

Let's say that you plan to buy $10,000 of IBM. What choices do you have when you enter? If IBM is trading at $50, you can buy 200 shares all at one time or 100 shares now and another 100 tomorrow or next week. You could buy in lots of 50 or 25 over a single day or spread the order out over a week. Is one method better than another?

AN AVERAGE PRICE OR A BETTER PRICE?

It's always safe to get an average price. If you're concerned that you'll buy IBM at $50 today and it will drop to $45 by the end of tomorrow, then you could just wait. Most likely, you're not sure that it will drop. If the employment report comes out favorably and the economy looks strong, then IBM could even jump to $60 by the end of today.

If you don't know what might happen in the next two days but you have a strong opinion that IBM will be going up, then average into the position. *To get an average price, you buy equal amounts over equal time intervals.* If you plan to buy 200 shares, then you buy 50 this morning, 50 this afternoon, 50 tomorrow morning, and the last 50 at tomorrow's close. You now have a reasonable approximation of an average price.

When you're trying to get an average price, breaking up your order into small pieces and feeding it into the market is the simplest way. You don't need to do it one share at a time. If you separated your 200-share order into eight parts of 25, you would get very close to the average.

THE MAGIC NUMBER IS 4

Whenever you are thinking of scaling into the market, remember that the *magic number is 4*. If you are trying to get an average price, you need to break your order into at least four equal parts. If you are trying to get a better than average price, then you cannot divide your order into more than three equal parts. *Four or more equal parts gets you close to an average price, three or less gives you a chance to get a better than average price.*

The best scenario is to buy your entire position at one time at the lowest price. We would all like that, but it's unrealistic. Therefore, you decide how long you have to enter your position, a few hours or a few days, and look for opportunities during that window. Let's say that prices are trading in a range from $35 to $40 and you expect good news to move prices through the $40 level to $50. It's Monday morning and you think this will happen by the end of the week after dividends are announced. The price is now $38. What are your choices?

1. You could buy one-third of your position now, one-third on today's close, and one third sometime tomorrow, for an average price.

2. You can wait for prices to test the low of $35, placing a buy order for your entire position at $35.50. However, what happens if you are right and prices move straight up to $50, never pulling back to $35? You've missed the move.

3. You can buy one-third now, one-third at $35.50, and one-third at $40.10 on a break above $40. That's a bit better because you are sure of getting two-thirds of your position at $39.05. If prices drop instead of rally, you have two-thirds of your position at $36.25. The only time you have a full position is if the price pattern is exactly as you predict—first declining to support, and then rallying up through resistance.

How realistic is case 3? Not very. If we knew how prices were going to move, we wouldn't need all this planning. It's difficult to forecast where prices will be in a few days; it's even more difficult to predict the pattern prices will take to get to that goal. There is a very small chance you will be able do both.

Try the average price method. In the example above you might buy two of the three parts by averaging into the trade, and then add the third part on a breakout through $40 in order to have a confirmation. In that case you raise your average price, but have the comfort of knowing that you were right about your prediction.

Some traders would wait for the breakout before entering any of the position. They get a worse price but a better chance of success. Other traders would enter the entire position between $39.75 and $39.90 looking for the breakout and trying to get *free exposure* from the jump through $40—a little more risk, but a lot more reward.

ENTERING TRADES

Let's look at the different ways that you can enter a trade. We'll cover entering your entire position at one time, scaling down, averaging into a trade, and adding additional positions on profits.

Entering Your Entire Position at One Time

Entering your entire position at one time is the simplest method and the easiest to follow. Entering at one time could get you the best or the worst price. Over the long term it probably averages out. You should keep a record of the current price at the time you get the buy or sell signal in order to compare it with the actual price you received when you entered the trade.

Entering at one time should serve as a benchmark. That is, you need to prove to yourself that another entry technique is better before you use it.

Scaling Down

Scaling down is a traditional investing technique that hides the fact that you entered at the wrong price. The way it works is that you buy 100 shares of Cisco at the current price of $20 because it has declined to a support level. You think it has reason to rally back to $30. Instead, Cisco drops through support to $18. Instead of closing out the trade because it's going the wrong way, you buy another 100 shares, giving you an average price of $19. Cisco continues to fall to the next support level at $15, and you buy another 100 shares. Your average price is now $17.67 and your loss is $2.67 on 300 shares; however, if the price gains only $3 you have a profit. Let's look at the good and bad points of this method:

- You need to decide the final size of you position in advance. You can't keep buying as prices move lower. At some point you'll run out of money.
- Let's say you will add to your position twice so that your initial entry is one-third of your potential investment. If prices immediately move higher, then your analysis is correct and you profit on one third of your available investment but never add more. If prices move lower, then you've figured this wrong. You continue to add to your position and increase your losses.
- Your greatest profits come from prices dropping after the first entry, stopping right after you've bought your maximum investment, then turning up, and continuing up. The success of the method is based on bad timing.
- You don't have a stop-loss; therefore, you have no risk protection. Where do you get out and say that you were wrong?

There is something wrong with a trading plan based on the expectation that you will be wrong. If you couldn't figure out where the first entry should be, then why would you be right even after you are fully invested at a lower price?

Scaling down is a technique that works when markets always go up and your broker has told you to buy at a bad price. If you're a trader, you get out when you're wrong.

Averaging into a Trade

Unlike scaling down, *averaging into a trade* is a plan to enter the entire position but assumes that we can't know the best single point to enter. In order to get an average price, we enter equal amounts at equal time intervals. Four or more entry points will get you close to an average price over a fixed time interval. Once a trading signal occurs and you start your averaging, you always execute the entire size with one exception: If an exit condition occurs before you are entirely in the position, then you stop entering and exit.

This method is safe unless you are a fast trader and entry timing is critical. Then you must enter the entire position at one time.

Adding Additional Positions on Profits

The opposite to scaling down is *adding additional positions on profits*. This is also called *pyramiding*. The most common ways to add positions on profits are:

- Add as soon as you have profits.
- Add on secondary entry signals (for example, a new breakout from a continuation pattern).
- Add on a pullback to a support level following new profits.

The quantity that you add is very important. Your choices are:

- Add as much as you can using your profits.
- Add a percentage of your profits.
- Add a smaller amount on each new signal (a *normal pyramid*).
- Add the same amount as your original entry size (an *equal pyramid*).
- Add an increasing amount on each subsequent entry (an *inverted pyramid*). In this case you must draw from additional capital.

Adding when you have profits capitalizes on a good trading decision. It's also a good way to turn a profit into a loss. When you add to your position, it takes a smaller reversal to eat up all your profits. The inverted pyramid is the worst case, but all pyramiding is risky. Every time you build your position the risk of loss increases as the end of the move gets closer.

Common Trading Sense

If you want to add to your position, common trading sense goes as follows:

1. Add smaller amounts at each secondary entry point.
2. Each secondary point should be a valid signal (e.g., a breakout) or a clear timing point.
3. Your exit point must be adjusted so that the new entry cannot turn the entire trade into a loss.
4. Don't add more than twice after the initial entry. Your risk becomes too great.

EXITING TRADES

There are also choices when you exit a trade. It isn't necessary to get out of the entire position at one time; however, you still may find that a hasty exit is the safest strategy.

Exiting the Entire Position at One Time

As with the entry, this is the simplest method and serves as a benchmark. If you want to try another approach, you should prove to yourself that the other method is better than exiting all at one time.

Scaling Out with Profits

This method allows you to target an average exit price, but spread out the levels at which you will exit. You can never be sure where prices will stop before turning. This method of fanning your target price level will let you capture more profits and reduce risk. Follow these rules:

1. Calculate your profit target for the current trade. This should be based on volatility so that it's closer when prices are quiet and farther when the market is active.

2. Fan out your profit target into at least three separate prices, where the three prices average to your original profit target. For example, if you entered IBM at $50 looking for $55, then exit one-third of your trade at $54, $55, and $56, or even better, exit at $53, $55, and $57. The sooner you start getting out of your trade, the sooner you have profits in your pocket and lower risk. Once you've taken profits at $53 and $55, you only have one-third of your position at risk. If prices reversed back to your entry point of $50, you would still have most of your profits. If you only get one-third at $53 you've done better than if prices had reached $54 and then reversed back to $50.

3. You can take profits on different amounts at different prices as long as they all average to your original target. Instead of taking one-third of your profits at three levels of equal separation, you might take 20 percent at $53, 50 percent at $55, and another 30 percent at $56, giving you an average of $55.

We can only estimate where we think prices will go. Fanning out your target is a realistic and sound strategy. You don't need to be exact about the amounts and prices, just so they come close to you target.

When you have three levels to exit a long position, you also can exit any one of those levels if you think that volatility is falling and the price move is stalling. If you're wrong and prices start up again, you will take your profits at two more levels. Getting out a bit early on one of the parts won't matter in the final profits, but it's a good move if prices start down.

Scaling Out with Losses

Reducing the position as prices move against you will control the size of your loss, but there are some complications that need to be considered:

1. You can only scale out of your trade when prices move against you if you also plan to scale back into the trade. You believe that the trade is still sound but your entry price was bad. You reduce your risk until prices reach a support level or begin to rise.

2. If you remove part of the position and then prices reverse and become profitable, you are profiting with a smaller position than the one on which you lost. You need to know in advance where you will add back your positions.

3. You can always plan to add back the positions when the current holding becomes profitable. That's a confirmation that prices are moving the right way.

4. Scaling out and back in works best for long-term trend-following systems that have an orderly pattern in the generation of profits and losses. In that case it is similar to "trading the equity curve." When the trend isn't working, your equity is dropping and you lighten up on your position. When your equity starts to rise, then the trend is successful and you add back to your position. If you don't plan to add back to your position then you should get out of the trade completely.

TRADING GAME TIPS

You made the wrong trade. Every trader makes mistakes, even *buying* when you meant to *sell*. Don't try to manage the position; just get out. It's the wrong trade, and you can't manage it correctly. It will distract you from other trades and eat up your time. Close out the trade as soon as possible, and get on with your life.

The time of day to trade. There are two reasons to select the time of day to trade. Volume varies considerably during the day. The *greatest volume* is near the open; the *second greatest volume* is at the close. After the open the order flow steadily drops until its low point in the middle of the day. Many of the traders are off the floor—some actually eat lunch. During the middle of the day orders dribble in. If one large order hits the market, it could push prices higher or lower but have very little meaning with regard to price direction.

The open and close are the two most likely times to show the high or low of the day. If prices open and start to drop, then the open is most likely to be the day's high. The middle of the day is the next most likely time to be a high or low. Prices drop from the open and quiet at midday while there is little activity. When traders come back onto the floor and activity increases, they may move prices higher again. Then the midday price becomes the low. If they move prices lower, then the close becomes the low.

Questions

1. What is the best technique for getting the average price on a buy order of 1,000 shares over two days?

2. If you are trying to get the best price, in how many parts should you divide and execute your order?

3. What are the greatest advantages and the greatest disadvantages of scaling down?

4. What is the name of the technique that requires buying equal amounts as you increase your profits? Explain the risk of this method.

5. Explain the reasoning behind scaling out of a profitable position (as a short-term trader).

CHAPTER 17

Volatility and Portfolio Management

Other than price itself, volatility is the most important single piece of information for the technical trader. *Volatility equals risk.* The larger the prices swings, the greater the volatility and the greater the risk.

Volatility can be used to decide where to take profits and where to place your stop-loss order. It also is used to determine the number of shares to buy.

The goal of a trader is to *achieve the highest return for the lowest risk.* Volatility will be used to measure the risk.

MEASURING VOLATILITY

Volatility is a measure of price movement. Volatility can be measured and interpreted in a variety ways, but one meaning is universally understood: *Higher volatility means higher risk.*

Four Basic Volatility Measures

Before we can use volatility, we need to measure it. The four most common methods (shown in Figure 17.1) are:

1. The *change in price* over N days (Figure 17.1a):

$$\text{Volatility(today)} = \text{price(today)} - \text{price}(N \text{ days ago})$$

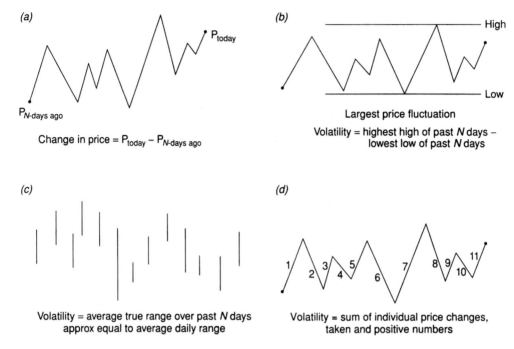

FIGURE 17.1   Four volatility measures. (*a*) Change in price, (*b*) largest price fluctuation, (*c*) average true range, and (*d*) sum of absolute price changes.

2. The *largest price fluctuation* (price range) over the past N days (Figure 17.1*b*):

Volatility(today) = highest high of the past N days
− lowest low of the past N days

Using an Excel spreadsheet, you can substitute *max* for the *highest high* and *min* for the *lowest low*.

3. The *average true range* over the past N days (Figure 17.1*c*):

Volatility(today) = average of the daily true range from N days ago to today

where average true range can include the previous closing price if there is a gap opening. This is explained in the next section.

4. The *sum of the absolute price changes* over the past N days (Figure 17.1*d*):

Volatility(today) = sum from today to N days ago of
absolute value(price(current day) − price(previous day))

Adding absolute price changes gives you the length of the path taken by prices over the past *N* days.

True Range. The *true range* measures the daily trading range so that it includes yesterday's closing price when there is a gap opening. This is an important feature when measuring volatility. For example, if Amazon closed yesterday at $10 and opened today at $11, traded up to $12 without going lower than $11, and then closed at $11.50, we would have open, high, low, and closing prices of $11.00, $12.00, $11.00, and $11.50. If you measure volatility using the daily trading range then we have the high of $12.00 less the low of $11.00, giving a range of $1.00. However, that doesn't reflect the real volatility because prices jumped from yesterday's close of $10.00. The volatility is really $2.00, not $1.00.

The true range is the largest of the three combinations:

1. High(today) – low(today)
2. High(today) – close(previous day)
3. Close(previous day) – low(today)

If the prices today (*T*) and the prices yesterday (*T* – 1) are:

  (*T*): high $55.00, low $53.00, close $53.50
  (*T* – 1): high $51.00, low $48.00, close $51.00

then today's true range is $4.00 while the normal range calculation is $2.00.

Which of the Four Volatility Measures Is Best?

You will find that each of the four ways to measure volatility will be useful:

- In securities, most risk is measured simply by taking the standard deviation of the daily price changes.
- When you are deciding where to take profits based on volatility, you'll want a multiple of the average true range.
- When you want to compare one market to the other or find the relative volatility of the stock you are trading, the most descriptive measure is the sum of the price changes.
- Using the total path of price movement recognizes that a stock that trades from $15 up to $20, back to $15, and up to $20 again is more volatile than one that trades from $15 to $20 only once (see Figure 17.2).

FIGURE 17.2   The price path tells the most about volatility. Although both price paths have the same high and low, and start and end at the same points, (*b*) is more volatile than (*a*) because of its more frequent fluctuations.

(a)   (b)

The Theory of Stock Market Volatility

Traditional thinking by securities analysts is that in the stock market, *price volatility is lognormal*. That is, when prices increase, the volatility also increases at a more or less predictable rate. We can see that in most charts where the stock traded in a wide range (see Figure 17.3). Charting services such as TradeStation provide the ability to display a *semilog* chart at the click of a mouse. The importance of this lognormal relationship is that *risk increases as price increases*. Your trading method must accept larger risk at higher prices.

An Example of a Lognormal Calculation.   For those of you who have used log tables or can program formulas into Excel, the following example may be helpful. We use the spreadsheet math function *natural log*, Ln, to change actual prices to lognormal prices. Over the long term and under average market conditions, the relationship between actual price changes and volatility is expected to be:

$$\frac{|\text{price}(T) - \text{price}(T-1)|}{\text{Ln}(\text{price}(T))} \approx \frac{|\text{price}(S) - \text{price}(S-1)|}{\text{Ln}(\text{price}(S))}$$

where the vertical bars (||) represent the absolute value (the positive value) of the number inside the bars.

This formula says that the absolute value of the change in price on day T divided by the natural log of the price on day T is approximately equal ($\approx$) to the change in price on any other day, S, divided by the natural log of the price on day S.

For example, if the price on day T is \$20 and the price on day S is \$40, then the natural log of prices on those days are Ln $(20) = 2.99$ and Ln $(40) = 3.99$. If the volatility is \$1.00 when $P = 20$, then the volatility is expected to be \$1.23 when $P = \$40$. In equation form:

$$\frac{\text{Volatility at price}(T) = 20}{\text{Ln of price}(20)} \approx \frac{\text{volatility at price}(S) = 40}{\text{Ln of price}(40)}$$

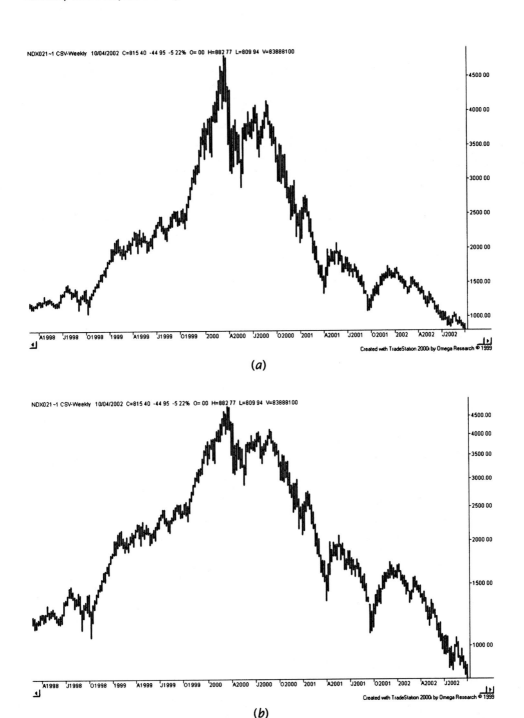

(a)

(b)

FIGURE 17.3   Comparing Nasdaq on different charting scales. (*a*) Equal prices scale (top), (*b*) semilog scale (bottom). The equal scale shows extreme volatility at the highest prices during the first half of 2000; the semilog scale shows only a small increase in volatility similar to the more volatile weeks when prices reached relative lows during the price decline. The semilog scale confirms the theory that prices have a predictable increase in volatility as they move higher.

If the volatility at $20 is $1, then the volatility at $40 is $1.23. Note: When using a spreadsheet for your calculations, the function Ln is not the same as the function Log.

HOW TO MAKE YOUR TRADING ADAPT TO CHANGING VOLATILITY

Enough of the theory. The best way to use volatility to improve your trading is to make your profit-taking objectives and your stop-loss targets get closer and farther away as volatility decreases and increases.

Changing Profit Targets Based on Volatility

If AOL is trading in a $1 range each day, you might want to target a short-term profit of $2. That would be reasonable if prices moved in one direction for about three or four days. If AOL was much more volatile, ranging $4 in one day, then an equivalent profit target would be $8. More important, if volatility dropped to $0.50 then a profit target of $2 would take much longer to reach and you'll want to set your goal at $1.

When you set your profit target by finding a resistance level on a chart, the volatility of prices tells you where to look. Don't pick a minor resistance level that's $1 above the current price when the market volatility is $2 a day, and don't expect a profit of $10 when prices only range $0.50 each day.

Changing Your Stops to Reflect Volatility

The same principle applies to stop-loss orders. If the stop is inside the normal daily trading range of AOL, then you can be sure that you'll be stopped out. How far away should you place your stop? Look for a support level at about 3 times the volatility below where you enter your long trade and place your stop-loss on either side of that level—depending on whether you are looking for *free exposure* or *confirmation*.

If you're a technical trader and you are not using charts, then you can set your profit target and stop based entirely on volatility. If you have just entered a long position in AOL at $15 and the stock has been trading in a $1 daily range, then:

$$\text{Profit target} = \text{entry price} + (\text{profit factor} \times \text{daily range})$$
$$= 15 + (2 \times 1)$$
$$= 17$$

$$\text{Stop-loss} = \text{entry price} - (\text{stop factor} \times \text{daily range})$$
$$= 15 - (3 \times 1)$$
$$= 12$$

You'll note that the profit target is 2 times the volatility and the stop is 3 times the volatility. The profit target is closer than the stop-loss. This is the normal pattern when you're a short-term trader. You want to be sure you capture profits as often as possible. To do that, you'll need to take a larger risk on each trade. If you make your stop closer than your profit target, then you're sure to be stopped out more often and end up as a loser. The closer order is most likely to be hit.

VOLATILITY EXTREMES

We have seen in previous chapters that if there is extremely high volatility or extremely high volume, then a price reversal follows soon after—prices cannot keep going the same direction on increasing volatility.

The problem with knowing that prices will reverse and being able to trade that pattern successfully is the risk. High volatility is high risk, and the only way to offset that risk is by trading a much smaller position. In some markets, such as the 1987 stock market crash, the potential profits weren't worth the risk. Even in less extreme markets you may feel that the risk is just too great. That's called common sense. First look at the risk and then the reward. If you are in doubt, don't trade.

Principles of Volatility

Two important principles of volatility are:

1. High volatility is associated with high risk.
2. Low volatility is associated with lack of direction.

Although we know that high volatility is intuitively risky, we might forget the risk of low volatility. Low volatility occurs when there is low participation in the market. Investors don't expect anything important to happen, and short-term traders disappear because they need the volatility to be profitable. These are the signs of a stock that's going nowhere. The public votes with its money. No one is voting.

A High-Volatility System

A system that was once very popular is a good example of how volatility can be used to trade. It has (or *had*) good reliability but high risk. It profits from a continuation of a volatile day that shows clear direction. You can find examples in Figure 17.4:

1. Buy a high-volatility day if prices close in the upper 90 percent of the range.
2. Sell a high-volatility day if prices close in the lower 10 percent of the range.
3. Close out the trade shortly after the open of the next day.
4. Do not enter the trade on Friday.

How big is a high-volatility day? You could set an absolute value of $3 for a stock trading at $20, or $10 for a stock trading at $100, but you'll do best with something that adapts to changes in volatility.

If you take the average volatility, for example, the average of the 65-day true range, you get the typical volatility over the past calendar quarter. If

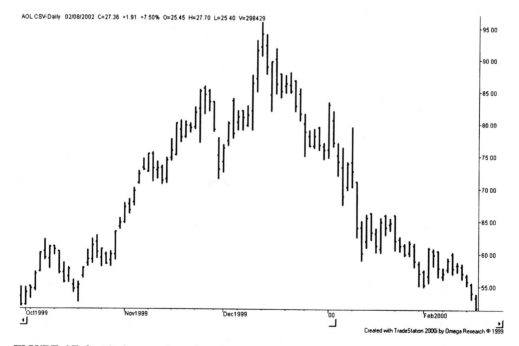

FIGURE 17.4   Find examples of trading high volatility. When prices get volatile, you can buy if the close is near the high or low and liquidate the trade on the next open.

today's true range (the range including the previous close) is more than twice the average, then we have a high-volatility day. The average true range allows the volatility to change over time. We don't need to rethink normal volatility every few weeks. Remember that trading during high volatility is always risky.

VOLATILITY AND YOUR PORTFOLIO

The volatility of each stock in your portfolio measures the risk of that stock. All things being equal, high-priced stocks have greater volatility than low-priced stocks. To give ourselves the best chance of profits when we're trading more than one stock or futures contract, we want to equalize the risk of our positions. In that way we improve diversification and minimize risk. It's all about controlling the risk.

Institutional money managers use *portfolio optimization* to balance the assets for clients. This is done with a mean-variance solution, such as quadratic programming, typical of Modern Portfolio Theory. The portfolio optimizer balances the volatility and cross-correlations of each component and calculates the weights that give you the best return-to-risk ratio.

Correlations and Diversification

Creating a formal portfolio is a process that is too complicated for our purposes. We do need to realize that trading two bank stocks does not give you the diversification of trading one bank stock and a pharmaceutical company, or Intel and pork bellies.

Don't forget that real diversification reduces risk and gives you a better chance of being successful. Trading in two different stocks or futures markets is much safer than trading in only one. Trading in three or four is even better. More than four begins to be less important.

It's Not the Markets, It's the Money

On most days you can get diversification from trading stocks in unrelated sectors or industrial groups. News will affect these groups differently. Energy may be strong on concerns about instability in the Mideast, while health care is weaker because of pending political legislation that limits reimbursement.

However, *in a crisis*, such as 9/11, *all markets move together*. It's not the fundamentals or the value of the stock, it's the people who own the shares who decide to get out. Money seeks a safer place. Stocks drop on widespread selling and bonds rise on widespread buying. No amount of correlation analysis or diversification will save you from a price shock in which all markets move the same way.

Mistaking Luck for Skill

Don't be fooled by anyone who shows that they profited from a price shock. They were simply lucky. *You can't predict a price shock.* You simply had a windfall profit or an unfortunate loss. Be grateful if it is a profit and get out of the position. The market is out of control.

Major price shocks occur infrequently, but are fatal to many traders. Even the smartest minds are not immune. There are only two ways to minimize your losses:

1. *Don't hold a position longer than necessary.* Get into a trade when you think that prices are going to move soon. Get out as soon as possible. You don't want to be holding a position in any one stock more than 30 percent of the time. Less is better.

2. *Try to make as much as possible by investing as little as possible.* The less you have exposed, the less you have at risk.

When a price shock occurs, the ones who survive are those who had the least exposure. By holding positions only 30 percent of the time, there is a 70 percent chance you will be out of the market when a price shock occurs. In addition, if you have only a small position, then a loss will not be a disaster. The combination is as good it gets.

You may trade for years before experiencing a major price shock, but history is clear. They occur every few years, they are violent, and they leave many traders in ruin. Don't be one of them.

BALANCING YOUR PORTFOLIO

You start by selecting stocks and/or futures markets that offer low correlation. You then measure the volatility of those items that you're trading. It makes most sense to calculate the volatility over the same number of days that you expect to hold the trade. Therefore, if your typical holding period is 10 days, then calculate the average true range of that stock over the most recent 10 days. You will find it easier to calculate the volatility for each stock on a spreadsheet.

Method 1: Trading an Equal Number of Shares

One of the easiest ways to trade is simply to buy or sell an equal number of shares in each stock. It is also the worst way. When you trade an equal number of shares, those stocks with higher volatility or higher price will overwhelm everything else.

Example 1
Company ABC trades at $100 and has average daily volatility of $5.00. Company XYZ trades at $10 and has an average daily volatility of $0.50. If you buy 100 shares of each stock you will risk:

1. $5.00 × 100 = $500 per day in ABC.
2. $0.50 × 100 = $50 in XYZ.

If each stock moves the same percentage, then the returns of ABC will be 10 times the returns of XYZ. Your success rides entirely on the results of ABC. Can you correct this by buying equal dollar amounts of ABC and XYZ?

Method 2: Trading Equal Dollar Amounts

The most popular advice is to trade equal dollar amounts of each stock. On the surface, this solves many of the problems. Let's assume you have $1,000 in investment capital.

Example 2
We will continue to use the high-priced ABC and the low-priced XYZ. We buy $500 worth of ABC trading at $100, or 5 shares. We buy $500 worth of XYZ trading at $10, or 50 shares. On a typical day, ABC gains $5.00 and XYZ loses $0.50. In dollars, ABC gains $5.00 × 5 shares = $25. XYZ loses $0.50 × 50 shares = $25. When stocks move in opposite directions and the profits and losses exactly offset one another, you have a *perfect hedge*.

The purpose of diversification is to profit from everything in your portfolio when you're right, and to lose as little as possible when you're wrong. When the volatility of stocks is directly proportional to their price, then buying equal dollar amounts works well. This is the ideal price-volatility relationship, and may be reasonable for long-term analysis. However, neither life nor the market is perfect.

It Sounds Good, but It Doesn't Work. Trading equal dollar amounts works in theory but not in practice. Not all stocks have the same volatility at the same price. Some stocks are simply more volatile than others. A high-tech company trading on the Nasdaq at a low price typically will be much more volatile than a public utility trading on the New York Stock Exchange at a high price. Intel at $16 is one and a half times as volatile as Cinergy at $32.

Example 3: An Actual Volatility Relationship with Equal Dollar Allocation
We have both Gold Fields (GOLD) and Merck (MRK) in our portfolio. MRK is trading at a higher price and has greater volatility than GOLD, but they are not in the classic percentage relationship. GOLD is trading at $10 with average daily volatility of $0.50, and MRK is trading at about $55 with average daily volatility of $1.00. We still have $1,000 to trade. If we trade equal dollar amounts, then we buy $500 worth of GOLD, or 50 shares, and buy $500 worth of MRK, or 9 shares.

On a typical day Gold loses 50 × $0.50 = $25 and MRK gains 9 × $1.00, or $9. You have a net loss of $16. This happens because the volatility is not in proportion to the price of the stock.

The mistake is that the long-term volatility relationship doesn't reflect what's happening in the market now. We don't care about the average 10-year volatility when we're holding the trade for the next five days. Your risk is related to the holding period of your trade, not to the long-term analysis of the market.

Method 3: Allocation by Volatility

Let's look again at two different stocks, a large, stable company BIG, trading on the NYSE, and a new, hi-tech company NEW, trading on the Nasdaq. NEW is more volatile than BIG relative to its price. BIG trades at $100 and has an average daily volatility of $3.00 (3 percent), and NEW trades at $25 and has an average daily volatility of $1.00 (4 percent). How many shares of BIG and NEW do you buy so that your total risk is equal? We'll need to do some arithmetic to get the answer.

Finding the Allocations Based on Volatility. For an investment of $10,000 we want to buy *B* shares of BIG and *N* shares of NEW. We know that:

1. The sum of the share prices times the units (*B* and *N*) is equal to the investment; therefore:

$$10,000 = (100 \times B) + (25 \times N)$$

2. The volatilities should be equalized by the number of shares; therefore:

$$B \times 3.00 = N \times 1.00$$

We can find the values of B and N by first solving Equation (2) for $N = 3 \times B$ and substitute that answer into Equation (1). Equation (1) becomes:

$$10,000 = (100 \times B) + (25 \times 3 \times B)$$
$$10,000 = (100 \times B) + (75 \times B)$$
$$10,000 = 175 \times B$$
$$B = 57$$

Substituting $B = 57$ back into Equation (2) and solving for N, we get $N = 171$.

On a typical day we may have BIG drop 3.00×57 shares = $171 loss, while NEW rises 1×171 = $171 gain. The net is zero and the portfolio is perfectly balanced. Note that $171 \times 25 + 57 \times 100 = \$9,975$, which leaves room to trade another share of NEW. However, that would put the volatility ratio out of balance, and you wouldn't have balanced risk when something goes wrong.

Calculating Volatility for a Larger Number of Stocks. If you are trading a larger number of stocks, then solving all these equations will get tedious. Instead, you can use a spreadsheet to create a volatility table. The trick to using the volatility table is to arbitrarily pick a target volatility that is big enough to assign shares to each stock. A large target volatility will mean that you would have a large investment, which isn't true, but we'll fix that at the end of the calculation.

The *target volatility* is the amount of risk you will take each day for each stock. In the following example the target volatility is $5,000 per day. If the stock has a daily trading range of $1, then we would trade 5,000 shares of that stock.

Based on a daily target volatility of $5,000, the following table shows how many shares we would trade and how much of an investment it would take to trade that position:

	Current Price	Volatility	Shares Needed at Volatility of $5,000/Day	Capital
Stock *A*	$30	$0.75	6,667	$200,010
Stock *B*	$10	$0.50	10,000	$100,000
Stock *C*	$100	$1.00	5,000	$500,000
Stock *D*	$50	$1.00	5,000	$250,000

Therefore, if we traded the four stocks, A, B, C, and D, each with a daily risk of $5,000, we would trade 6,667 shares of A, 10,000 shares of B, 5,000 shares of C, and 5,000 shares of D, for a total investment of $1,050,010.

Of course, we don't want a daily risk of $5,000 and we don't have a million dollars to invest, but we can scale this to any investment level. If we are willing to take a risk of $500 each day in each market, then we can then invest one-tenth of the amount, $105,001, and trade one-tenth of the number of shares in each stock. We can divide that by 10 again and invest only $10,500 by trading 66, 100, 50, and 50 shares of stocks A, B, C, and D. It's a backwards way of solving the problem, but it's easy.

When you create a portfolio you start with the question, "How much am I willing to risk?" From there you find out how much you need to invest, and then you decide how much profit you can expect. You always start with the risk. If you can't get enough profit for the risk you are taking, then don't trade.

ADDING FUTURES TO THE PORTFOLIO AND ADJUSTING FOR VOLATILITY

Using volatility makes it easy to include futures and stocks in the same portfolio, although the calculation may be a little more complicated. Let's say we have a $100,000 investment with the high-priced stock ABC and the low-priced stock XYZ as before. Company ABC trades at $100 and has an average daily volatility of $3.00. Company XYZ trades at $25 and has an average daily volatility of $1.00.

We want to add a futures contract in crude oil (CRUDE). CRUDE is trading at $25 and has volatility of $1.50 per day.

We know that one contract of crude oil futures is an obligation to trade 1,000 barrels of oil; therefore, a $1 move in the oil price, from $25.00 to $26.00, will net a profit or loss of $1,000. If crude has a volatility of $1,500 per day, that translates into a risk of $1,500 per day ($1.50 volatility × $1000 per $1 move = $1,500 risk) while a single share of ABC at $3.00 per day is $3.00 and a single share of XYZ is $1.00 per day of volatility.

Equalizing the Risk of Futures and Stocks

The next step is to equalize the risk of the futures contract and stocks in the same $100,000 portfolio. We want equal volatility; therefore, if ABC, XYZ, and CRUDE are the units to be traded (ABC and XYZ in shares and CRUDE in contracts), then each stock or futures contract has risk equal to:

Risk = share price (or futures price) × daily volatility × number of units

If the risk is to be equal, then:

$$\text{Risk(ABC)} = \text{Risk(XYZ)} = \text{Risk(CRUDE)}$$
$$\text{ABC}(\times 1) \times 3.00 = \text{XYZ} (\times 1) \times 1.00 = \text{CRUDE} \times 1000 \times 1.50 \qquad (1)$$

We also know that the total capital (if fully committed) should be:

$$\$100,000 = \text{ABC} \times \$100 + \text{XYZ} \times \$25 + \text{CRUDE} \times \$3000 \qquad (2)$$

Note that the margin of $3,000 is used for futures instead of the share price. We start the solution by solving one pair of equations:

$$\text{ABC}(\times 1) \times 3.00 = \text{CRUDE} \times 1000 \times 1.50$$
$$\text{CRUDE} = 3 \times \text{ABC} / 1500$$

We then solve the next pair of equations:

$$\text{ABC}(\times 1) \times 3.00 = \text{XYZ} (\times 1) \times 1.00$$
$$\text{XYZ} = 3 \times \text{ABC}$$

Substituting ABC for XYZ and CRUDE:

$$100,000 = (\text{ABC} \times 100) + (3 \times \text{ABC} \times 25) + (3 \times \text{ABC} / 1500) \times 3000$$
$$100,000 = (100 \times \text{ABC}) + (75 \times \text{ABC}) + (6 \times \text{ABC}) = 181 \times \text{ABC}$$
$$\text{ABC} = 552.5 \text{ (rounded down to 552)}$$

Then

$$\text{XYZ} = \text{ABC} \times 3.00 = 552.5 \times 3.00$$
$$\text{XYZ} = 1657$$

$$\text{CRUDE} \times 1500 = \text{XYZ} = 1657$$
$$\text{CRUDE} = 1.10$$

Verifying the results, we see that the daily dollar volatilities are nearly equal for the two stocks and as close as possible for the futures contract:

$$\text{ABC} \times \$3.00 \times 552 \text{ shares} = \$1,656$$
$$\text{XYZ} \times \$1.00 \times 1657 \text{ shares} = \$1,657$$
$$\text{CRUDE} \times \$1.50 \times 1000 \text{ conversion} = \$1,500 \text{ (due to rounding)}$$

The capital used is

$$\text{ABC} = 552 \times \$100$$
$$\text{XYZ} = 1657 \times \$25$$
$$\text{CRUDE} = 1 \times \$3,000$$
$$\text{TOTAL} = \$99,625$$

ACCOUNTING FOR THE CORRELATIONS

A proper trading portfolio allocation considers both volatility and correlation. That is, you want to trade more of those stocks that have the least similarity to one another. The combination of equalizing risk (volatility) and diversifying among noncorrelated markets results in a portfolio that maximizes returns with respect to risk. However, that is only true in a *passive* (buy-and-hold) portfolio.

When trading, we should be looking at the correlation in daily returns, not prices. For example, if we are long the S&P and prices drop 1 percent then the return is a loss of 1 percent. Because the price of the S&P dropped at the same time, the daily return and the price are correlated.

If we are short when the S&P drops 1 percent then our return is a positive 1 percent while the S&P price posts a 1 percent loss. It doesn't matter if the S&P price went up at the same time bond prices went up. What does matter is whether we were profitable on both the S&P and the bonds.

If we consistently return profits on the S&P and bonds on the same days, and then lose in both markets on the same day, we are 100 percent correlated. It doesn't matter in which direction prices are moving.

Substituting Prices

If you're just starting out and don't have a history of trading performance, then you have no choice. You can only look at the correlation in prices. We will assume that if prices move in a similar way, we would have made similar trades.

Cross-Correlations

We can find the correlation in prices by downloading the price history from a website (e.g., *MSN Money Central*) or from most quote machines using the *export* feature. From there you can load the prices into a single spreadsheet and use the function *correl* to create the cross-correlation Table 17.1. Each cell gives the correlation of the stocks in the corresponding row and column. If we look at all of the cells in the cross-correlation table, we can see:

- The highest correlation is 0.60 between SP500 and WMT.
- The next highest is SP500 and MRK at 0.15.
- There are four negative correlations.
- There are four other lower correlations.

Anything above 0.20 is considered *moderately correlated*. Any correlation factor over 0.50 is *strongly correlated*.

Big Money Moves the Same

Although Wal-Mart may have been rising or falling during the past few months, it moves in the same direction as most other large-cap stocks on most days. That's because traders can buy and sell the S&P futures contract, Spyders (SPY), S&P Mutual Funds, or other S&P index clones.

When they buy or sell the index, the arbitrageurs (or program traders) enter to make sure the spread between the index and the actual stocks comprising the index does not get out of line. You can't have the futures price going up 10 full points while the actual stock prices don't change. Therefore, whenever there is significant buying in the index, that buying also forces all the stocks in the index higher, regardless of the individual personalities of those stocks.

In the absence of news specific to a particular company, *Big Money treats all stocks in a similar manner*. It buys and sells baskets of stocks.

Negative Correlations

We should not assume that a negative correlation in stocks means that prices actually move in the opposite direction. It is safest to consider it as *uncorrelated*; that is, some days it moves with the other markets and other days it doesn't. On extreme days, when you need the diversification the most, it is safest to expect all the markets to be correlated and move together.

In Table 17.1, the negative correlations in Raytheon and Gold Fields were the result of September 11. Traders immediately recognized that defense stocks would be the first to benefit, and cash gold prices rose because in-

TABLE 17.1 **Cross-correlation table.** Four stocks, Wal-Mart, Merck, Gold Fields, and Raytheon, are compared with the S&P 500. Except for Wal-Mart and the S&P, the correlations are very low, showing good diversification.

	SP500	WMT	MRK	GOLD	RTN
SP500	1.00				
WMT	0.60	1.00			
MRK	0.15	0.10	1.00		
GOLD	−0.17	−0.15	0.05	1.00	
RTN	−0.13	−0.05	0.12	0.09	1.00

vestors traditionally move money to hard currency, a safe haven in a crisis. Gold stocks benefit from the rise in gold prices. On normal days they may move the same way as the bulk of stocks. Under a different economic scenario, such as an unexpected increase in interest rates, those stocks may react exactly the same as others in the S&P. You cannot count on them offering diversification all the time, but they can help out once in a while.

Adjusting Your Portfolio for Correlations

If the correlation between two markets is very strong, then treat it as one market when deciding how much to trade. If the average correlation in your portfolio is above 0.20, then your only choice is to trade less of your capital, thereby reducing your risk exposure in the event of a price shock. When trading on your own, simply choose those stocks that are fundamentally different. It's safer that way.

TRADING GAME TIPS

You don't learn anything by making money. In case you've had a difficult time with this trading game, take heart from the fact that losing money teaches you more than making money. If you made money by luck, then you didn't review your trades to find out what went wrong. Losing makes you evaluate your work carefully. In the end, you'll have a better understanding.

Do the analysis yourself. Long before we found out that market analysts had a conflict of interest, promoting those stocks in which their company had a financial interest, we should have known that you must analyze the market yourself. You can't make a trade unless you know why and understand the risk and reward. Don't believe anyone. Even your friend, who bought something last week, will try to sell you on it. Don't do it. Study the market and choose your own trades.

Be proactive. Some of you will miss a trade because you're waiting to see how it does tomorrow. You're too late. You need to act today. Place the order and put a stop at a safe place. You want to be in early to get the *free exposure* when prices jump. *Anticipate, don't react.*

Reversing your position. It often turns out that the trade you expect to be the most profitable is the largest failure. When a clear signal fails, it becomes likely that a large reversal will follow. Don't be slow about reversing your own position. Don't take the bad signal as a personal insult—take it as an opportunity for a larger profit.

Recheck the correlation between stocks in your portfolio. If the stocks are moving together too often and you have all profits and all losses on the same days, then change some of the stocks that you're trading. Stay on top of your portfolio.

Questions

1. What is the best single word that describes a price shock?

2. Give three ways that you can protect yourself from a price shock.

3. What happens to the correlation between stocks, and even futures markets, when there is a major price shock? Why?

4. We know that any one day can be more or less volatile then the next. Under normal conditions, do prices get more volatile when they go up or down? Specifically, what about IBM, the Euro, crude oil prices, and Treasury notes?

5. To find the "true range" of the day, you need to find the largest of what three values (using high, low, and closing prices)?

6. As a short-term trader using profit targets and stop-loss orders, which would be closer, the profit-target or the stop-loss order?

7. What does low volatility imply with regard to price movement?

8. If you are trading three stocks, A, B, and C, with corresponding daily volatilities of $1, $2, and $3, what percentage of your total capital would you place in each one to minimize risk?

9. You are trading two stocks, A and B, and gold futures. Stock A has a daily price range of $3, stock B has a daily range of $4, and gold has a daily range of $3/ounce. The gold contract is 100 troy ounces. How many shares of A and B do you need to trade so that each stock has the same risk as gold?

CHAPTER 18

Dow Theory

*The more things change
the more they remain the same.*

We've nearly come to the end of this course in technical trading. We started by studying charts and trends and looked at retracements, momentum, and overbought/oversold indicators. Finally, we studied how volatility can be used for trading, risk control, and balancing your portfolio. However, Dow Theory, the most well-known of all technical methods, was conspicuously missing.

Dow Theory is a grand plan. It tries to identify the big picture and offer broad rules for deciding on the direction of prices. We have been very specific in these chapters, carefully measuring trendlines and breakouts, calculating profit levels, and looking for technical divergence. It seems to be the right time to decide if Dow Theory makes any sense after 100 years.

DOW THEORY

Charles Dow determined that the stock market moved as the ocean, in three waves, called *primary, secondary,* and *daily fluctuations.* The major advances and declines, lasting for extended periods, were compared to the tides. These tides were subject to secondary reactions called *waves,* and the waves were comprised of *ripples.* In 1897 Dow published two sets of averages in the *Wall Street Journal,* the *Industrials* and the *Railroads,* in order to advance his ideas. These are now the *Dow Jones Industrial Average* and the *Transportation Index.* Figure 18.1 shows the past 20 years of history for the three most important averages. Dow Theory now uses these three averages, the Industrials, the Transportation Index, and the Utilities.

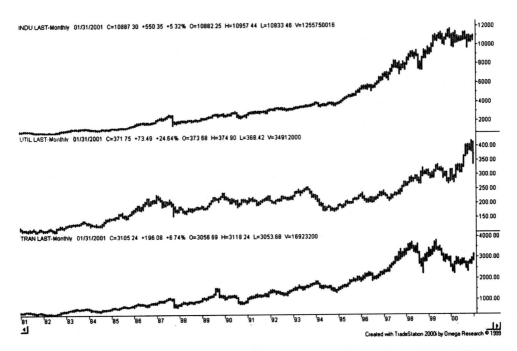

FIGURE 18.1   Dow Industrials, Utilities, and Transportation Indices, 1981–1999.
Dow originally created the industrial and railway averages to hide the large, erratic price moves caused by price manipulation and lack of liquidity. Dow Theory has been adapted to use the current versions of the major indices, the Industrials (top panel), the Utilities (center panel), and the Transportation Index (bottom panel).

THE BASIC TENETS OF THE DOW THEORY

There are six fundamental principles of the Dow Theory. We'll look at each in turn.

1. The Averages Discount Everything (except "Acts of God")

At the turn of the century (that is, 1900) there was considerably less liquidity and regulation in the market; therefore, manipulation was common. By creating averages, Dow could reduce the frequency of "unusual" moves in a single market, those moves that seemed unreasonably large or out of character with the rest of the market.

If you averaged 30 stocks, then one odd move would only be ⅓₀ of the total, reducing its importance to somewhere near insignificance. The average also represented far greater combined liquidity than a single stock. The only large moves that would appear on a chart of the average price were price shocks, or "Acts of God."

2. There Are Three Classifications of Trends: Primary Trends, Secondary Swings, and Minor Day-to-Day Fluctuations

The primary trend, also called the *wave*, is the trend on a grand scale. It is a bull or bear market. It is a major move over an extended period of time, perhaps a few years. A clear bull market can be seen in the S&P weekly chart (Figure 18.2) from 1984 to mid-1987 and again on the monthly chart (see Figure 18.3) from the end of 1987 to early 1998 or into 2000, depending upon whether you consider the decline in 1998 too large to be included in the extended bull market.

Bull and Bear Market Formation (for Monthly or Weekly Prices).   Bull and bear markets are determined using a traditional breakout signal based on large swings in the index value. The *bull market signal* is at the point where

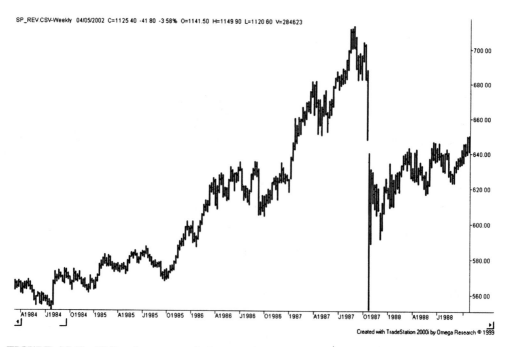

FIGURE 18.2   S&P primary trend. On a weekly chart, a major bull market (the *primary trend*) can be seen from 1984 through September 1987.

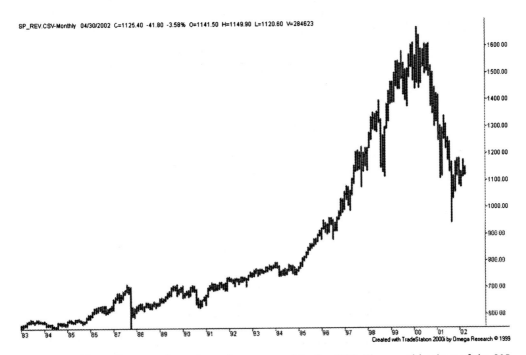

SP_REV.CSV-Monthly 04/30/2002 C=1125.40 -41.80 -3.58% O=1141.50 H=1149.90 L=1120.60 V=284623

FIGURE 18.3   A longer view of a primary trend in the S&P. The monthly chart of the S&P shows the major bull market (the *primary trend*) beginning at the end of 1987 and continuing into 2000. Some analysts would consider the 1998 price drop as the end.

prices confirm the uptrend by moving above the high of the previous rally. The *bear market signal* occurs on a break below the low of the previous decline (see Figure 18.4).

It is commonly accepted that a bull or bear market begins when prices reverse 20 percent from their lows or highs. In order to get an upward break-out signal needed for a new bull market, we would want to look at support and resistance levels separated by about 10 percent based on the value of the index. This 10 percent would be considered the *minimum swing value* discussed in Chapter 7, Event-Driven Trends.

Bull and Bear Market Phases.   In Dow Theory the primary trends are thought to develop in three distinct phases, each characterized by investor action. It is particularly easy to see these phases in the Nasdaq bull market of the late 1990s and the subsequent bear market (see Figure 18.5). Because most of us have experienced this recent market cycle, we should find the final phase of the bull market, in 2000, as a sad and chilling event.

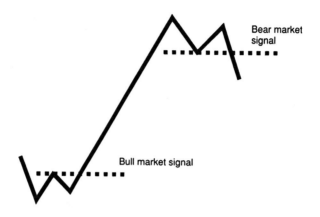

FIGURE 18.4 Bull and bear market signals. Bull
and bear markets are recognized using traditional
breakout signals, but on a larger scale. A bull market
begins when prices rise above the previous resistance
level after trading at low levels. The bear market begins
when prices break below a previous support level. With
primary trends the size of the swing must be large,
perhaps 10 percent.

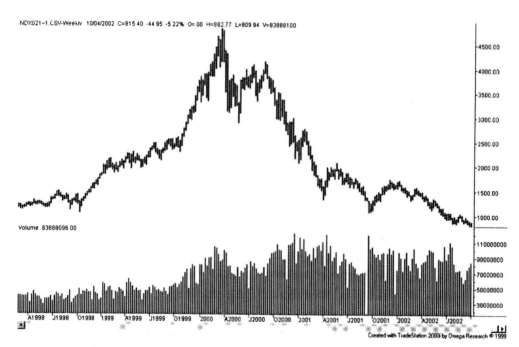

FIGURE 18.5 Nasdaq from April 1998 through June 2002. A clear example of a bull and
bear market with a classic pattern of volume.

The Bull Market

- *Phase 1* is the *accumulation* phase, where cautious investors select only the safest stocks to buy. They limit purchases to deeply discounted stocks at depressed prices and consider only primary services and industries, most often buying utilities and high-yielding stocks.
- *Phase 2* is characterized by increasing volume, rising prices, and an improving economic picture. A broader range of investor enters the market convinced that they have seen the bottom of the market. Secondary stocks become popular.
- *Phase 3* has a final explosive move, the result of excessive speculation and elation of the general public. Everyone is convinced that profits will continue, and buying becomes indiscriminate. Investors borrow to buy stocks. Value is unimportant because prices keep rising. Companies don't need to have positive earnings to be scooped up.

The Bear Market

- *Phase 1* is the *distribution* phase. Professionals begin selling while the public is in the final stages of buying. Stocks go from stronger to weaker hands. The change of ownership is forced by less experienced investors coming to the party late and paying what turn out to be unreasonably high prices.
- *Phase 2* is the *panic* phase. Prices decline more than at any other time during the bull market and fail to rally. The news talks about the end of the bull market. The public sees an urgency to liquidate. Investors who borrowed money to invest late in the bull market, trading on margin or leverage, now speed up the process. Some are forced to liquidate because their portfolio value has dropped below the critical point.
- *Phase 3* is the final sustained erosion of prices, affecting even the strongest stocks. All news is viewed as negative. Pessimism prevails. It's the summer of 2002.

Secondary Trends (Secondary Reactions Using Weekly or Daily Prices). Secondary reactions are also called *corrections* or *recoveries*. Corrections in bull markets are attributed to the prudent investor taking profits. This profit phase can have an erratic start but is considered over when prices rise above the previous secondary rally. The bull market is back in force when a new high occurs (see Figure 18.6).

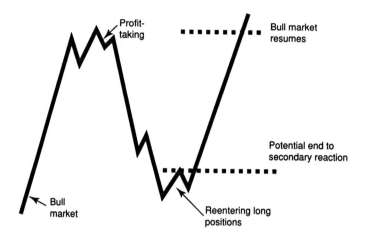

FIGURE 18.6   Secondary trends and reactions. A reaction is a smaller swing in prices that ends when a new high reinstates the bull market. Reactions are identified using smaller swings than those used for bull and bear markets. If the bull market is still intact, a trader can buy the breakout confirmation at the end of the reaction.

Lines may be substituted for secondary movements. In Dow Theory, a line is a sideways movement lasting from 2 to 3 weeks to months, trading in about a 5 percent range.

Characteristics of a Secondary Reaction

- There are a number of clear downswings.
- The movement is more rapid in the reversal (down during a bull market) than in the primary move.
- They last from three weeks to three months.
- If the volume on the drop is equal to or greater than the volume just prior to the decline, then a bear market is likely. If volume declines during the drop, then a reaction is confirmed.
- The "atmosphere" surrounding the decline is important. If there is a lot of speculation, then a bear market may develop.

The Perception of Who Is Winning and Losing.   It is interesting to note that declines in stock prices are always attributed to investors *taking profits*. We would all be quite wealthy if that were really the case. There are a large number of traders who will buy and sell for small profits and small losses.

Phase 3 of the bull market clearly states that there is a large surge of public buying near the top of the market. Are these the investors who are taking profits after the bear market is in full glory? It's not likely.

Minor Trends (Using Daily Prices). In Dow Theory, minor trends are the only trends that can be "manipulated." They are usually under six days in duration. Because they are considered market noise they are seen as frequent up and down movements.

3. The Principle of Confirmation

For a bull or bear market to exist, two of the three major averages (DJIA, DJT, DJU) must confirm the direction. Although a lot has changed since Dow devised this rule, the purpose is to assure that the bull or bear market is a widespread economic phenomenon and not an industry-related event.

4. Volume Goes with the Trend

Volume must increase as the trend develops, whether a bull or bear market. Volume will be greatest at the peak of a bull market and during the panic phase of a bear market.

5. Only Closing Prices Are Used

Dow had a strong belief that the closing price was the most important. It was the "evening up" at the end of the day. Although liquidity was a problem during Dow's time, any stock price can be pushed around during a quiet period. There is always high volume on the close of trading, and investors with short and long time frames come together to decide the fair price.

6. The Trend Persists

A trend should be assumed to continue in effect until its reversal has been definitely signaled. This rule forms the basis of all trend-following principles. It applies the trend to a long-term price move, and it suggest that trends persist. It is difficult to anticipate the end of a trend because a trend can continue longer than expected.

INTERPRETING TODAY'S MARKETS USING DOW THEORY

Is the S&P in one of the bull or bear market phases defined by the Dow Theory? In Figure 18.7 we can see two distinct bull market patterns. The first, beginning 1983 ended abruptly in October 1987 when prices plunged. Before that, the steadily rising prices accompanied by a clear increase in volume marked the classic Phase 2 of a bull market. Not every pattern has a smooth transition.

Transition from Bull to Bear in the S&P

After 1987, S&P prices continued higher, but that advance was not confirmed by volume. Only in 1994 did the general public seem to recognize that the economy was strong. Prices began to move up faster.

In mid-1997 we see a drop in volume as prices become more volatile, even though they continue higher at the same pace. A sharp drop in mid-1998 can be called a secondary reaction, although it was big enough to scare away some investors.

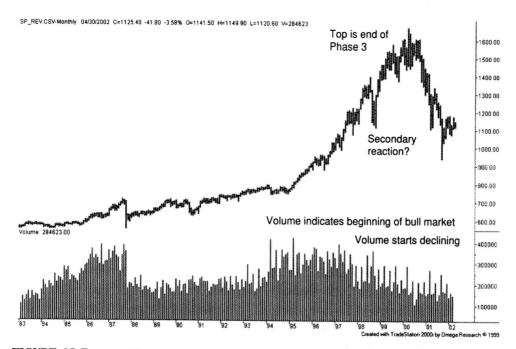

FIGURE 18.7   Dow Theory applied to the S&P. Most of Dow's principles apply, but each major move has its own special pattern.

After the secondary reaction in 1998, volume continues to drop while prices rise. We might justifiably (and using hindsight) call that a divergence. Rising volume confirms a price move; declining volume does not. However, there was still a year and a half of significant profits to be made before the top was reached.

In 2000 we see a price peak on continued lower volume. Prices declined faster than they rose. At the price of 1320, after a 20 percent retracement from the highs, we are told that the bear market has "officially" started. Volume is still dropping, but it doesn't look like a buying opportunity.

EVOLUTION IN PRICE PATTERNS

A change has occurred in the market because of the ability to trade the S&P 500 index directly rather than individual stocks. S&P futures have become an active vehicle for both speculation and hedging. If you think that stock prices are about to fall because of a pending interest rate announcement by the Fed, you can protect your portfolio by selling an equivalent amount of S&P futures. Afterward, when you have decided that prices have stabilized, you can lift your hedge and profit from rising prices. It's an easy and inexpensive way to achieve portfolio insurance.

When institutions and traders buy or sell large quantities of the S&P futures, that price can drop while the share prices of the stocks that comprise the S&P Index may not have fallen yet. Enter the big business of *program trading*. If you have enough capital and the difference between the S&P futures price and the S&P cash index is sufficiently large, you can buy the S&P futures and sell all of the stocks in the S&P 500 cash index. It is a classic arbitrage that brings prices back together.

How does program trading, or just the trading of S&P futures, affect the price patterns of individual stocks? The answer is that all the stocks in the S&P Index move together at the same time. It doesn't matter whether IBM is fundamentally stronger the GE, or that Xerox is at a resistance level and Ford is at support, or even if Enron is under investigation. When you buy the S&P you buy all of the stocks at the same time.

Today's technical trader must keep one eye on the individual stock and the other eye on the index. Exxon may have moved above its recent resistance level but stops because the S&P Index is at its own resistance level, and there are more traders watching the S&P than Exxon. In today's market, you can anticipate when a stock will find support and resistance by looking at the S&P chart rather than at the stock chart.

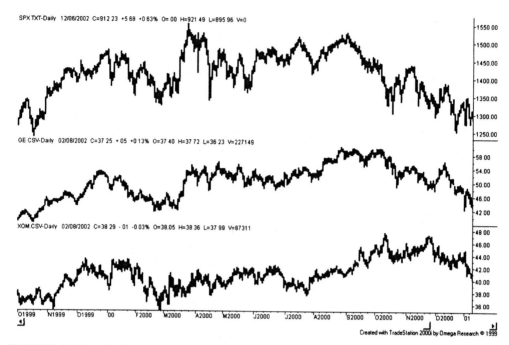

FIGURE 18.8   Similar patterns in the S&P, GE, and Exxon. There is a clear similarity in the up and down patterns of the three markets. Heavy trading in the S&P index forces arbitrage that keeps all stock prices within the index closely aligned to the index price. Unless there is a strong fundamental reason for one stock moving either up or down, they will all show a pattern very similar to the S&P index.

Figure 18.8 shows the S&P 500 index, GE, and Exxon over the same period from October 1999 through December 2000. The overall patterns of the three markets are remarkably similar, with most tops and bottoms occurring at the same time. How likely is it that the fundamentals of each company would result in a similar price pattern? Not likely.

During times where there is no news, the stocks all move together. When there is positive news for a specific company, it will gain over other stocks, but it will still meet resistance where the S&P as a whole meets resistance. This change in the way stocks are traded reduces the ability to get diversification by trading across sectors and increases your risk. Short-term traders will not be as affected as those holding positions longer.

Will Your Trading Method Withstand the Test of Time?

Dow Theory has withstood the test of time. Will your method of trading still work after five years? It will if you focus on the bigger picture. As a long-term trader you'll want to stay with the trend that reflects economic policy. As a short-term trader, you need to look past trends and concentrate on volatility and overbought/oversold situations. Combine your style of trading with the time frame that complements those methods.

Above all, practice risk control. Start with a small commitment and build as you improve. Figure out the risk of a trade before you get excited about the potential reward. You need to control your risk in order to keep trading. Treat it as a business, not a game.

Questions

1. In Dow Theory, what are the three waves of stock market movement called?

2. Why did Dow use averages?

3. Why did Dow want confirmation of more than one index?

4. What is the price pattern that gives you a bull market signal?

5. In Dow Theory, what are the terms describing the first phases of a bull or bear market?

6. In Dow Theory, how do you tell the difference between a secondary reaction in a bull market and a downturn signaling a bear market?

7. In Dow Theory, what happens to volume in a bull market? In a bear market?

Review Questions

The following questions are a review of the entire course and draw on knowledge from across chapters. The answers appear in the final chapter. You can score yourself. There are 210 points possible for 94 questions. All questions have points shown. Keep your answers brief.

If you score greater than 145, points then you are a solid "A" student.

1. What is technical analysis? (2 pts)

2. State three important positives and two negatives for using technical analysis? (5 pts)

3. When viewing a daily and weekly chart of the same stock, what would be the most obvious difference in the price patterns? (2 pts)

4. What are the obvious differences between the way prices behave when prices are low compared to when prices are high? (2 pts)

5. What is a price shock? (2 pts)

6. How can you plan to make money from a price shock? (2 pts)

7. What is market noise? (2 pts)

8. What are three ways of measuring price volatility? (3 pts)

9. When trading individual stocks, why would you want to know the direction of the S&P? (2 pts)

10. In Figure R1.1, show at least seven different one-day price patterns (e.g., gaps), but no more than two of any one type. Mark them directly on the chart. (7 pts)

FIGURE R1.1

11. In Figure R1.2, show one each of three continuation patterns (e.g., triangles). (3 pts)

FIGURE R1.2

12. On Figure R1.3, identify 20-, 40-, and 60-day moving average lines. (3 pts)

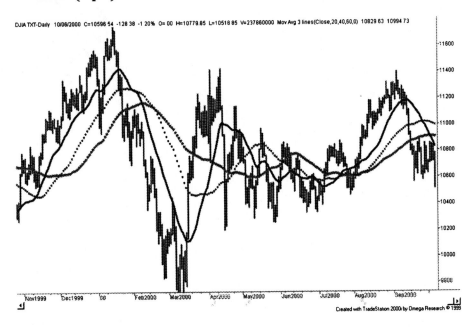

DJIA TXT-Daily 10/06/2000 C=10596 54 -128 38 -1 20% O= 00 H=10779.85 L=10518 85 V=237860000 Mov Avg 3 lines(Close,20,40,60,0) 10829 63 10994 73

FIGURE R1.3

13. If you wanted to see the price trend more clearly, would you use a daily, weekly, or monthly chart? Why? (2 pts)

14. What causes the lag in trend techniques such as a moving average? (3 pts)

15. What does *conservation of capital* mean when applied to a moving average system: (*a*) investing a smaller amount, (*b*) a few large losses and many small profits, or (*c*) many small losses and a few large profits? (1 pt)

16. When applying a trend method to a stock or futures contract that you haven't seen before, which is likely to make more money: moving average, exponential smoothing, linear regression, or breakout system? (2 pts)

17. On Figure R1.4, draw the major downtrend line and uptrend line. Show where you would have gotten a perfect buy and a perfect sell signal. On the right part of the chart, show the point of confirmation where the topping formation is over. (5 pts)

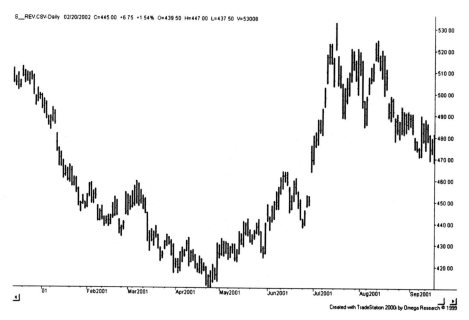

FIGURE R1.4

18. On Figure R1.5, prices are about to start down. Draw and identify where the two major support levels would be located, and where the next two minor support levels would be located. They may be a combination of trendlines, retracements, and the 200-day moving average. (5 pts)

FIGURE R1.5

19. Which is not true: Trending techniques are not useful for fast trading because (*a*) market noise interferes with identifying the trend, (*b*) transaction costs are too high, or (*c*) you cannot apply profit-taking? (1 pt)

20. Why is it more likely that a long-term MA will work and a short-term MA will not (for example, using T-notes)? (3 pts)

21. When does profit-taking work best: (*a*) anytime you have more than a 10 percent profit, (*b*) in a noisy market, or (*c*) as a long-term trend follower? (1 pt)

22. As a chartist, how do you draw a upward-sloping channel? (2 pts)

23. How would you use an upward sloping channel for trading? (2 pts)

24. What are Bollinger bands? (2 pts)

25. If you were a mean reversion (countertrend) trader, how would you use Bollinger bands? (2 pts)

26. From the perspective of trading, what is the primary difference between a bar chart and a point-and-figure chart? (2 pts)

27. When does a standard buy signal occur using point-and-figure charts? (2 pts)

28. What is the purpose of a stop-loss? (2 pts)

29. If you are basing your trading on support and resistance breakouts and you get a buy signal, where would you place your initial stop-loss order? (2 pts)

30. As your trade becomes profitable, how would you change your stop-loss? (2 pts)

31. Which triangle formation is more likely to appear in the middle of a prolonged downtrend: (*a*) ascending, (*b*) descending, or (*c*) symmetric? (1 pt)

32. When the price breaks the head-and-shoulders neckline moving down, where is the traditional target price level? (2 pts)

33. What are the three most popular retracement levels (in percent)? (2 pts)

34. Write the first seven numbers in the Fibonacci series. (2 pts)

35. If a volume spike occurred on a highly volatile day with prices dropping, would you expect the next day's price to (*a*) continue lower, (*b*) move sharply higher, or (*c*) neither 1 or 2? (1 pt)

36. If prices have been moving higher, name five technical points that you would look for to indicate a likely change of direction? (2.5 pts)

37. Fill in the table below with the trend and strength of the trend using "up" and "down" for the trend direction, "weak" and "strong" for the strength, and "none" for no trend. For example, if the trend is down but weak, enter "weak down." (4.5 pts)

	Price		
Volume	**Increasing**	**Unchanged**	**Decreasing**
Increasing			
Unchanged			
Decreasing			

38. What is momentum? (2 pts)

39. Is a 10-day momentum (*a*) smoother, (*b*) noisier, or (*c*) the same as price movement? (1 pt)

40. If prices are increasing or decreasing $1 each day, what is the maximum value a 10-day momentum may have? (2 pts)

41. A one-day momentum has which special quality: (*a*) smoothing prices, (*b*) limiting price movement, or (*c*) removing the trend? (1 pt)

42. The MACD is most reliable when used for which of the following: (*a*) trending signals, (*b*) overbought and oversold signals, or (*c*) bullish and bearish divergence? (1 pt)

43. Describe the pattern needed in prices and an oscillator in order to get a bullish divergence. (2 pts)

44. On an MACD oscillator chart, which is faster: (*a*) the MACD line, (*b*) the signal line, or (*c*) the trend line? (1 pt)

45. Using the MACD, the sell signal comes following a bearish divergence, when which two lines cross in what direction? (2 pts)

46. When momentum reaches high values which of the following happens: (*a*) it immediately reverses, (*b*) it remains at high levels for

long periods of time, or (*c*) it remains at high levels for an uncertain period of time? (1 pt)

47. What is the most recent value of the five-day momentum value given the following prices: $52.50, $52.75, $53.00, $52.80, $52.75, $52.90, $53.10, $53.40, $54.00, $53.50? (2 pts)

48. Which of the following is false: Market sentiment is (*a*) a driving force behind market moves, (*b*) difficult to measure, or (*c*) used as a leading indicator for a change of price direction? (1 pt)

49. In your own words, what does the 10-day raw stochastic measure? (2 pts)

50. In order to create the *slow-K* and *slow-D* from the raw stochastic value *K*, what do you do? (3 pts)

51. For the stochastic chart to be useful, the stochastic value needs to be in the extreme zones (e.g., above 80 and below 20) when: (*a*) all of the time, (*b*) about 50 percent of the time, (*c*) about 20 percent of the time, or (*d*) rarely. (1 pt)

52. Which of the following is false: The stochastic is most useful as (*a*) a trending indicator, (*b*) an entry timing indicator, or (*c*) an over-bought and oversold indicator? (1 pt)

53. The Relative Strength Index (RSI) is created from which ratio: (*a*) high and low prices, (*b*) first differences of high and low prices, or (*c*) upward and downward price changes? (1 pt)

54. True or false? It is best to use a very fast stochastic (e.g., under 10 days) in order to get more divergence signals? (1 pt)

55. True or false? It is possible to create a very smooth trendline with a small lag by double smoothing if you first start with price differences instead of prices. (1 pt)

56. To find the true range of the day, you need to find the largest of what three values (using high, low, and closing prices)? (2 pts)

57. When trading (not holding a stock for an indefinite period), which entry technique is the least desirable: (*a*) scaling down, (*b*) averaging in, or (*c*) buying your entire position at one time? (1 pt)

58. In Figure R1.6, using technical analysis, explain why you think prices will go higher or lower. Draw any trendlines or formations necessary and explain the basis for your conclusions below the chart. Reference the volume and MACD charts as needed. (10 pts)

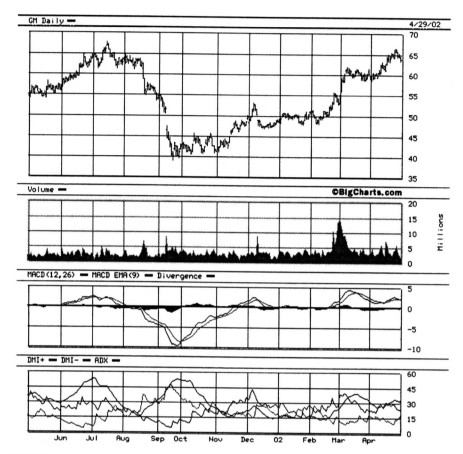

FIGURE R1.6

59. Which statement is false? The best protection from a price shock is (*a*) having a trading system that is correctly positioned for a price shock, (*b*) being out of the market as much as possible, or (*c*) using the lowest leverage when trading. (1 pt)

60. You have $10,000 in capital and want to trade four stocks that are risk-adjusted by volatility. If you wanted to use all of your capital, how many shares would you trade of each stock if the current prices and volatilities were in the table? (10 pts)

	Price	Volatility	No. of Shares
Stock *A*	$10.00	$0.50	
Stock *B*	$50.00	$1.00	
Stock *C*	$50.00	$1.50	
Stock *D*	$100.00	$5.00	

61. You have $1 million to trade the S&P and T-notes. Because of the risk you want to invest only 50 percent of your capital in the market and you want to equalize the risk between the two markets. Based on the following information, how many contracts do you trade of each market? T-note prices and volatility are in 32nds. (8 pts)

	Price	Volatility	Conversion Factor	Margin	No. of Contracts
S&P	1100.00	20.00	250	20,000	
T-notes	102/00	/24	1000	3,000	

62. When targeting a level to take profits, is it best to (*a*) exit the entire trade at one point, (*b*) scale out at multiple levels looking for an average price, or (*c*) wait for a trend reversal? (1 pt)

63. Which of the following are true? In Dow Theory, the index was used because (*a*) markets were manipulated, (*b*) volume was low, or (*c*) trends were undependable for individual stocks. (1 pt)

64. In Dow Theory, to what do the (*a*) tides, (*b*) waves, and (*c*) ripples refer? (1 pt)

65. In the principle of confirmation, why did Dow think it necessary to have two of the indices confirm the bull or bear market? (2 pts)

66. In Dow Theory, the formation in which prices are at their lowest level and remain there preceding the period of increased volume is called what? (2 pts)

67. When we using a trend, are we (*a*) predicting where prices will go, (*b*) assuming that the trend persists, or (*c*) expecting prices to change direction? (1 pt)

68. Is profit-taking best used (*a*) with any technical method, (*b*) with longer-term positions that generate large profits, or (*c*) with short-term trading? (1 pt)

69. The phenomenon of a price trend is not caused by which of the following: (*a*) periodic news releases, (*b*) anticipation of news, or (*c*) public opinion (market sentiment)? (1 pt)

70. Figure R1.7 shows DELL (top) and CPQ (second). You want to create a market neutral strategy, one that is long one stock and short the other with equal risk based on volatility. You have $1,000 to invest. In

which one would you be long and which one would you be short? Support your answer with technical analysis based only on these charts and indicators (DELL MACD is in the third panel and CPQ MACD is in the fourth panel). (10 pts)

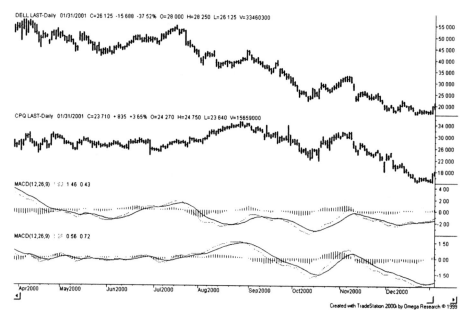

FIGURE R1.7

71. When a company announces earnings greater than the previous quarter and greater than a year ago, prices will do which of the following: (*a*) always rise, (*b*) rise if the overall market is stronger that day, or (*c*) decline if earnings are lower than anticipated? (1 pt)

72. Why would there be a similarity between the price movements of Exxon-Mobil and those of Wal-Mart? (2 pts)

73. State one situation in which diversification conspicuously fails. (2 pts)

74. Trend-following methods typically have which of the following: (*a*) an equal number of profitable and losing trades, (*b*) a larger number of losing trades, or (*c*) a larger number of profitable trades? (1 pt)

75. An MACD oversold signal is best at which of the following times: (*a*) when the MACD value reaches historic lows, (*b*) anytime the MACD goes negative and then the signal line crosses the MACD line, or (*c*) at the same time prices make a new low? (1 pt)

76. True or false? You would use a price order (limit order) when you want to buy at a lower price. (1 pt)

77. True or false? A stop order becomes a market order when the price is touched. (1 pt)

78. Yesterday's closing price was $51.00 and you have placed an order to "buy 51.50 stop" to protect your short position. The stock opens the next day at $52.00, trades down to $51.00, and then closes higher at $52.50. What price did you receive on your stop order? (2 pts)

79. If you are using a long-term trend-following system, then you expect your average profits to be which of the following: (*a*) about the same as your average losses, (*b*) greater than your average losses, or (*c*) less than your average losses? (1 pt)

80. When trading a stock relating to a physical market (Gold Fields and physical gold, Oil Services and crude oil), give one positive and one negative reason for analyzing both the stock and the physical commodity at the same time. (3 pts)

81. Why is trading futures riskier than trading stocks? (2 pts)

82. Why would you choose to reverse a trade (e.g., change from long to short) rather than simply close out your position and wait for another opportunity to go long? (2 pts)

83. Anticipation is most important when you are doing which of the following: (*a*) using a trend-following method, (*b*) entering a trade, (*c*) trading quickly, (*d*) expecting a price shock? (1 pt)

84. At what time of day are trading signals less dependable: (*a*) at the open, (*b*) midday, (*c*) at the close, or (*d*) just before the close? (1 pt)

85. Which is not true? Your trading risk is directly related to (*a*) the amount of capital in use, (*b*) the volatility of the stocks, (*c*) the amount of leverage used, or (*d*) the amount of diversification in your portfolio. (1 pt)

86. If you discover that you are holding a losing stock position because of an order error, it is best to do which of the following: (*a*) close-out the trade as soon as possible, (*b*) manage the position using technical analysis, or (*c*) sue the brokerage firm because it was their error? (1 pt)

87. You are long Treasury notes when the Fed unexpectedly announces that it will cut rates by ½ point. Your best move is which of the following: (*a*) stay with the trade because you are on the winning side, (*b*) take your windfall profit by closing out your trade, or (*c*) reverse your position to take advantage of an overreaction to the news? (1 pt)

88. What does the phrase "you don't learn anything by making money" mean? (3 pts)

89. What is wrong with using the conclusions of another analyst when deciding on your trade? (3 pts)

90. The price of GOLD closed at $13.50 yesterday. You have no position and you place an order to "Buy 1000 GOLD 14.25 stop." The stock opens today at $14.15 and has a high of $14.90 and a low of $13.80. What is your fill? (2 pts)

91. The price of MRK closed at $55.00 yesterday. You are long and want to take profits higher. You place an order to "Sell 2000 MRK 56.60." The stock opens at $56.90 and immediately trades down to $55.75. It ends the day with a high of $56.90 and a low of $55.50. What is your fill? (2 pts)

92. June S&P closed at 1090.00 yesterday. You are short and want to protect your profits with a stop-loss. You enter an order to "Buy 5 SPM 1105.00 stop." The market opens at 1106.50, trades down to 1102.00 and closes higher at 1110.00. What is your fill? (2 pts)

93. June CL closed at $24.50. You are long and place an order to "Sell 10 CLM 23.90 stop MOC." The market opens at $24.60, has a high of $24.70, a low of $23.80, and closes at $23.95. What is your fill? (2 pts)

94. When a support line is broken, what does it become? (2 pts)

Chapter 2   Charting the Trend

1. What is the reason for drawing a trendline?

   To get an objective assessment of the direction of the trend.

2. What is the intended relationship between interest rate changes and stock market changes?

   As interest rates decline, the stock market rises.

3. If you wanted to see the trend on a chart more clearly, would you use a daily, weekly, or monthly chart? Why?

   A monthly chart because the trend is clearer when viewed over a longer time period, removing the noise.

4. How could you have a chart where the trend was both up and down?

   It can be up in the long term and down in the short term. It depends on your time frame.

5. In the S&P monthly chart shown in Figure 2.12, draw the major uptrend lines as they develop. Is there a point (or points) at which you would have gone short?

   The first uptrend line, *A*, connects the low on the day after the 1987 crash (point 1) with the lows at the end of 1991 (point 2). The low of the October 1987 crash (point 1) is considered a false penetration. The second uptrend, *B*, connects points 2 and 3. The third uptrend, *C*, is more extreme and drawn after lows at 3 and 4 are in place. The fourth and most extreme trendline, D, is drawn after point 6 is established. Penetration of trendline C after point 6 may be a sell signal; however, you may choose to wait for a penetration of trendline C, which does not happen. Trendline D is then confirmed by points 7 and 8, and a sell signal comes near the top when prices break below 1500.

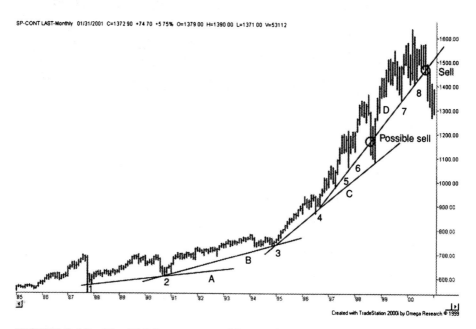

FIGURE 2.12 **The S&P futures monthly continuation series** shows the sustained bull market of the 1990s and the peak in 2000.

6. Using the chart of Cisco during 1998 shown in Figure 12.3, draw the trendlines and outline the (ideal) trades you would have made based on the price penetration of the trend.

> The first trendline, A, can be drawn after the lows at 1 and 2 are established. At point 3 we can buy as prices come near trendline A. We redraw the trendline, B, using point 4 after the lows at points 5 and 6 are set. We then get a potential sell signal after the high at point 7 based on a penetration of trendline B. Prices rally to point 8 and we can draw the first downward trendline, C. Another sell signal comes when prices fall through trendline A after the high at C. At that point the previous penetrations of trendline A appear to be a false penetration based on extreme volatility.

FIGURE 2.13 **Daily Cisco prices from February through October 1998.** A strong uptrend followed by a difficult, volatile period makes finding the trendlines more challenging but makes trading more exciting.

Chapter 3 Breakout Trends

1. What is a breakout?

   A price penetration through a horizontal support or resistance line.

2. Why does a breakout occur after a sideways price pattern?

   Events change or there is an anticipation of events changing.

3. If you buy when an upward breakout occurs, what is your initial risk in the trade?

   The distance between the entry point and the support line where you would get a sell signal.

4. What is a false breakout?

   A false breakout occurs when prices penetrate the support or resistance line during the day but close inside the original support and resistance lines. A false breakout may also be one day that closes outside the sideways range but returns to that range on the next day

5. Explain when you would get a sell signal from a 20-day rolling breakout.

When prices close below the 20-day low. If you are using an intraday breakout, it's when the low of today is below the low of the previous 20 days.

6. Explain why a technical trader might choose to use an N-day breakout instead of drawing classic trendlines on a chart.

An N-day breakout is well-defined and can be tested historically. It can be calculated quickly using a spreadsheet; therefore, it will allow you to trade more stocks or other markets for added diversification.

7. How would you combine a penetration of a classic downward trendline with a breakout method?

You would wait after the downward trendline is broken by an upward price move, identify the next sideways pattern or the next higher resistance level from which you would draw a horizontal resistance line, and then buy when that resistance line is broken by an upward price move.

8. Is the distribution of the length of trends random?

No. There are more trends that are of longer length than expected in a normal distribution. The distribution of trend lengths has a fat tail.

Chapter 4   Calculating the Trend

1. Using the following S&P index prices from November 2002:

908.35, 915.36, 923.76, 902.57, 894.73, 876.19, 882.95, 882.53, 904.27, 909.81, 900.36, 896.74, 914.15, 933.79, 930.55, 932.87, 913.31, 938.87, 936.31, 934.53

(*a*) What are the last three values of a 10-day moving average?
(*b*) Is the trend going up or down?
(*c*) What would be the next price in order to change the direction of the trend?

(*a*) The last three values of the 10-day average are 917.472, 920.676, and 923.148
(*b*) The trend is up.
(*c*) Any price lower than 923.16 will turn the trend down.

2. Which trend will change direction first—a 10-day moving average or a 20-day moving average?

   The 10-day moving average.

3. With percentage smoothing, the most recent price changes are given (*a*) less importance, (*b*) the same importance or (*c*) more importance than previous price changes?

   (*c*) More importance.

4. If today's closing price is $50, yesterday's trendline value was $40, and you are using a percentage smoothing of 10 percent, what is today's trendline value?

   $41.

5. When the slope of a regression line is greater than zero, are prices rising or falling?

   Rising.

6. What is the daily slope of a regression line that rises 10 points in 5 days?

   2.

7. When the slope values today and yesterday are both 1.5, are prices rising, unchanged, or falling?

   Rising.

8. If yesterday's slope value was 1.5 and today's slope value is 1.0, are prices rising, unchanged, or falling?

   Rising at a slower rate.

9. Using a moving average to trade, when do you get a buy signal? A sell signal?

   You buy when the trendline turns up and sell when the trendline turns down.

10. Using a breakout system, the previous 10-day high was $30.50 and the previous 10-day low was $28.50. Prices break out to the upside and you buy 100 shares at $31.00. What is the risk of your trade in dollars?

    $250, the distance from your entry to the breakout low price.

11. Which of the four trending methods, moving average, smoothing, breakout, or slope,

    (*a*) Is usually most reliable?

    (*b*) Has the smallest losses?

    (*c*) Has the largest losses?

    (*a*) Breakout, (*b*) moving average and smoothing, (*c*) breakout and slope.

12. If the moving average method produced good profits when you checked its performance on the history of IBM, but none of the other trending methods were profitable, would you trade IBM using the moving average? Why?

    No. To have high confidence in a trending method, all the trending techniques should work.

13. You've just read an advertisement for a trend system that has 80 percent profitable trades and very low risk. What's wrong with that statement?

    A trend system has two profiles, one with small losses (small risk) and a small percentage of profitable trades, the other with large losses and a large percentage of profitable trades. There is no trending system that has mostly profits and low risk. You also may question the number of trades in the results (5 or 500?), the total time period of performance (one week or 10 years?), and whether the performance was generated by a computer or was the result of actual trading.

Chapter 5   The Trading Game

1. Why do you want to choose at least three stocks from three different market sectors?

    For diversification.

2. In the price shock of 9/11, which way did GM move and which way did Raytheon move? Why?

    GM fell and Raytheon rose. Raytheon is a defense contractor and would immediately benefit from any antiterrorist policies.

3. If the price of Amazon.com is $10 and you wanted to go long 100 shares at $12, what order would you place?

    Buy 100 AMZN 12 stop.

4. IBM is trading at $38. You own 500 shares at $40 and want to buy an equal amount if it drops to $36. What order do you place?

   Buy 500 IBM 38.

5. You want to buy 250 shares of GE if it rises to $45 and closes above that level. What order do you place?

   Buy 250 GE 45 stop MOC.

6. The December S&P futures contract has been in a narrow, sideways range for three weeks, trading from 950 to 990; therefore, you want to go long above 990 or short below 950 to take advantage of any new direction. What order do you place?

   Buy 1 SPZ 991 stop OCO Sell 1 SPZ 949 stop.

7. You bought 200 GE at $30 and the price is now $28. What is your profit or loss?

   $400 loss.

8. You sold 1 contract of TYZ at 108-16 and the price is now 108-00. What is your profit or loss?

   $500 profit.

Chapter 6   Channels and Bands

1. Once you've drawn an upward trendline, how do you draw the upward channel line?

   The upward channel line is drawn parallel to the trendline using the highest high price between the points used to draw the trendline.

2. When would you redraw the upward channel line? What point would you use to redraw it?

   You redraw the upward channel line after a significant penetration of the previous channel line, and two or three days following the penetration to be sure that it was not a false breakout. You use the new highest high to draw the new channel line parallel to the original trendline

3. If you are trading a channel, where would you buy and where would you sell?

   Buy in the lower 20 to 25 percent of the channel, and sell in the upper 20 to 25 percent of the channel.

4. If you've bought near the bottom of the channel, where are the two places you would exit the trade?

Take profits in the upper zone, and take a loss if prices penetrate the upward trendline heading lower.

5. If prices move above the channel line for only one day, and then fall back below the channel line, explain why you would or would not redraw the channel line.

You may redraw it because the penetration shows that volatility is increasing; you may not redraw the channel line because the price reversal indicates a false breakout that may be driven by a one-time news event.

6. How do you construct a 3 percent band around a 10-day moving average?

You multiply the moving average value by 1.03 to get the upper band and divide the moving average value by 1.03 to get the lower band.

7. How would you trade a percentage band?

In the same way as any other channel, selling in the upper zone and buying in the lower zone

8. What are two advantages of Bollinger bands over percentage bands?

(*a*) They adapt quickly to changes in volatility.
(*b*) They represent specific *confidence* levels. You can expect 5 percent of the highs and lows to penetrate the bands.

9. If prices penetrate through a 5 percent band too often, what can you do?

Increase the size of the band.

10. What are two disadvantages of a larger band?

Higher risk and fewer trades.

11. When does profit-taking work best? Anytime you have more than a 10 percent profit, in a noisy market, or as a long-term trend follower?

In a noisy market. Profit-taking should be based on price volatility, or support and resistance levels; therefore, 10 percent is arbitrary. Long-term trend followers cannot take profits because they need the few, very large profits to offset many losses.

Chapter 7   Event-Driven Trends

1. What is the key element that distinguishes a moving average trend from a swing trend?

    The moving average is time-driven; a swing is event-driven. A swing has no time element.

2. If the swing direction is up, the high price is $50, and you are using a 3 percent swing value, at what price would the swing direction turn down?

    $48.50.

3. If prices make a swing high of $30, a swing low of $25, and a swing high of $31, at what price would you get a swing sell signal?

    Below $25.00.

4. Would you get more point-and-figure signals using a box size of $1 or 50¢?

    50¢.

5. If you had a point-and-figure box size of $1, and prices have just declined from $48.00 to $41.50, at what price would you begin a new column of X's.

    $45.00.

6. Using a $1 box size, we plot a column of X's with the highest box filled at $28, followed by a new column of O's and then another column of X's. What is the lowest price that would give you a *buy* signal?

    $29.00.

Chapter 8   Controlling the Risk of a Trade

1. The best place for a stop-loss is (*a*) as close as possible, (*b*) based on how much you can afford to lose, or (*c*) a support or resistance level.

    (*c*) A support or resistance level.

2. What is the closest point at which you would place a stop-loss order? Why?

    About 1½ times the daily volatility; otherwise, you are likely to always get stopped out due to market noise, even when the trend doesn't change.

3. When you enter a new long position, where would you place your initial stop-loss?

    At the point where you would get a sell signal.

4. If you have just entered a long position, when would you raise your stop-loss for the first time?

> Following a new high (secondary buy signal) a pullback that forms a new, higher support level. The new support level becomes your stop-loss point.

5. What is the advantage of using a stop close-only order on your long position?

> The stop is not executed unless prices close below the stop-loss level. It prevents exiting on a false breakout to the downside.

6. Why would you use a fast and a slow trend instead of just a slow trend?

> The combination has smaller risk, and smaller profits, but the net result could be as good as a single trend.

7. If you've placed your stop-loss at $35 for your long position (entered at $40) and a price shock causes a sudden, large drop to $25, what are you likely to get as your exit price?

> $25.

Chapter 9   One-Day Chart Patterns and Reversals

1. Define an upward gap.

> The low of the day is greater than the high of the previous day.

2. When is a gap most likely to occur?

> When a news release occurs after the market is closed, the gap occurs on the next open.

3. Name four gaps most often found on a chart. Briefly explain how to recognize each.

> (a) A *common gap* occurs most often and may be found within a cluster of price activity. It does not have any special features other than the gap from the previous day.
>
> (b) A *breakaway gap* (up) occurs when prices jump out of a trading range or another formation, such as a descending triangle. Prices do not retrace back into the previous pattern.
>
> (c) A *runaway gap* occurs in the middle of a trend and is seen as an acceleration of the current trend.
>
> (d) An *exhaustion gap* occurs just after the top of a steep move and usually marks the end of the current trend.

4. If today's price action is much more volatile than the previous month and the high is much higher than the high of the same period, would we call the pattern a *spike* or a *wide-ranging day*?

> A wide-ranging day because we need to see the next day trade much lower to be a spike, but any exceptionally volatile day can be a wide-ranging day.

5. Define an *island reversal bottom.*

> A cluster of days separated by a gap down at the beginning and a gap up at the end, where the body of the "island" is below the previous and subsequent price movement.

6. When are reversal patterns most reliable? (*a*) After a sustained move in one direction, or (*b*) after a highly volatile move?

> (*a*) After a sustained move in one direction.

7. Why would a five-day run day pattern be considered *not* timely for trading?

> Because you need to wait five days after it occurs to identify the pattern.

8. After a sustained upward price move, there are two inside days. What does this tell you?

> It shows a drop in volatility that indicates a lack of direction. The event that caused the upward move is over. If nothing new happens to stimulate a continuation of the upward move, expect a reversal.

Chapter 10   Continuation Patterns

1. How does a continuation pattern help you trade?

> It confirms the direction of the trend.

2. At what points in a trend is a symmetric triangle most likely to occur?

> At the beginning and end, where the direction of the trend is uncertain.

3. Which triangle is most likely to occur in the middle of an upward trend, a symmetric, ascending, or descending triangle?

> Ascending, it leans in the direction of the trend.

4. Describe a flag in an uptrend.

> It is a downward-leaning formation bounded by two parallel lines.

5. What is the difference between a pennant and a triangle?

A pennant is an irregular formation. It does not have a horizontal support or resistance line, nor is it symmetrical.

6. During a downtrend, which way does a wedge point?

   Down.

7. What should you do if a descending triangle is formed during an uptrend?

   Exit your long position. The upward trend is likely to be over.

Chapter 11   Top and Bottom Formations

1. True or false? It is best to sell a "V" top on the day it makes its spike at the top of the move?

   False. You don't know that it's a "V" top until one or two days after the spike.

2. Define an island top.

   A formation at the top of a run that begins with a gap up and ends with a gap down.

3. Which is riskier to trade, (*a*) selling a double top or (*b*) buying a double bottom?

   (*a*) Selling a double top because prices tend to be very volatile. Double bottoms can occur in much quieter trading.

4. The price of a stock falls through support at $30, and then forms a double bottom with a low of $21. After better economic news, prices rally and break through resistance at $30. You buy. What is your price objective?

   $39.

5. If the volatility of a double top was $10 and prices moved through support at $40, the point where the double top was confirmed, what would be your maximum profit target? What would be a more realistic target and why?

   $30. A more realistic target would be $32.50, because volatility will decline as prices fall.

6. Describe the classic calculation for a head-and-shoulders top profit target.

   The distance between the neckline and the top of the head projected downward from the point where prices break the neckline after the right shoulder is formed.

Chapter 12   Retracements, Reversals, Fibonacci Numbers, and Gann

1. What are the three most likely percentage retracement levels?

    100 percent, 50 percent, and 61.8 percent.

2. What significance would you put on a 100 percent retracement?

    The reason for the prior move had disappeared.

3. Write the first six numbers of the Fibonacci summation series.

    1, 1, 2, 3, 5, 8, 13.

4. In the Fibonacci summation series, for large numbers in the series, what is the ratio of the *N*th value to the previous value?

    1.618.

5. If prices moved from a low of $35 to a high of $55, then retraced to $45, and started to move higher, a Fibonacci ratio of .618 would tell you to expect prices to reach what level?

    $57.36.

6. If a high occurred on December 4, a low 20 days later, and another high 15 days after the low, in how many days would you expect a new high or low according to the Fibonacci ratio .618?

    About 22 days later.

7. In a Gann square, the key support and resistance levels are supposed to fall where?

    On the horizontal, vertical, and diagonal lines crossing through the center of the square.

8. As you move outward in Gann's square or hexagon, the various support and resistance levels represent (*a*) an increase in, (*b*) unchanged, or (*c*) a decrease in volatility?

    (*a*) An increase.

Chapter 13   Volume, Breadth, and Open Interest

1. What interpretation do you place on falling prices and falling volume?

    It is a weak downward trend, not heavily supported by traders.

2. Would you say that volume trends are (*a*) clear and easy to interpret or (*b*) require smoothing to avoid erratic values?

(*b*) Require smoothing to avoid erratic values.

3. If volume was high and prices closed unchanged, would you consider the risk of trading (*a*) low, (*b*) normal, or (*c*) high?

(*c*) High.

4. A volume spike usually corresponds with what price pattern?

A local top or bottom.

5. How do you calculate On-Balance Volume?

If prices are higher, add the total volume; if prices are lower, subtract the total volume.

6. Of all the volume patterns and indicators, which appears to be the most definitive?

The volume spike.

7. If prices are falling, what would the market breadth need to do in order to confirm the decline?

Fall.

8. In futures trading, if a new buyer meets an old seller, what happens to the open interest?

It remains unchanged.

Chapter 14   Momentum and MACD

1. If the last five prices of IBM were $40.25, $40.75, $41.25, $40.75, and $41.50, what is the value of the five-day momentum?

1.25.

2. Which one of the 20-day or 40-day momentum lines can potentially have the highest value?

40-day.

3. When two consecutive momentum values are 1.50 and 1.50, are prices (*a*) increasing, (*b*) unchanged, or (*c*) decreasing?

(*a*) Increasing.

4. When two consecutive momentum values are 2.50 and 1.50, are prices (*a*) increasing, (*b*) unchanged, or (*c*) decreasing?

> (*a*) Increasing but at a slower rate.

5. If you are using momentum as a trend indicator, at what point does the trend turn up?

When the momentum value crosses zero going up.

6. If you are using the MACD as a trending indicator, when do you get a *sell* signal?

> When the MACD crosses the slower signal line heading down.

7. How would you improve the reliability of a standard MACD trending sell signal?

> By selecting only those sell signals above a minimum MACD value.

8. Describe an MACD bearish divergence.

> Two consecutive price peaks are rising, while the two corresponding MACD peaks are declining.

9. What would make you consider one bullish divergence as *stronger* than another?

> The stronger one has prices declining further and/or the MACD low points rising more than the other.

10. If you were anticipating a *bearish divergence* and planned to make two sales, when would you sell?

> (*a*) When prices made a new high and the MACD was lower.
> (*b*) When the second MACD high comes within 10 to 15 percent of the previous MACD high while prices are above the previous price peak.

Chapter 15 Overbought/Oversold Indicators and Double Smoothing

1. When contrary opinion indicates that the market is oversold, do you (*a*) buy immediately, (*b*) sell immediately, (*c*) use a timing indicator to give you a specific buy signal, or (*d*) use a timing indicator to give you a specific sell signal?

> (*c*) Use a time indicator to give you a specific buy signal.

2. What is the greatest disadvantage of the Bullish Consensus indicator?

   It is not timely.

3. Explain the raw stochastic in words.

   It is the position within the recent high-low range, expressed as a percentage of the range relative to the lowest price of the range.

4. Name the three stochastic calculations from fastest to slowest.

   The raw stochastic, %K, the three-day smoothing of %K called %K-slow or %D, and the three-day smoothing of %D called %D-slow.

5. What is the primary difference between the stochastic calculation and momentum values?

   The stochastic is scaled between 0 and 100. The momentum values can be as large as the greatest price move within the calculation period.

6. Explain the chart pattern that gives you a bullish stochastic divergence signal.

   Two consecutive price lows are declining, and the two corresponding stochastic values are rising. The first crossing of the faster and slower stochastic upward, after the divergence formation, will give a buy signal.

7. In a stochastic bearish divergence, the second stochastic peak should be lower than the first by at least what value?

   5 percent.

8. The Relative Strength Index is a ratio of what two values?

   The sum of the upward price changes divided by the sum of the downward price changes over the same time interval.

9. Explain the steps need to create a double-smoothed trendline using a 10-day momentum.

   (*a*) Create the 10-day momentum.
   (*b*) Smooth the value of the 10-day momentum using a selected percentage.
   (*c*) Smooth the value of step b using another selected percentage.

10. What is the advantage of double smoothing?

   It produces a smooth trendline with less lag than a comparable moving average.

Chapter 16 Managing Your Entry and Exit

1. What is the best technique for getting the average price on a buy order of 1,000 shares over two days?

   Divide the order into four or more equal parts and enter the buy orders spread out over equal time periods. The more parts, the closer to the average.

2. If you are trying to get the best price, in how many parts should you divide and execute your order?

   One.

3. What are the greatest advantages and the greatest disadvantages of scaling down?

   The greatest advantage is that you will get a better average price. The greatest disadvantages are that there is no limit to the risk and you will miss the price move by only having part of your position set.

4. What is the name of the technique that requires buying equal amounts as you increase your profits? Explain the risk of this method.

   Pyramiding (an equal pyramid). The risk is that you have the largest position when prices reverse, and you can lose all of your profits in a very small move.

5. Explain the reasoning behind scaling out of a profitable position (as a short-term trader).

   Price movement can be unpredictable in the short term. Scaling out over a range of prices allows you to target an average price but accept the fact that price movement may fall short of that target, or go significantly farther. Scaling out gets the same average result if all levels are reached, and captures some profits and reduces risk if prices fall short of your target.

Chapter 17 Volatility and Portfolio Management

1. What is the best single word that describes a price shock?

   Unpredictable.

2. Give three ways that you can protect yourself from a price shock.

(*a*) Be out of the market.

(*b*) Trade with low leverage.

(*c*) Diversify so that you have less exposure to a market that experiences a price shock.

3. What happens to the correlation between stocks, and even futures markets, when there is a major price shock? Why?

> The correlation disappears because investors all react the same way—they pull their money and move to a safer investment. Therefore, every market reverses direction as money leaves. It's not the stock, it's the money flow that causes correlation.

4. We know that any one day can be more or less volatile then the next. Under normal conditions, do prices get more volatile when they go up or down? Specifically, what about IBM, the Euro, crude oil prices, and Treasury notes?

(*a*) IBM gets more volatile when it goes up. Volatility follows the standard lognormal relationship. Volatility is lower at lower prices and higher at higher prices.

(*b*) There is no "high" or "low" price for foreign exchange, there is only "equilibrium." That's where the price of one currency in terms of another currency (for example, the yen denominated in Euros, or the Swiss franc in U.S. dollars) is at a fair value. We can see this because volatility drops and prices move sideways in a narrow range. The currency price is stable. When an event affects either currency, the cross-rate will move higher or lower and the volatility will increase in either direction. That represents instability. If the event was temporary, then prices will return to the level of equilibrium. If it is a permanent change caused by an interest rate change, then prices will eventually settle at a new level of equilibrium.

(*c*) The marginal barrel of crude oil is controlled by OPEC; therefore, they are very influential in controlling price. OPEC sets a target price at, for example, $22 per barrel. That represents an artificial "equilibrium" in the same way as foreign exchange has an equilibrium level. When prices move either higher or lower, volatility increases. If OPEC changes the target level by a small amount, then prices take that level as equilibrium. If they change the target upward by a large amount, then the market fights with their decision and volatility increases until the issue is resolved.

(*d*) Treasury notes have a normal volatility relationship except that volatility is in direct proportion to the interest rate yield, not the Treasury note prices. Volatility increases as rates go from 5 percent to 6 percent, while Treasury prices go down from about 108 to 100. If you're using prices because you trade futures, then you'll need to change to yield to apply any long-term relative volatility measurement.

5. To find the "true range" of the day, you need to find the largest of what three values (using high, low, and closing prices)?

(*a*) Today's high minus today's low.

(*b*) Today's high minus yesterday's close.

(*c*) Yesterday's close minus today's low.

6. As a short-term trader using profit targets and stop-loss orders, which would be closer, the profit target or the stop-loss order?

The profit target.

7. What does low volatility imply with regard to price movement?

Lack of direction.

8. If you are trading three stocks, A, B, and C, with corresponding daily volatilities of $1, $2, and $3, what percentage of your total capital would you place in each one to minimize risk?

54 percent in A, 27 percent in B, and 18 percent in C.

9. You are trading two stocks, A and B, and gold futures. Stock A has a daily price range of $3, stock B has a daily range of $4, and gold has a daily range of $3/ounce. The gold contract is 100 troy ounces. How many shares of A and B do you need to trade so that each stock has the same risk as gold?

Gold has a daily volatility of $3 × 100 = $300; therefore, you need to trade 100 shares of A and 75 shares of B.

Chapter 18   Dow Theory

1. In Dow Theory, what are the three waves of stock market movement called?

The primary, the secondary, and daily price fluctuations.

2. Why did Dow use averages?

   Because low liquidity in individual stocks allowed for price manipulation. These were seen as "unusual" price moves that could be minimized using averages.

3. Why did Dow want confirmation of more than one index?

   To be certain that the price move was based on broad economic factors and not limited to a specific industry.

4. What is the price pattern that gives you a bull market signal?

   Prices go above previous resistance, where that resistance is about 20 percent above the major lows of the previous price move. A bull market signal is similar to a price breakout.

5. In Dow Theory, what are the terms describing the first phases of a bull or bear market?

   Accumulation for a bull market and distribution for a bear market.

6. In Dow Theory, how do you tell the difference between a secondary reaction in a bull market and a downturn signaling a bear market?

   A secondary reaction lasts from three weeks to three months, the size of the downturn is less than 20 percent, and volume declines during the price drop.

7. In Dow Theory, what happens to volume in a bull market? In a bear market?

   Volume goes with the trend. It increases in a bull market and increases in a bear market.

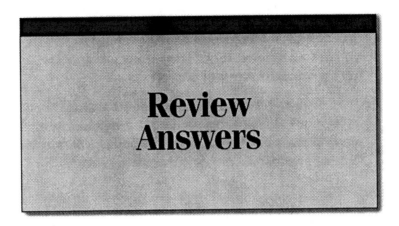

Review Answers

1. The analysis or forecasting of price movement using only price and volume; the study of price patterns.

2. Pros:
    (*a*) Allows, discipline, ability to assess expectations and, backtesting.
    (*b*) Creates an objective, not arbitrary, assessment of market direction.
    (*c*) Applies discipline to trading (to know when to take a loss) and risk control.

    Cons:
    (*a*) Lack of flexibility.
    (*b*) Inability to override with fundamentals.
    (*c*) Inability to analyze the market correctly.

3. The weekly chart is smoother. The trend is clearer on the weekly chart. The daily chart has more noise.

4. Higher prices have higher volatility; lower prices have low volatility and often lack direction. credit ½ point for answering, "Volume is different."

5. An unpredictable, very large, volatile price move.

6. You cannot predict a price shock; therefore, you can't plan to profit. Credit ½ point for answering, "Have profit-taking orders placed in the market."

7. The small, erratic, unpredictable price moves that occur frequently.

8. (*a*) The change in price over *N* days.
   (*b*) The highest high to lowest low over *N* days.
   (*c*) The sum of the absolute price changes over *N* days.
   (*d*) The average true range over *N* days.

9. The S&P gives the direction of the overall market. When the S&P has a strong trend, it is best to consider that trend, and its correlation to the marketplace, when trading individual stocks. Don't fight the big trend. Credit 1 point for answering, "In order to hedge."

10.

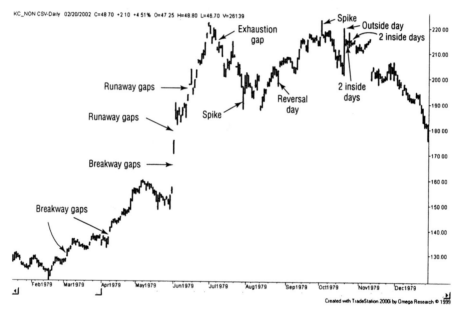

FIGURE R3.1

11. See Figure R3.2 on facing page.

12. See Figure R3.3 on facing page.

13. Monthly, because it smoothes price movement.

14. The *N*-day calculation, through day *t*, is plotted below day *t* rather than at the average point of the calculation period, $t - N/2$. Also, the effects of smoothing cause lag.

15. (*c*) Many small losses and a few large profits.

16. All of them would be expected to produce similar results, but with a different pattern. It's the risk and trading frequency that differ.

Figure showing answer for Question 11.

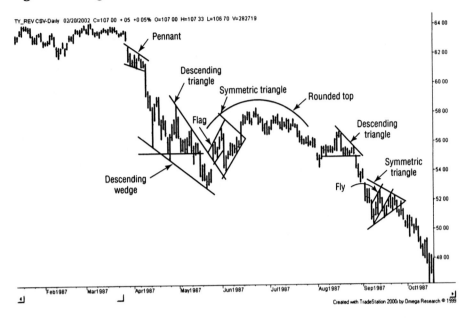

FIGURE R3.2

Figure showing answer for Question 12.

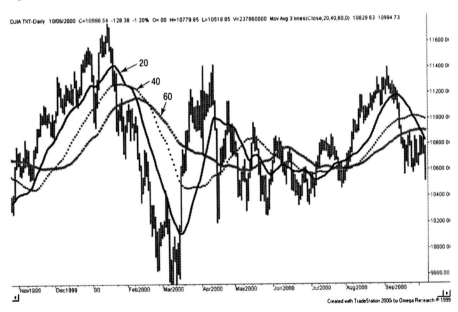

FIGURE R3.3

17.

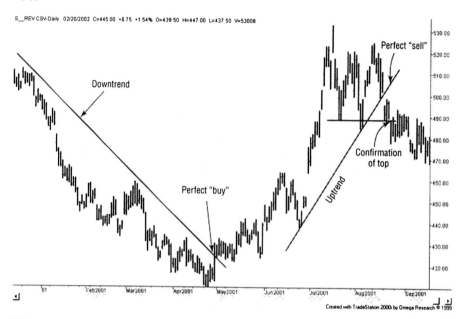

FIGURE R3.4

18.

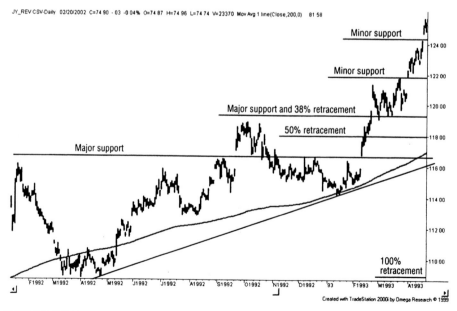

FIGURE R3.5

19. (*c*) You cannot apply profit-taking.

20. The long-term MA takes advantage of fundamental factors, primarily Fed interest rate policy, which can dominate the market for six months to two years. Short-term trends fight with market noise; therefore, they have many false signals. Credit 1 point for answering, "There is more data," and 1 point for answering, "There is less noise."

21. (*b*) In a noisy market.

22. An upward channel is drawn parallel to an uptrend line across the tops of the price movement. Also, draw a regression line through the center of prices, and then two parallel lines across the corresponding tops and bottoms.

23. Buy when prices near the bottom of an upward-sloping channel and sell when prices near the top of the channel. Credit 1 point for answering, "The breakout target is the width of the channel," and 1 point for answering, "Buy an upward breakout and sell a downward breakout."

24. Bollinger bands are 2-standard-deviation bands around a moving average. The calculation period is the same as the moving average.

25. As a countertrend trader you would sell when prices penetrated the top band and buy when prices penetrated the bottom band.

26. A bar chart advances to the right each day, the point-and-figure chart has no time component. Also, a bar chart is time-driven; a point-and-figure chart is event-driven.

27. When a box is entered that is higher than the box in the previous column of boxes.

28. To control your risk or losses.

29. Just above or below the resistance level that is outside normal volatility range. Credit 1 point for answering, "Two times the volatility below the entry."

30. Raise it after new support levels are formed, always keeping it away from the current daily volatility range. Also, raise it to the next secondary buy signal.

31. (*b*) Descending.

32. Below the neckline by the same distance as from the neckline to the top of the head.

33. 100 percent, 50 percent, and 61.8 percent.

34. 1, 1, 2, 3, 5, 8, 13.

35. (*c*) Neither 1 or 2.

36. Decline in volume, decline in volatility, nearby resistance—horizontal or downtrend trendline, overbought indicator, bearish divergence, testing a long-term moving average line, cross-market confirmation, high volatility top, rounded top, head-and-shoulders top, island reversal, reversal day, volume spike, gap down, MACD signal crossing.

37.

Volume	Price		
	Increasing	Unchanged	Decreasing
Increasing	Strong up	None	Strong down
Unchanged	Up	None	Down
Decreasing	Weak up	None	Weak down

38. Change in price over a time interval; speed.

39. (*a*) Smoother.

40. $10.

41. (*c*) Removing the trend.

42. (*c*) Bullish and bearish divergence.

43. Prices make lower lows and the oscillator makes higher lows.

44. (*a*) The MACD line.

45. The MACD crosses the signal line heading downward.

46. (*c*) It remains at high levels for an uncertain period of time.

47. $.75.

48. None.

49. The position of the closing price in the recent 10-day high-low range. Credit 1 point for answering, "Speed and relative price," and 1 point for answering, "Whether the price is overbought or oversold."

50. *Slow K* is a three-day average of *K*, *slow D* is a three-day average of *slow K*. Credit 1 point for answering, "Smooth."

51. (*c*) About 20 percent of the time.

52. (*c*) An overbought and oversold indicator.

53. (*c*) Upward and downward price changes.

54. False. A small number of days causes the stochastic to be erratic and bounce from extreme highs to extreme lows based on market noise. Signals are undependable.

55. True.

56. (*a*) High minus low.
   (*b*) High minus previous close.
   (*c*) Previous close minus low.

57. (*a*) Scaling down because you have the largest position when you lose and the smallest when the market moves quickly in a profitable direction.

58.

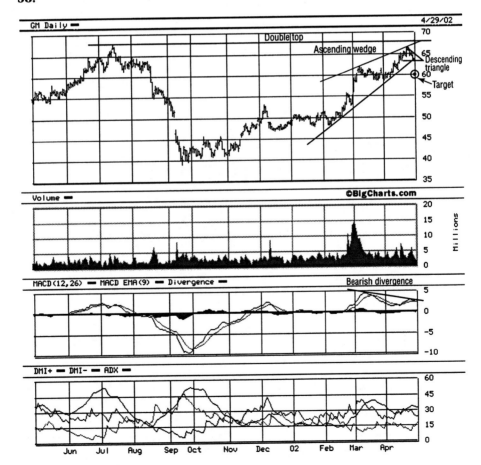

FIGURE R3.6

Explanation for either higher or lower answer:

Lower because of double top, bearish divergence, ascending wedge, descending triangle, lower volatility.

Higher because of medium-term uptrend, not overbought, higher volume on upward moves.

59. (*a*) Having a trading system that is correctly positioned for a price shock.

60.

	Price	Volatility	No. of Shares
Stock *A*	$10.00	$0.50	162
Stock *B*	$50.00	$1.00	81
Stock *C*	$50.00	$1.50	54
Stock *D*	$100.00	$5.00	16

61.

	Price	Volatility	Conversion Factor	Margin	No. of Contracts
S&P	1100.00	20.00	250	20,000	12.5
T-notes	102/00	/24	1000	3,000	83.0

62. (*b*) Scale out at multiple levels looking for an average price.

63. All are true.

64. (*a*) Bull and bear market, major trend, policy.
(*b*) Secondary trends or reactions, secular trends.
(*c*) Minor trends or noise.

65. To be sure it was a broad-based economic movement, not limited to one industry.

66. Accumulation.

67. (*b*) Assuming that the trend persists.

68. (*c*) Short-term trading, because it has the largest amount of noise and the trend does not persist.

69. (*a*) Periodic news releases.

70. Long DELL because of a bullish divergence, rising prices near a horizontal breakout, and a potential descending wedge bottom formation. Credit 5 points if you can justify another decision.

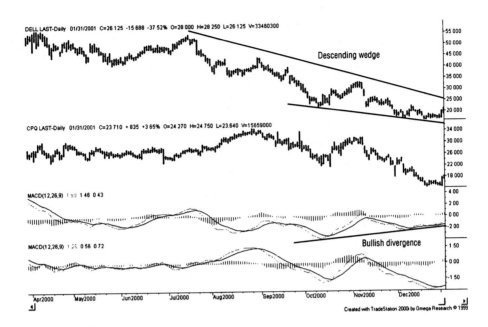

FIGURE R3.7

71. (*c*) Decline if earnings are lower than anticipated.

72. Because "big money thinks the same," pensions and institutions buy and sell across the board without distinguishing the specific attributes of a stock. They are setting or removing long-term long positions.

73. "When you need it most," during a price shock.

74. (*b*) A larger number of losing trades.

75. (*a*) When the MACD value reaches historic lows.

76. True.

77. True.

78. The open, $52.00.

79. (*b*) Greater than your average losses.

80. Positive: Strong correlation between the two gives signal confirmation. Negative: It doesn't always work, analyzing the stock itself is "pure," and the actions of management or company earnings do not necessarily relate to the underlying price of the physical market.

81. Leverage; you can buy $25,000 worth of crude oil for $3,000 margin.

82. A failed signal can be a strong indicator of direction, you were proved wrong in your choice of direction by virtue of a loss, or simply, "the trend changed."

83. (c) Trading quickly, because profits are smaller; therefore, you need to act faster.

84. (b) Midday, because it is less liquid.

85. (d) It is indirectly related to the amount of diversification.

86. (a) Close out the trade as soon as possible.

87. (b) Always get out of a windfall profit due to a price shock.

88. Profits tend to make you complacent. Losses teach you lessons in how to control risk and trade during difficult times.

89. You don't know their biases, what tools they've used, whether they have analyzed the market correctly, or potential conflicts of interest or hidden agendas.

90. $14.25.

91. $56.90.

92. 1106.50.

93. You are not filled.

94. A resistance line.

Index

Printed in the United States
96816LV00001B/25/A